IMAGES
of America

LAURENS

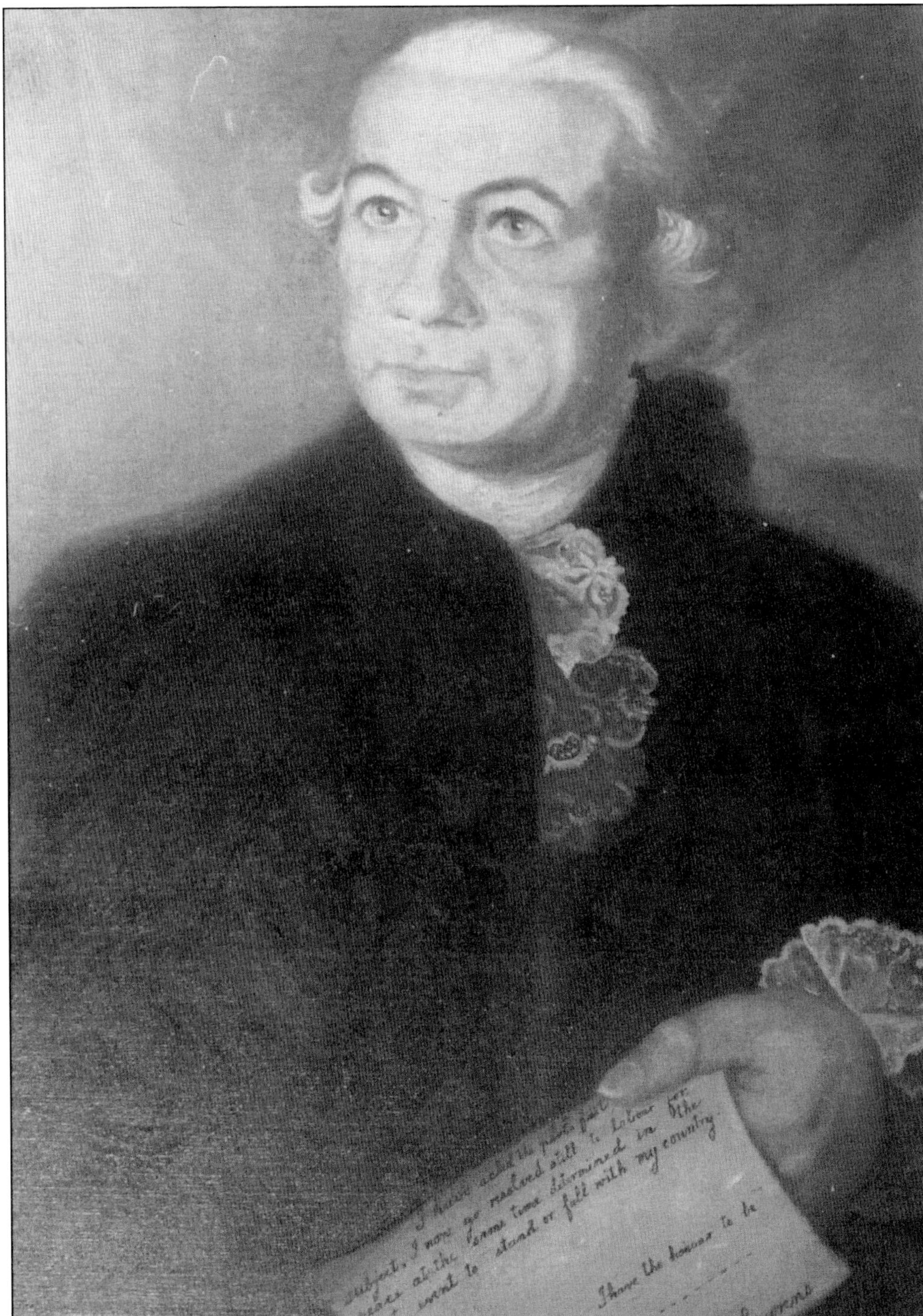

HENRY LAURENS. The town of Laurens derived its name from the sterling patriot, distinguished warrior, and sagacious statesman, the Honorable Henry Laurens of Charleston. It is generally agreed by local historians that the name was chosen by an early Laurens judge, Jonathan Downs. (Courtesy of the Laurens County Library.)

IMAGES
of America

LAURENS

Libby Rhodes

ARCADIA
PUBLISHING

ISBN 978-0-7385-0625-8

Published by Arcadia Publishing
Charleston, South Carolina

Printed in the United States of America

Library of Congress Catalog Card Number: 00-106091

For all general information contact Arcadia Publishing at:
Telephone 843-853-2070
Fax 843-853-0044
E-Mail sales@arcadiapublishing.com
For customer service and orders:
Toll-Free 1-888-313-2665

Visit us on the Internet at www.arcadiapublishing.com

This book is dedicated to my children,
Mason Charles Motes II and Katherine Willis Rhodes,
with the fervent hope that they will forever cherish the fact
that their roots are deeply implanted in Laurens.

Contents

INTRODUCTION

In the years following the Revolutionary War, immigrants and settlers arrived in Upstate South Carolina. They followed the Great Wagon Road from Virginia, Pennsylvania, and North Carolina in search of cheap lands. Some land sold for as little as 50¢ an acre. It was a turbulent period in the history of Upstate Carolina, as there were disturbances between Patriots and Tories. It also was a time of unrest between the Cherokees and settlers, resulting in the Cherokees losing their hunting grounds.

Settlers developed small communities in areas that were convenient to business establishments and meetinghouses, and these little villages eventually grew into trading centers. Laurensville was one such village that progressed steadily enough to be classified as a town. As to the exact time the town was named, historians were not able to ascertain because records of that era were destroyed by fire. However, a few remaining documents determined the date to be approximately between 1785 and 1790. It is known that Laurens was a part of the Ninety Six District, which had been carved out of Craven County.

Land on which the town of Laurens was located was originally a portion of a grant awarded in 1774 to John Rodgers and his wife, Margaret, from William Bull, the royal governor of the province of South Carolina in the name of King George III of England. Rodgers sold part of his property to Lewis and Samuel Saxon, who in turn sold 4 acres to the judges of Laurens County for the purpose of establishing a center for the town. Robert Goodloe Harper purchased 300 acres of the grant, and in 1880 the property surrounding the courthouse was sold for business establishments.

Squires Charles Allen, Jonathan Downs, John Hunter, and Thomas Wadsworth, the "Honorable Judges," gathered at a distillery, located near Hudgens' Factory and belonging to John Rodgers, for the purpose of choosing a site on which to locate the town. The members of one regiment wished the town to be located at Boyd's Cross Roads near High Point, and the members of the other regiment wished it to be situated 1 mile northeast of the present site. Rodgers's distillery was situated on a spring that was located between the two points. According to some accounts, the location of Laurens was an accident. The "Judges," having imbibed too freely of peach brandy, did not care to undergo the fatigues of a journey to either of the two points mentioned and accordingly went to the top of the hill and there placed stakes in a chinquapin thicket. Most likely the "Judges" chose the site because it was a central point located on Little River and practically surrounded by water. Also five roads that brought together the Upstate connected at the chosen location.

Laurens, the county seat of Laurens County, is located in that delightful portion of South Carolina known as the Piedmont region. The town is closely linked to many major Upstate towns with a distance of 38 miles from Spartanburg; 36 miles from Greenville; 60 miles from Anderson; 36 miles from Abbeville; 32 miles from Newberry; and 35 miles from Union.

The first courthouse constructed for the county was a log structure that was also used as a church and schoolhouse. The location and date of construction are unknown. Laurens, or "Laurensville" as it was called in the early days, soon developed into a flourishing town. Like most courthouse towns of that era, Laurens was laid off around the square with five radiating streets. A new courthouse was constructed in 1815 and was replaced in 1840 by the present structure with additions made in 1857. The Courthouse became the center of the Square. The residential area was circular and extended a mile from the square in all directions.

Log cabins and wooden structures that were then on the Square gradually disappeared and in their place were erected large, commodious, and beautiful brick store buildings. Wells were dug and watering troughs for horses were erected at both the front and rear of the Courthouse. When automobiles replaced the horse and buggy, marble water fountains replaced the troughs. The wells were discontinued when the streets were paved with bricks in 1907.

With the passing of years, the little town of Laurens continued to grow and attracted fancy confectionery and fruit stores; carriage, buggy, and wagon shops; cobblers; a tannery, with saddlery and harness shops; tailoring establishments; banks; livery stables; building contractors; flour and corn mills; medical practitioners; grocery stores; dry good stores; hardware stores; textile mills; a glass plant; and a variety of other shops, business concerns, and industry.

The arrival of the railroad promoted growth and served as yet another means of putting Laurens on the map and in touch with other areas of the state. Presbyterian, Baptist, Methodist, Episcopal, and African Methodist Episcopal churches were organized by the town fathers to minister the spiritual needs of the developing town. The town also erected educational facilities to serve the needs of Laurens children as well as young ladies and young men from throughout the South.

The traditions of the city as to culture, education, religion, hospitality, and all-around good citizenship have been well preserved, as the people of the city, which is generally known as the "Center of the Piedmont," are friendly toward each other and toward strangers and visitors. Laurens, one of the oldest towns in South Carolina, has continued to grow with the passing of years and remains one of the liveliest and most progressive towns in upper South Carolina. Many historical properties remain and represent several stages of architectural growth and development.

This book is simply a pictorial history of Laurens; a nostalgic journey from the town's beginning until the 1940s. It is a brief sketch of only a few of the dedicated, hard-working, and devoted men and women that helped to create a small Southern town. *Laurens* is intended to bring back a flood of memories of tree-lined streets; front porches; friends, neighbors, and relatives; a church bell ringing; a classroom in the Laurens Graded School; the bustling town square with its variety of drugstores and shops; a leisurely stroll down Main Street; and citizens of varying backgrounds, professions, and culture. The images portray life in a small town—a way of life that is fast disappearing.

One

Town Square and Surrounding Establishments

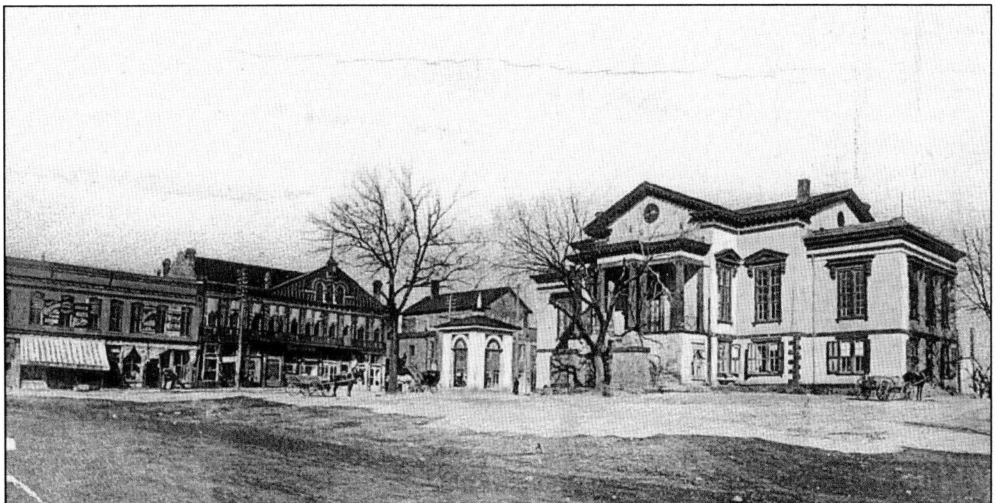

Center of Square. Architect Thomas C. Veal designed the Laurens County Courthouse, and Dr. John Wells Simpson was the builder. The Courthouse illustrates an example of Greek Revival architecture in rural South Carolina. The central portion was constructed in 1837–1838; wings to the northeast and southwest were added in 1858; and in 1911 additions were made to the wings, windows were remodeled, Palladian stairs were added, and the elliptical dome was constructed. The Laurens County Courthouse is the focal part of the Laurens Square. (Courtesy of Laurens County Library.)

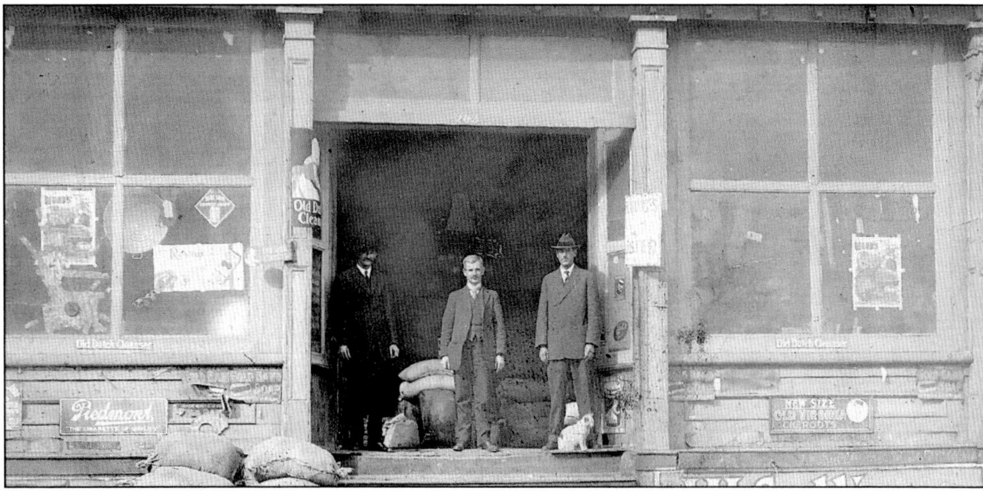

Oldest Merchant. At the time of his death in 1923, James Hewlett Sullivan was the oldest merchant in Laurens. The son of Captain Wash Sullivan of Sullivan's Township, he came to Laurens as a young man and first engaged in business as a member of Gray and Sullivan Firm with W.L. Gray. After the partnership was dissolved, he remained in business for himself until the time of his death. A trustee of the Methodist church, Sullivan was married to Mary Pelham Sullivan of Newberry and lived on West Main Street. (Courtesy of Rhodes collection.)

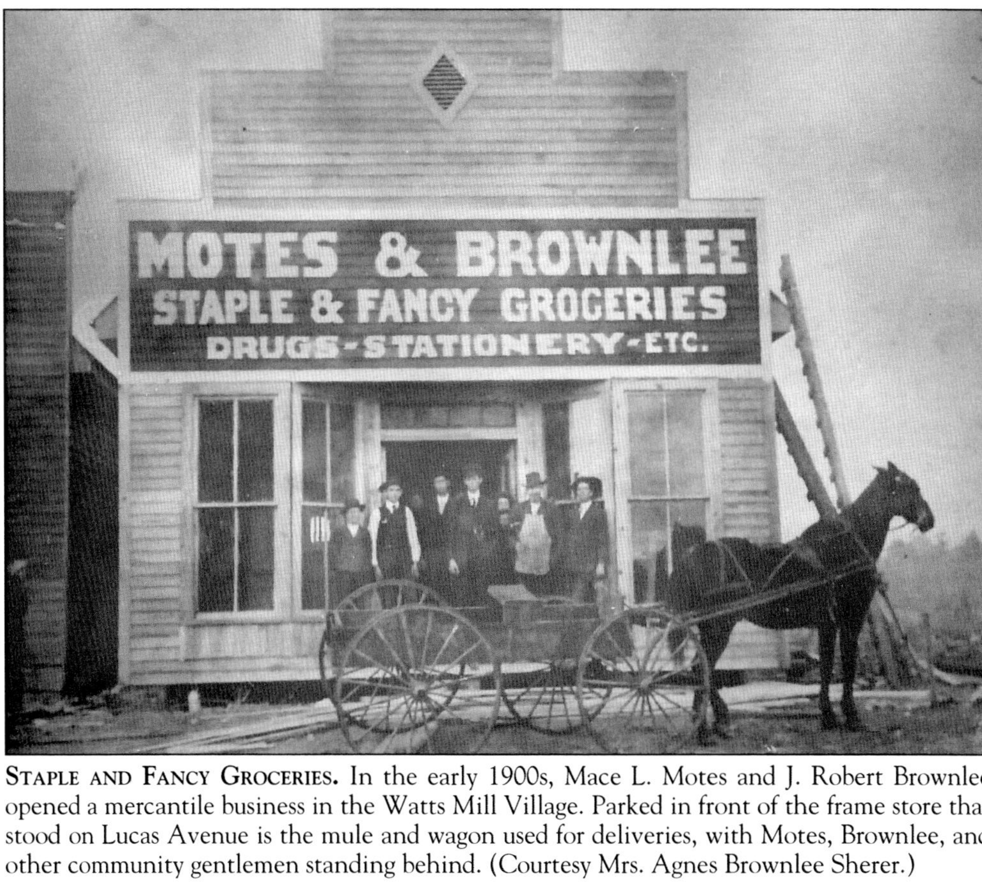

Staple and Fancy Groceries. In the early 1900s, Mace L. Motes and J. Robert Brownlee opened a mercantile business in the Watts Mill Village. Parked in front of the frame store that stood on Lucas Avenue is the mule and wagon used for deliveries, with Motes, Brownlee, and other community gentlemen standing behind. (Courtesy Mrs. Agnes Brownlee Sherer.)

ROBERTSON HOTEL. As the city of Laurens grew, several hotels sprang up just off the Public Square. A sheet from the Robertson Hotel register lists guests from Goldville (Joanna), Tumbling Shoals, Waterloo, Clinton, and as far away as Bristol, Tennessee. (Courtesy of Rhodes collection.)

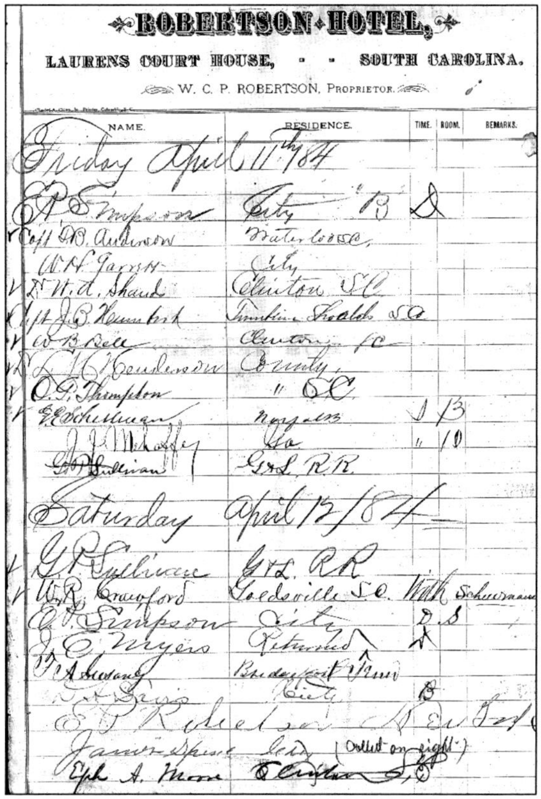

ROBERTSON HOTEL,

LAURENS COURT HOUSE, - - SOUTH CAROLINA.

W. C. P. ROBERTSON, PROPRIETOR.

NAME.	RESIDENCE.	TIME.	ROOM.	REMARKS.
Friday	April 11th /84			
Saturday	April 12/84			

BEN DELLA HOTEL. Located near the Public Square of Laurens, the Ben Della Hotel was one of several hotels in town. Since Laurens was the county seat and the courthouse was located here, gentlemen traveled from outlying communities on horseback or in horse and buggy to attend to legal, banking, and shopping business. (Courtesy of Mrs. Agnes Sherer Brownlee.)

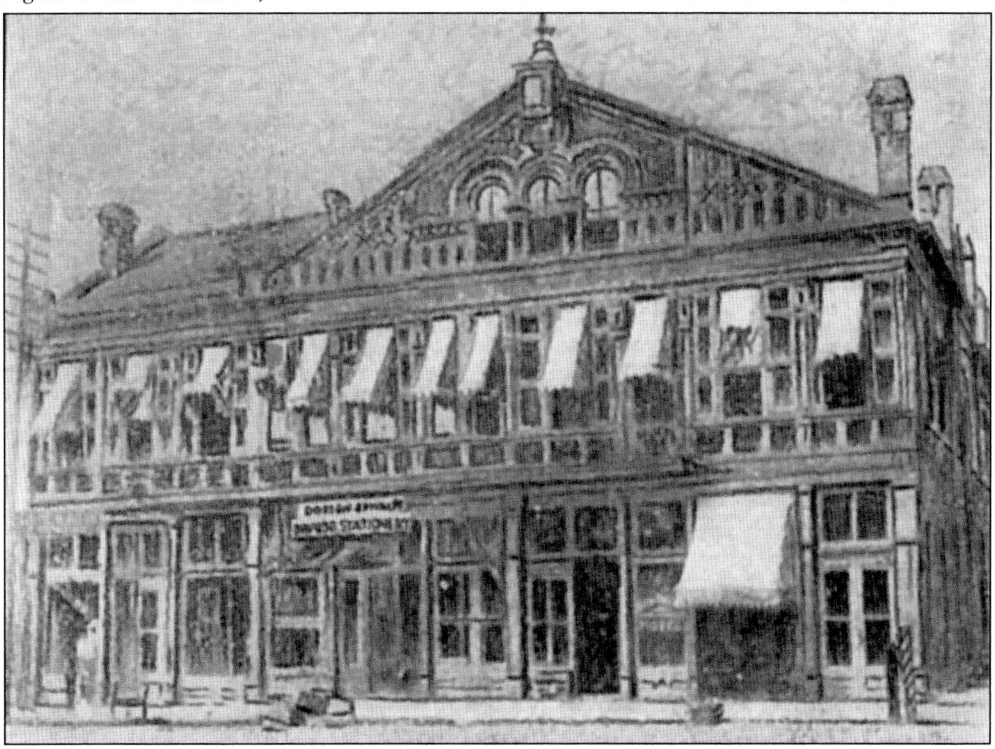

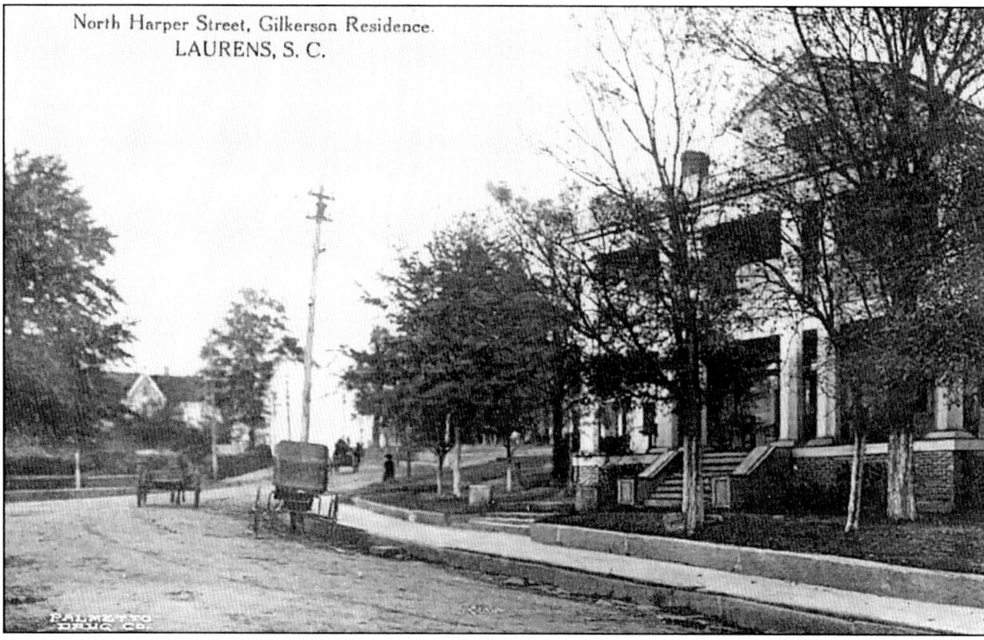

BLACK BEAR INN. The Black Bear Trail was a tourist route from the north to the south. The Black Bear Inn, a boarding house located on North Harper Street, was on the route and therefore became a popular stopping place for travelers. Some families that were associated with the house before it was torn down were the Garlingtons, Richardsons, and Brysons. (Courtesy of Mrs. Katherine Weathers Johnson.)

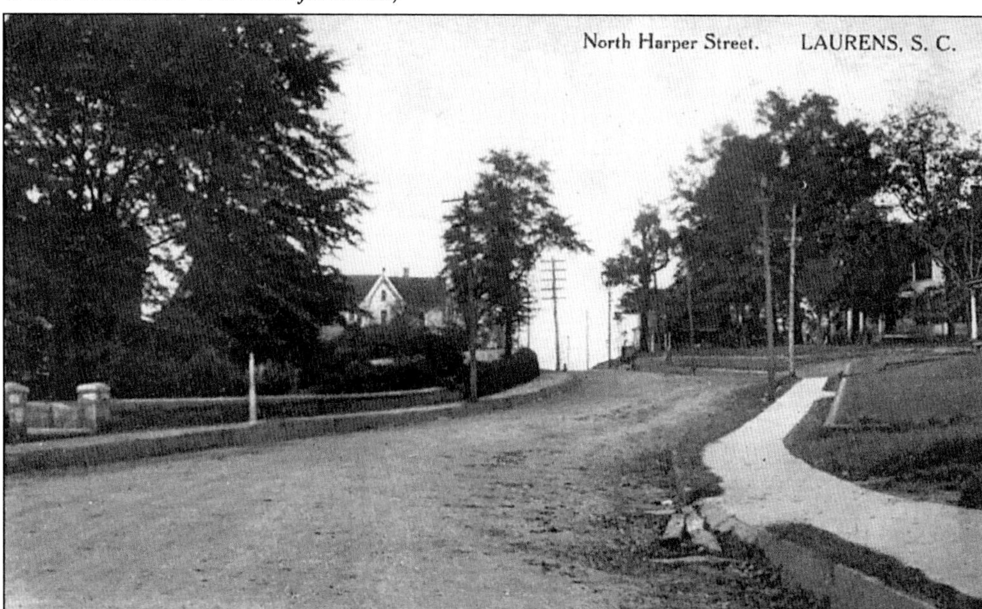

VIEW OF NORTH HARPER STREET. North Harper was one of four main streets leading from the Laurens Public Square. Shown before it was paved, the street, once lined with houses, led to the Laurens City Cemetery, the Little River Bridge, and Watts Mill. (Courtesy of Laurens County Library.)

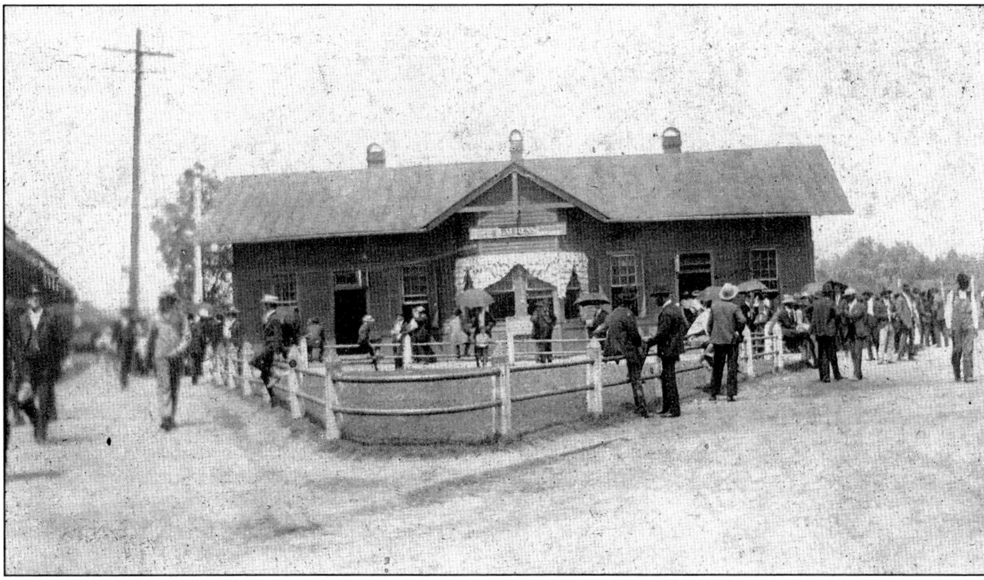

Earliest Depot. Factual information was not available for the photograph. However, according to several local historians, the building could possibly have been the first depot in Laurens and probably was located on East Main Street. (Courtesy of Mrs. Beatrice Babb Bradley.)

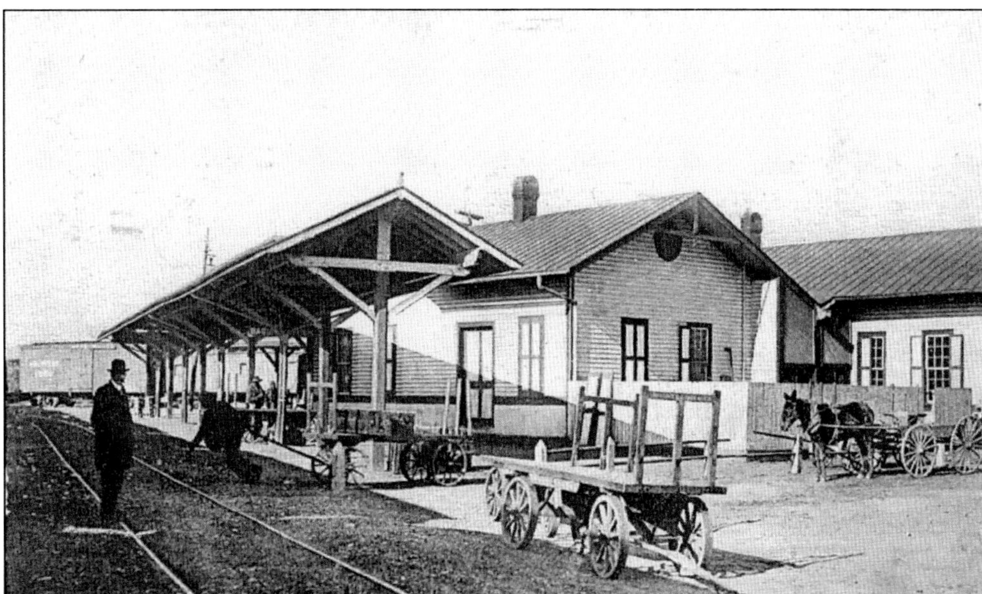

Railway Station. The wooden depot, located on East Main Street, served Laurens citizens, farmers, and merchants prior to the construction of the brick depot *c.* 1908. The railroad was an important factor in the growth of Laurens. (Courtesy of Laurens County Library.)

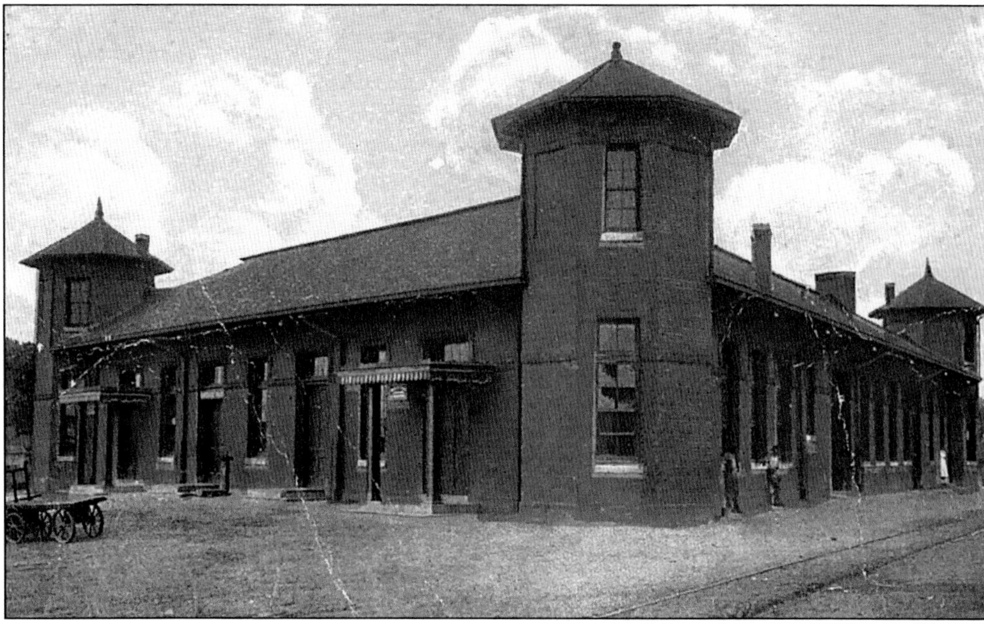

LAURENS DEPOT. Constructed around 1908, the unusual, wedge-shaped, brick, triangular station served the Charleston and Western Carolina (C&WC) as well as the Columbia, Newberry and Laurens lines (CN&L). The C&WC to Spartanburg was on the left and the CN&L was on the right of the building. (Courtesy of Laurens County Library.)

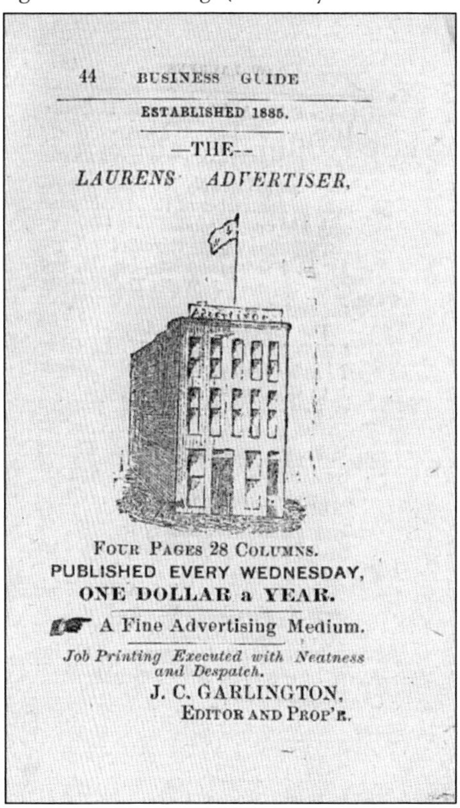

FIRST ISSUE IN 1885. Conway Garlington, editor of the *Laurens Advertiser*, published the first issue on August 5, 1885, as an eight-column, four-page newspaper. After several years of publication, the paper was purchased by Colonel B.W. Ball and was edited by Colonel Ball until his death. The paper was then edited by W.W. Ball, Mrs. Sara Ball Copeland, and Samuel E. Boney. Arthur and Allison Lee purchased the paper in 1910. The original *Advertiser* was located upstairs in a building on the North Side of the Public Square. (Courtesy of John Wells Todd IV.)

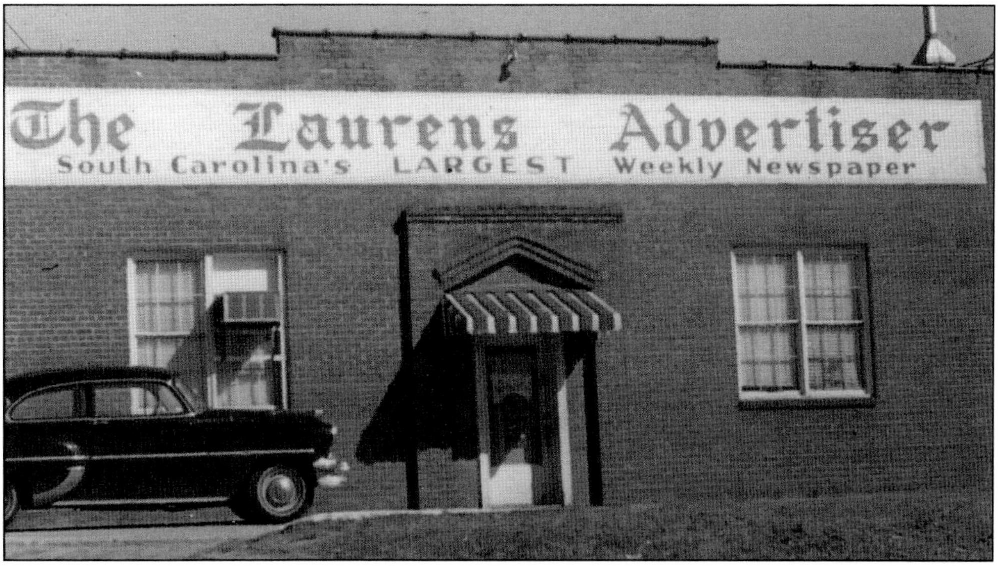

LAURENS ADVERTISER. At one time the *Laurens Advertiser* was located in a small brick building on Silver Street, just off the public square. Brothers Arthur and Allison Lee purchased the newspaper in 1910. Allison Lee served as owner and publisher until the newspaper was sold to W.J. Brown of Belton. (Courtesy of *Laurens County Advertiser* files.)

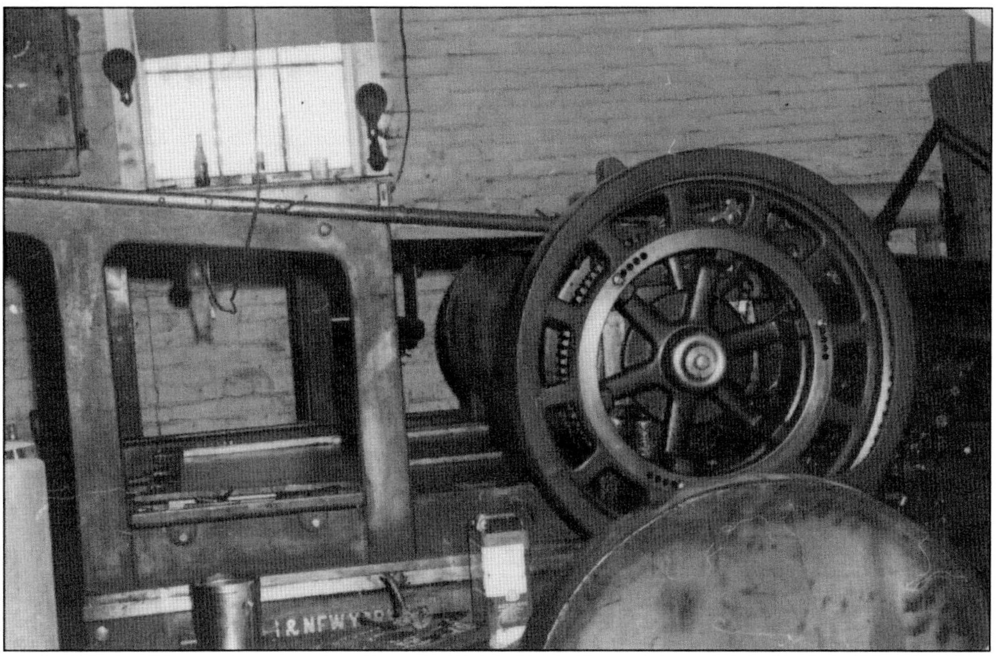

CONVENTIONAL LETTERPRESS. W.J. Brown, publisher and editor of the *Laurens Advertiser*, made possibly the greatest single changeover in the history of the newspaper when it moved from the conventional letterpress to the "offset" method of printing. Another milestone was passed when the *Advertiser* began bi-weekly publication. Under Brown's leadership, the name of the newspaper was changed to the *Laurens County Advertiser* to indicate that it was a countywide newspaper, not just for the city of Laurens. (Courtesy of *Laurens County Advertiser* files.)

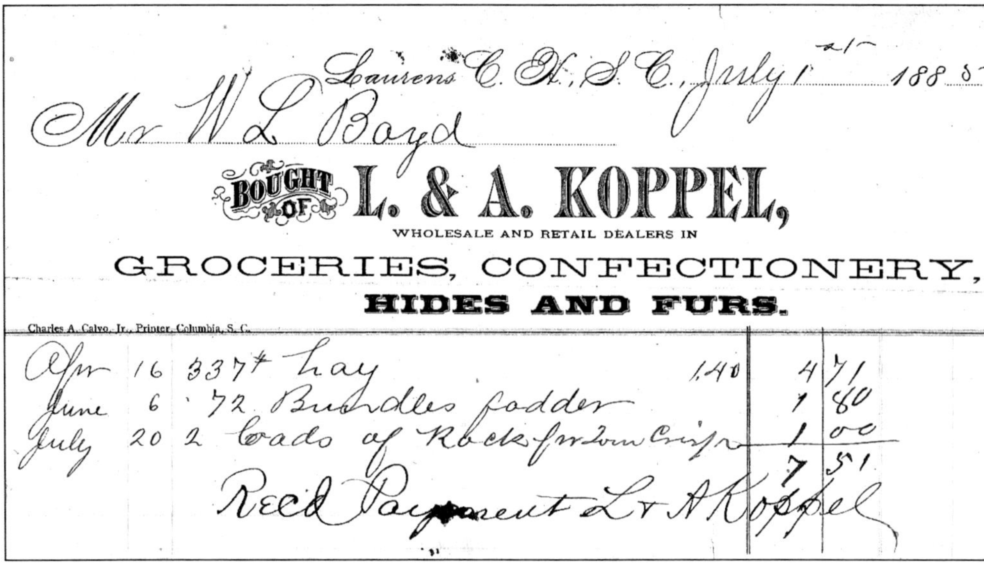
Laurens C. H., S. C., July 1st 1885
Mr W L Boyd
Bought of L. & A. KOPPEL,
WHOLESALE AND RETAIL DEALERS IN
GROCERIES, CONFECTIONERY,
HIDES AND FURS.
Charles A. Calvo, Jr., Printer, Columbia, S. C.

Apr	16	337# hay	1.40	4	71
June	6	72 Bundles fodder		1	80
July	20	2 Loads of Rocks for Town Crisp		1	00
				7	51

Rec'd Payment L & A Koppel

L. & A. Koppel. In 1885, the address listed for L. & A. Koppel, wholesale and retail dealers in groceries, confectionery, hides, and furs, is the Laurens Courthouse. The bill of sale shows that W.L. Boyd purchased hay and fodder, in all likelihood for his horses. (Courtesy of Rhodes collection.)

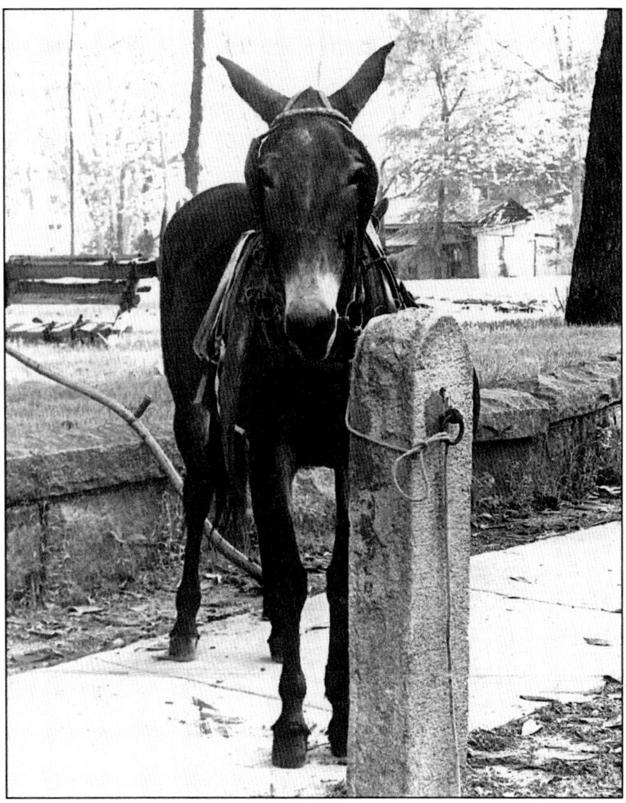

Granite Hitching Posts. Located on the town square and on the main streets leading from Laurens, hitching posts were necessary for visitors as well as Laurens residents. Horses and mules were familiar sights in the early days of "Laurensville." A few of the granite structures remain to remind residents of a by-gone era. (Courtesy of the Rhodes collection.)

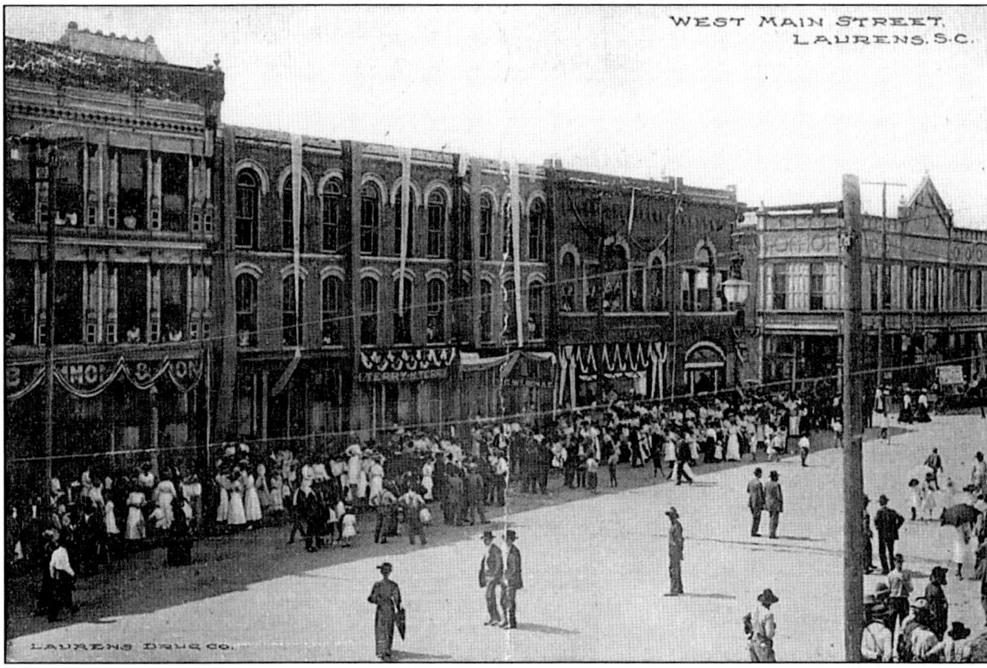

West Main Street. This postcard shows a West Main Street scene in Laurens. (Courtesy of Laurens County Library.)

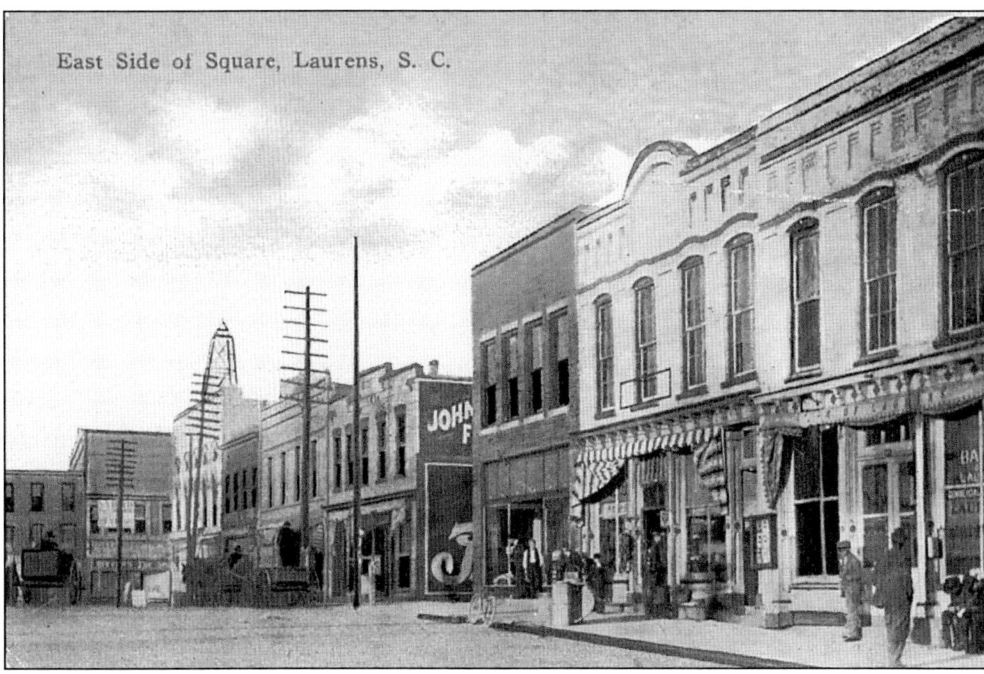

East Side of the Square. This postcard shows stores on the East Side of the Laurens Square. (Courtesy of Laurens County Library.)

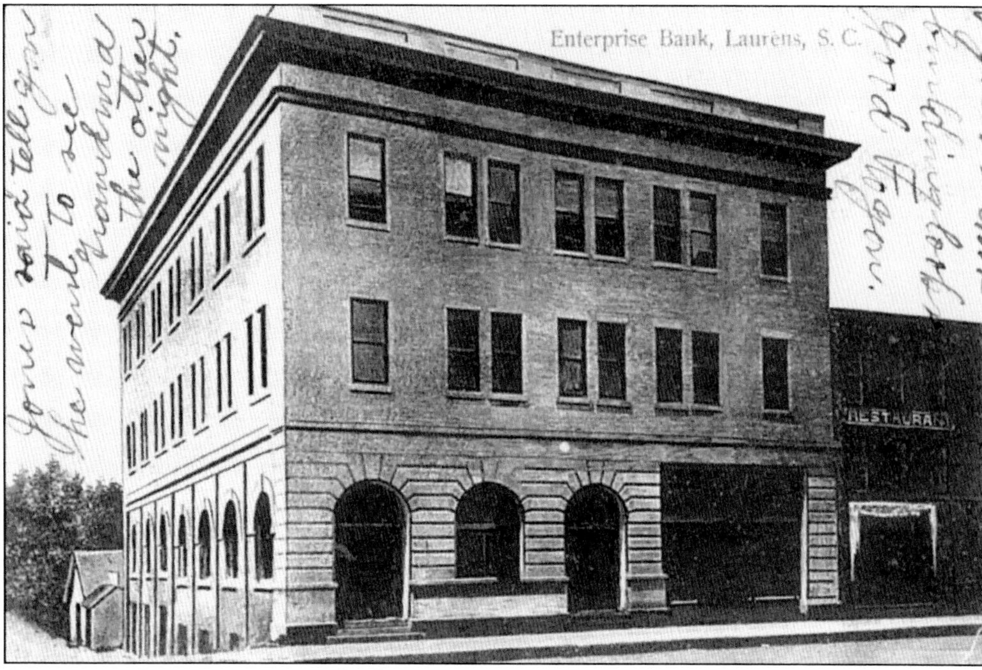

ENTERPRISE BANK. In 1901 Charles Houston Roper was instrumental in organizing the Enterprise Bank, located on the north side of the Square. He became the cashier of the financial institution, and N.B. Dial became president. When Dial was elected to the U.S. Senate, Roper assumed the presidency and remained in that capacity until the bank consolidated with the Peoples Loan and Exchange Bank. (Courtesy of Laurens County Library.)

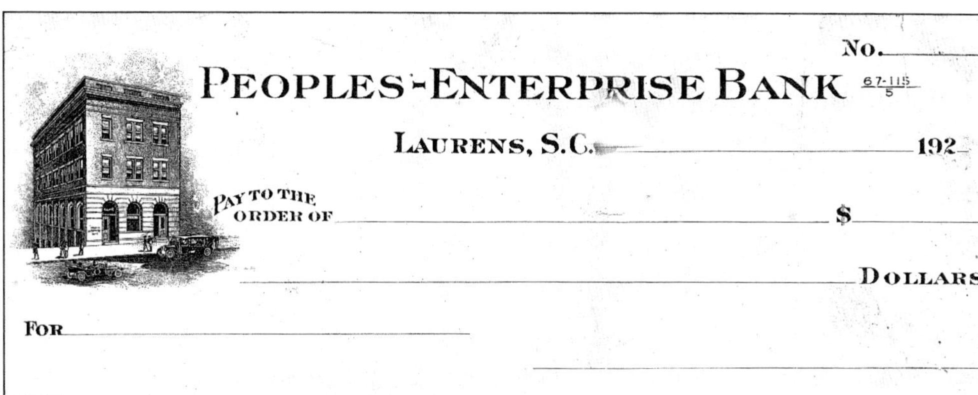

PEOPLES ENTERPRISE CHECK. This check from the Peoples Enterprise Bank from the early 1900s shows the Bank Building, located on the corner of Silver Street on the Square. (Courtesy of Rhodes collection.)

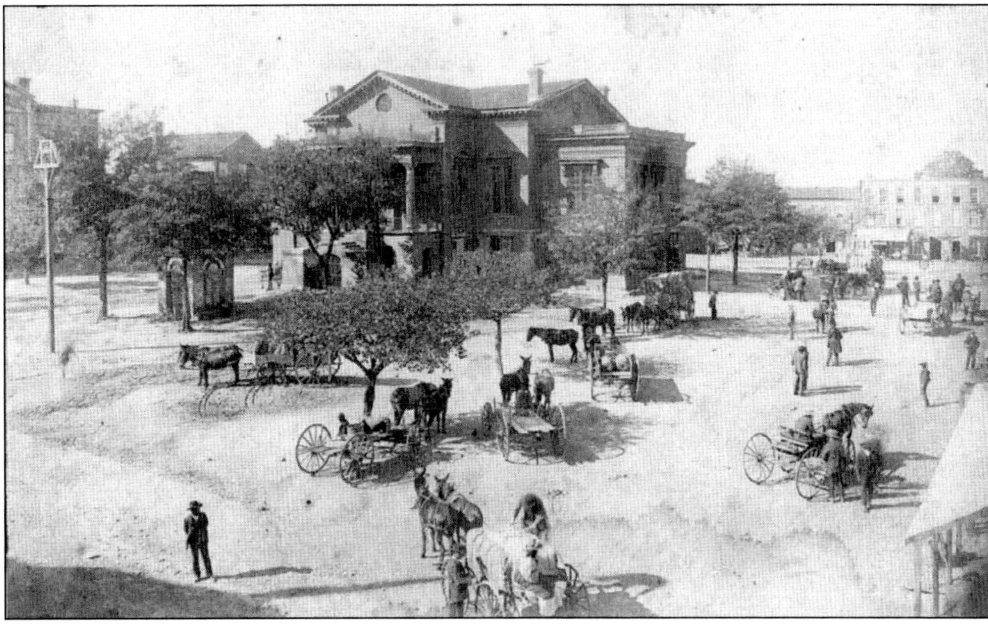

SATURDAY IN LAURENS. Citizens from the rural areas came by horse and wagon to Laurens on Saturday. The Square and Courthouse grounds were bustling with activity as people shopped, visited, and caught up on the news from town. (Courtesy of Laurens County Library.)

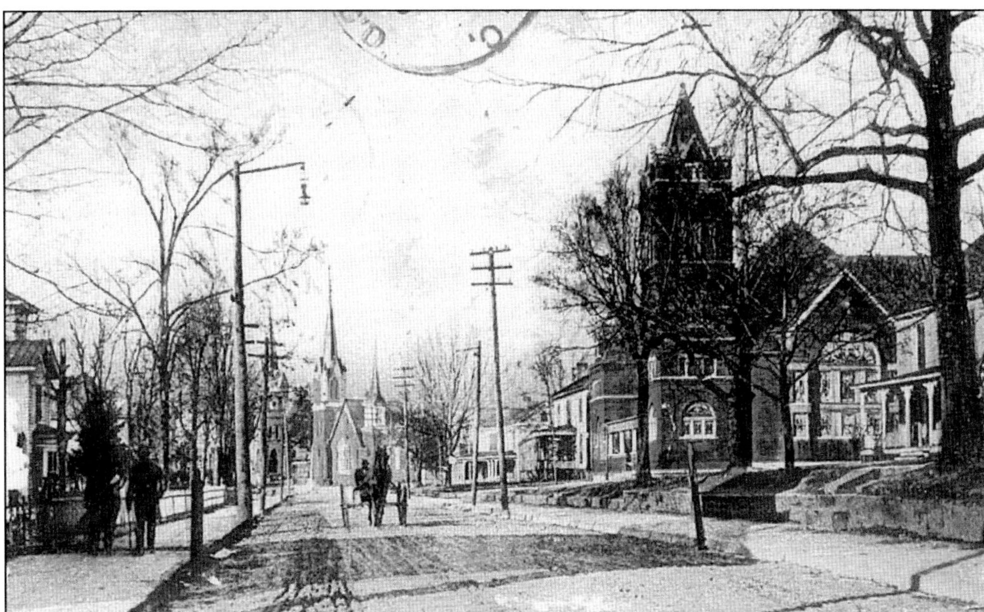

HEADED TO TOWN. A horse and buggy shown traveling down West Main Street moves past the churches and is heading to the Laurens Town Square. The steeple of the Presbyterian church can be seen in the background of the postcard. (Courtesy of Mrs. Katherine Weathers Johnson.)

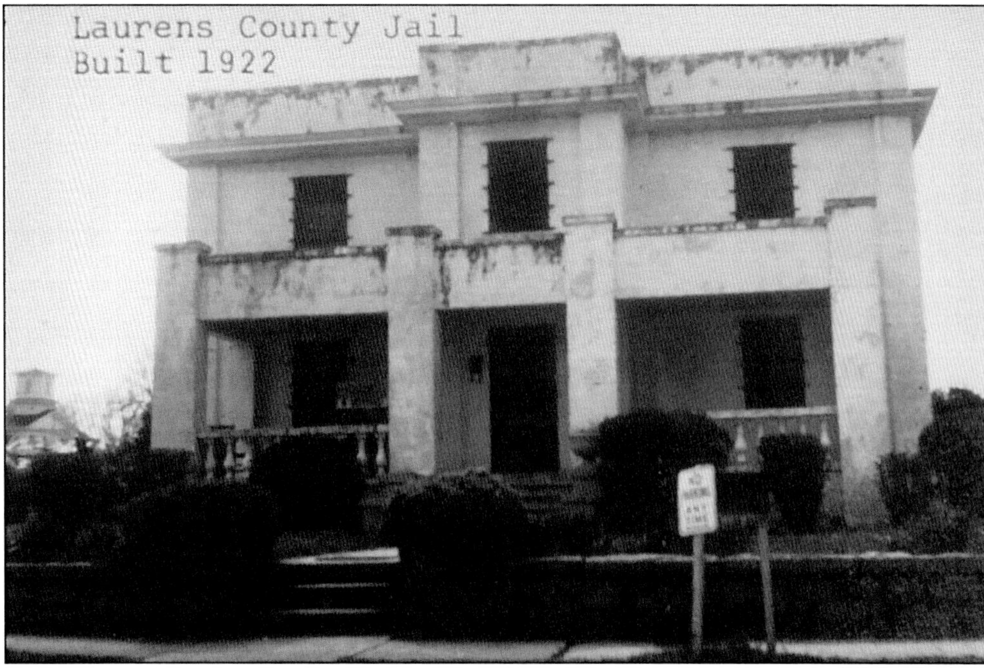

JAIL DESIGNED BY ROBERT MILLS. The third Laurens jail was built between 1826 and 1828 and was designed by the famed architect Robert Mills. The jail was renovated in 1921. Laurens County sheriffs and their families lived on the ground floor, and the cell blocks were located upstairs. There were beds to accommodate 24 male and 2 female prisoners. The kitchen and laundry room were housed in the basement. A clothesline and vegetable garden were located in the rear of the jail. (Courtesy of Laurens County Library.)

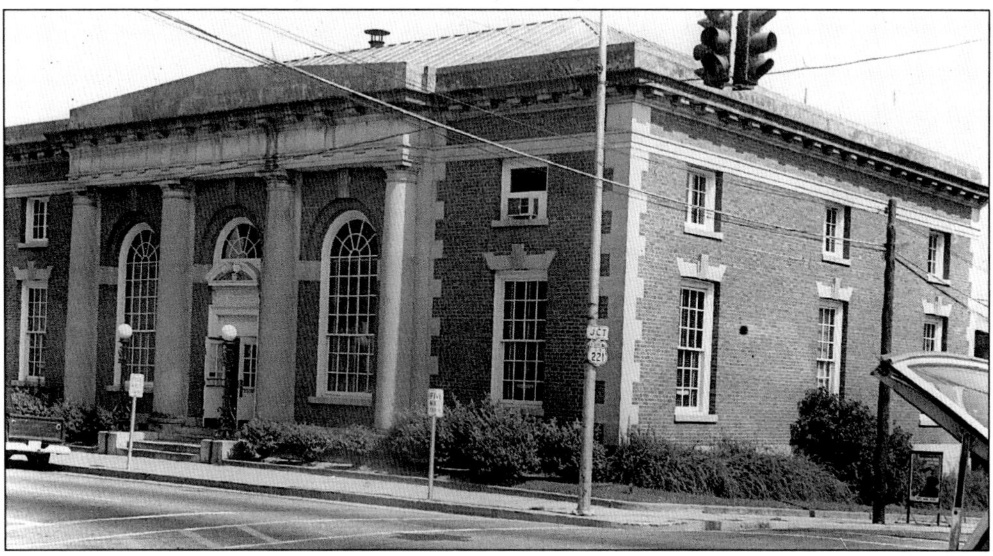

POST OFFICE. The Federal Building was constructed in 1913 on the corner of West Main and Caroline Streets. It replaced a small wooden post office, which was located on the Anderson property on West Main. The brick building remained in use until a new post office was constructed on North Harper Street in 1965, at which time the Palmetto Bank purchased the Federal Building and razed it for a parking lot. (Courtesy of Laurens County Library.)

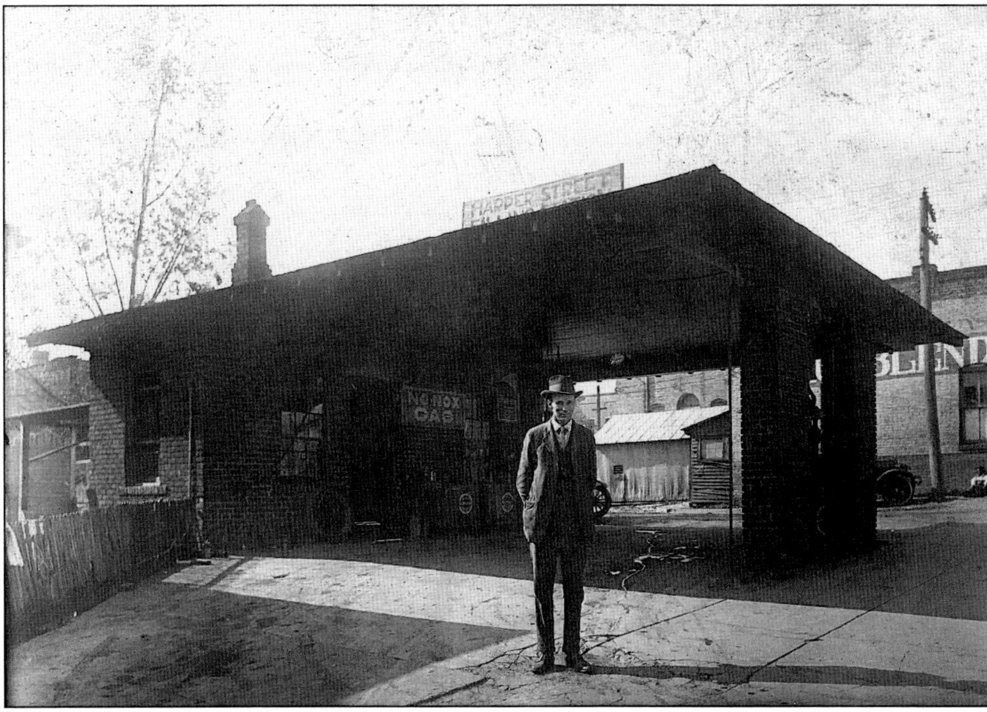

Service with a Smile. Service stations began replacing livery stables in the early 1900s, as many Laurens residents were purchasing automobiles. J.A. Taylor opened a station in 1925 and serviced vehicles on the corner of South Harper and South Streets for many years. (Courtesy of the late Wesley Taylor.)

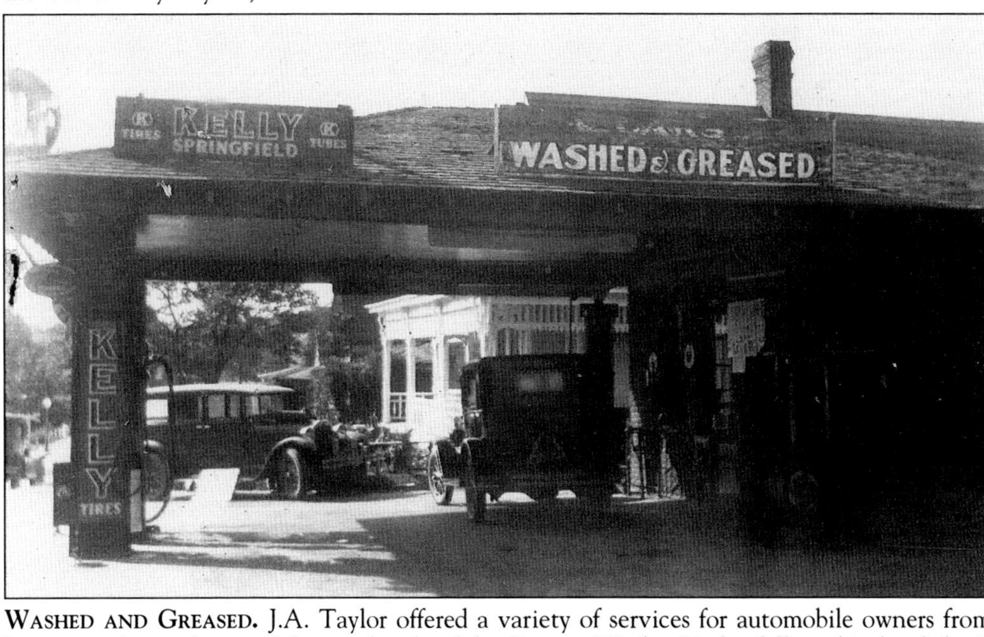

Washed and Greased. J.A. Taylor offered a variety of services for automobile owners from his station located just off the south side of the Square. Wesley Taylor followed in his father's footsteps and continued his reputation of good service, thus making the Taylors respected businessmen in the town of Laurens. (Courtesy of the late Wesley Taylor.)

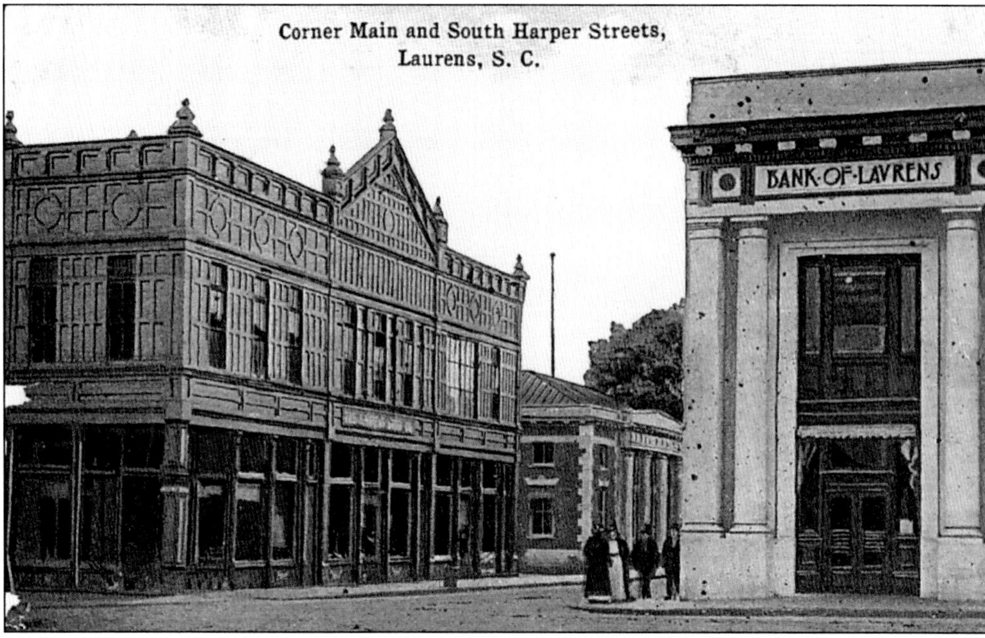

CORNER OF MAIN AND SOUTH HARPER STREET. The Bank of Laurens is the building on the right, standing on the corner of South Harper and Main Streets. (Courtesy of Laurens County Library.)

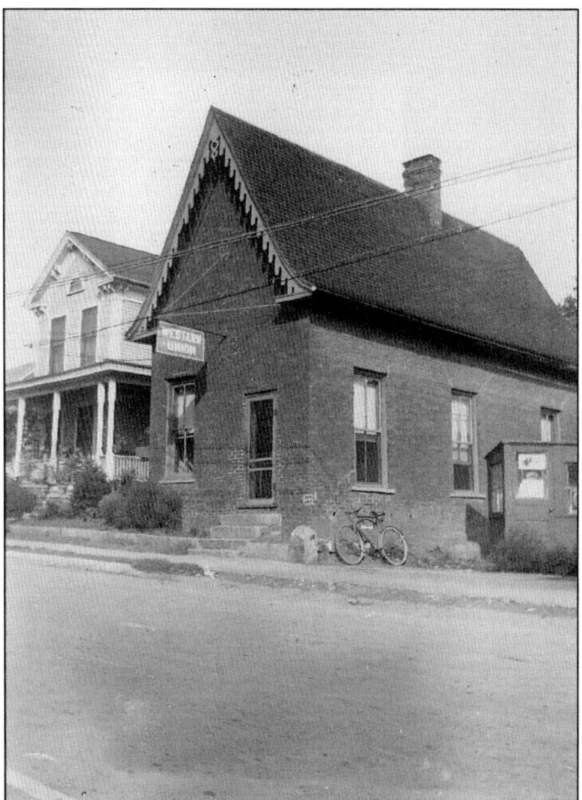

TELEGRAPH OFFICE. No longer standing, this quaint brick building located on West Main Street housed the telegraph office. Just off the Laurens Public Square, the office was a necessary utility to Laurens citizens and business establishments. Miss Sue Dean was the operator and is fondly recalled by many Laurens residents. (Courtesy of Miss Louise McCord.)

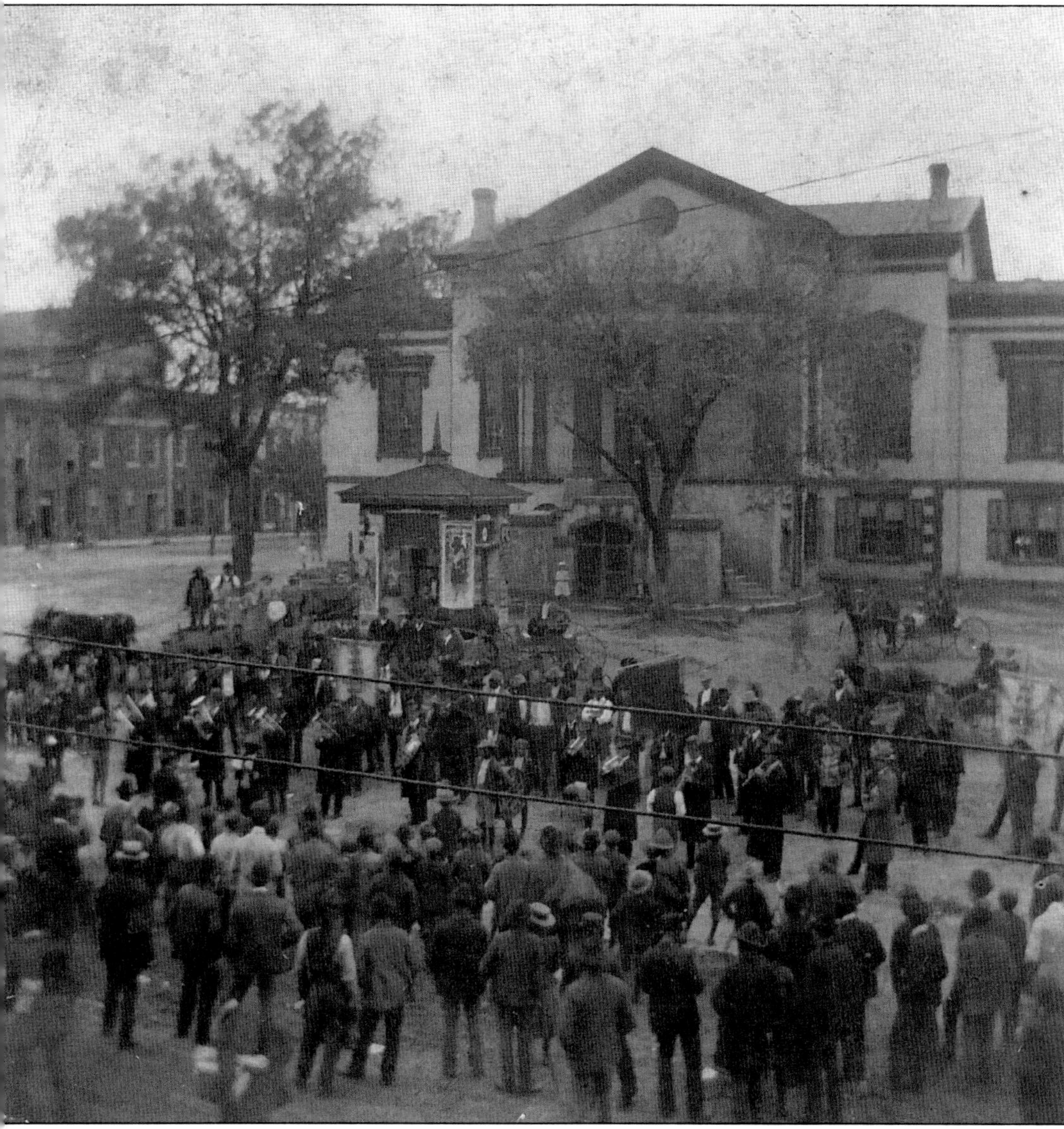

CROWD CONGREGATING AT THE COURTHOUSE. Laurens citizens are seen here congregating on the south side of the Laurens County Courthouse. The west side of the Laurens Square is seen through the branches of a young oak tree. Also one of the town wells is visible. (Courtesy of Mrs. Beatrice Babb Bradley.)

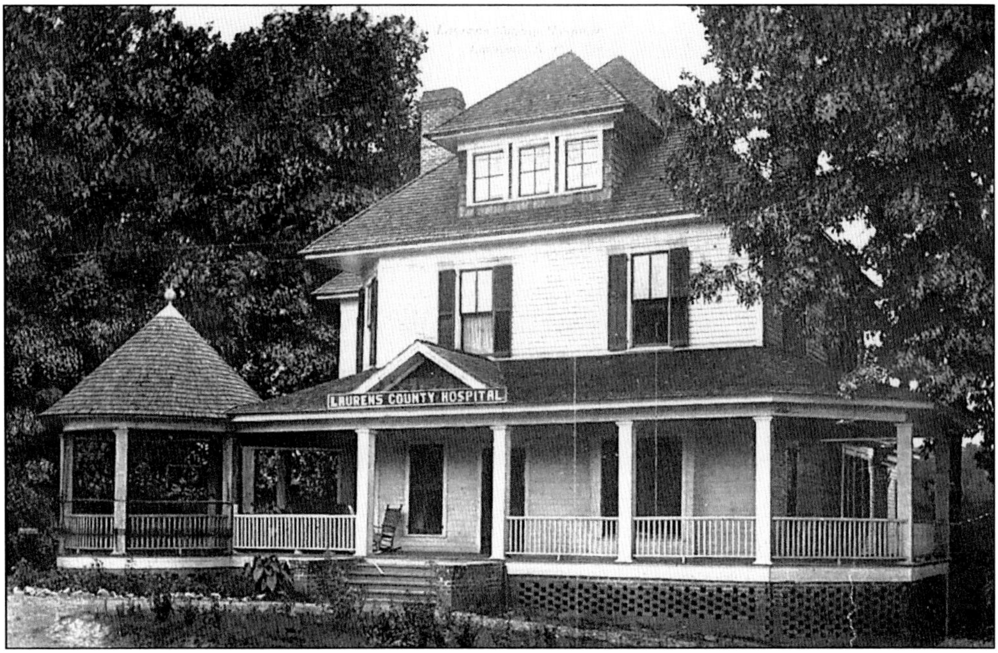

First Hospital. To serve the medical needs of the growing city of Laurens, Miss Julia Irby started the first hospital, housed in the Irby House on Chestnut Street. (Courtesy of the Laurens County Library.)

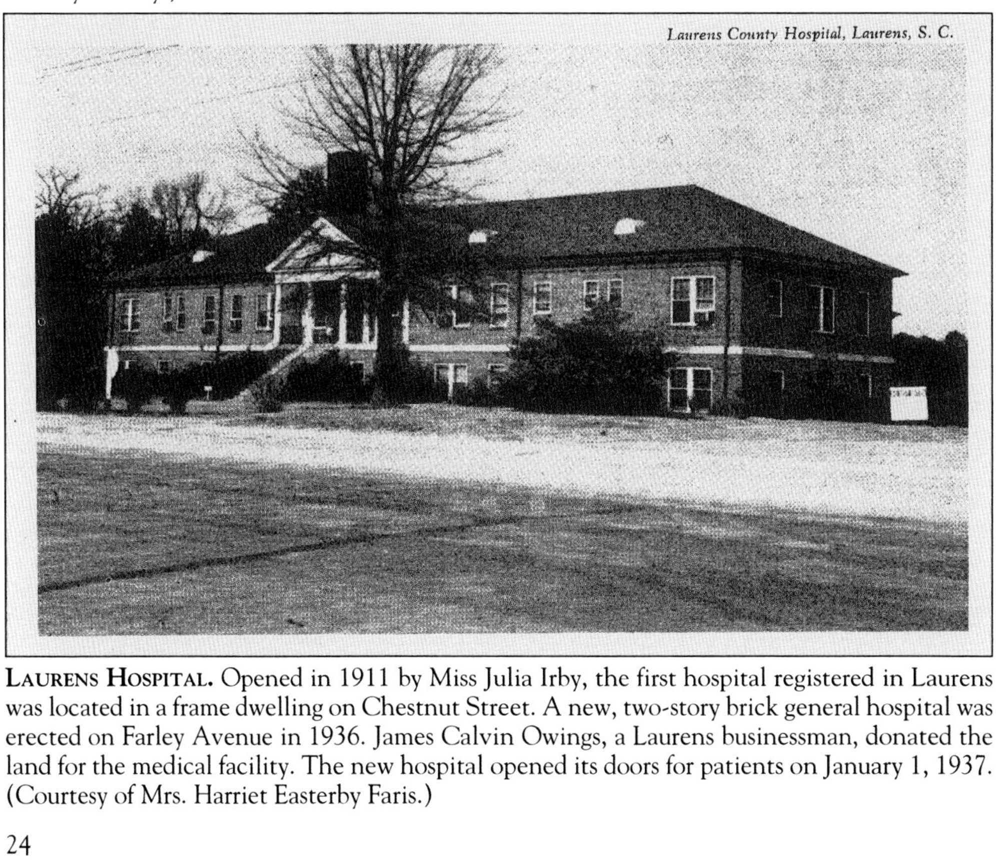

Laurens Hospital. Opened in 1911 by Miss Julia Irby, the first hospital registered in Laurens was located in a frame dwelling on Chestnut Street. A new, two-story brick general hospital was erected on Farley Avenue in 1936. James Calvin Owings, a Laurens businessman, donated the land for the medical facility. The new hospital opened its doors for patients on January 1, 1937. (Courtesy of Mrs. Harriet Easterby Faris.)

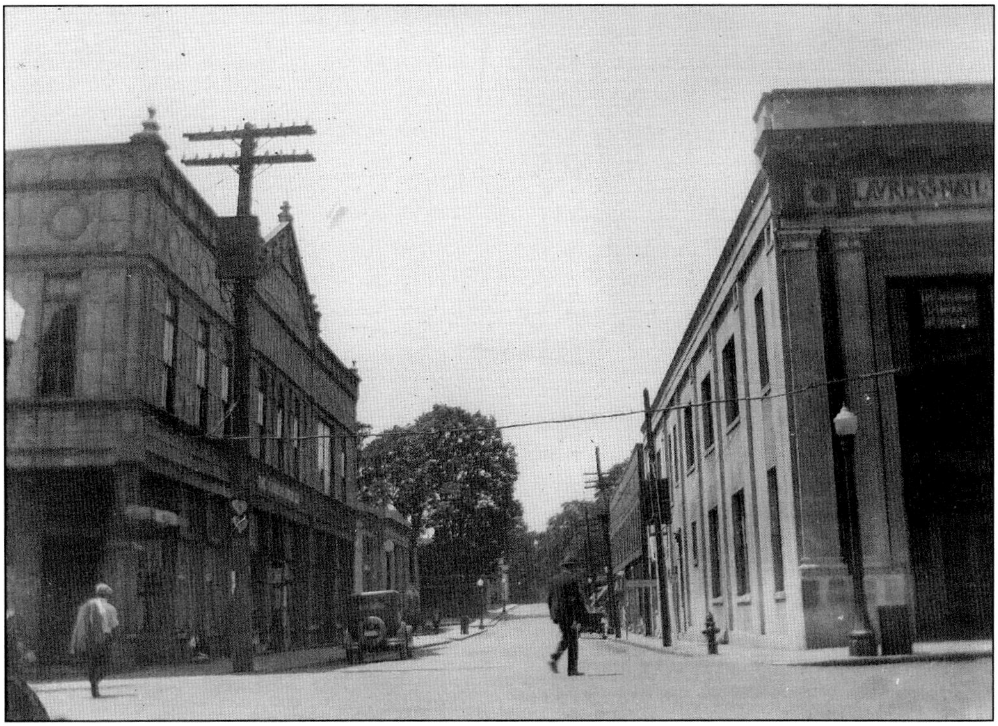

Street Corner. This photograph showing a pedestrian crossing the street at South Harper and Main was taken by the town's most popular photographer, Luther McCord. (Courtesy of Miss Louise McCord.)

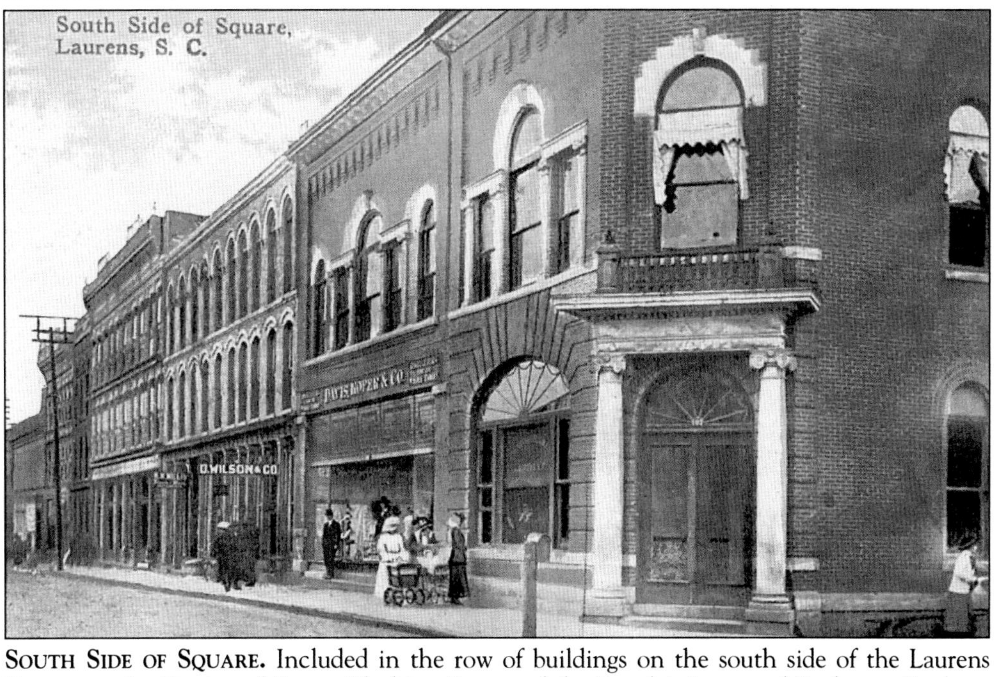

South Side of Square. Included in the row of buildings on the south side of the Laurens Square are the Davis and Roper Clothing Store and the People's Loan and Exchange Bank on the corner of South Harper Street. (Courtesy of Laurens County Library.)

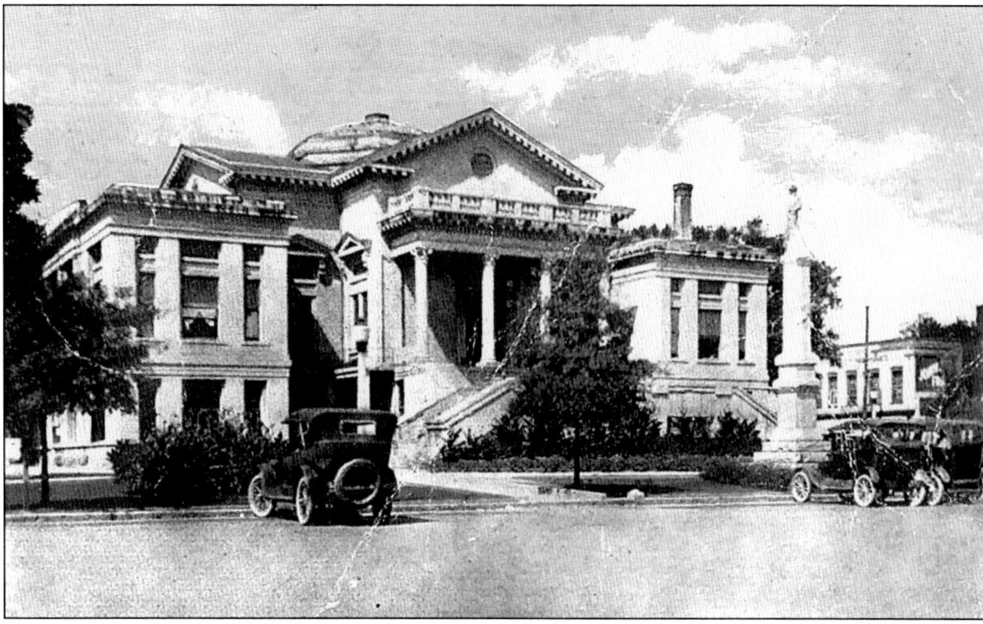

Automobiles on the Square. Automobiles replaced horse and buggies on the Laurens Square in the 1900s. With the advent of gas-powered vehicles, the Courthouse and Square became more accessible to rural residents. (Courtesy of the Rhodes collection.)

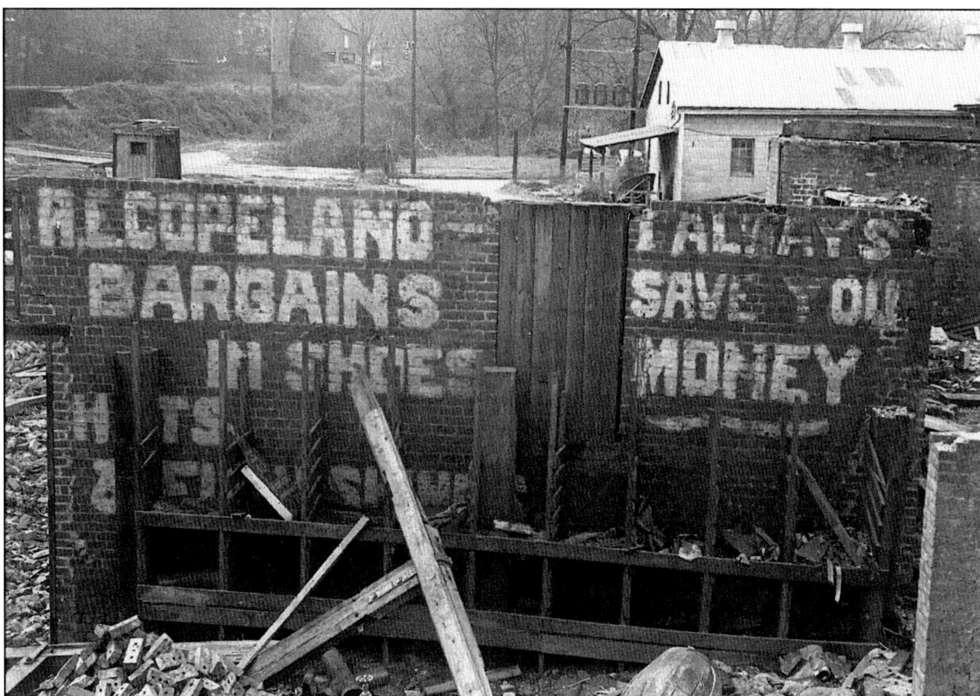

Discovery. While tearing down a building on Fleming Street some years ago, workmen discovered an advertisement from a store of the past, "R.L. Copeland, Bargains." (Courtesy of the *Laurens County Advertiser* files.)

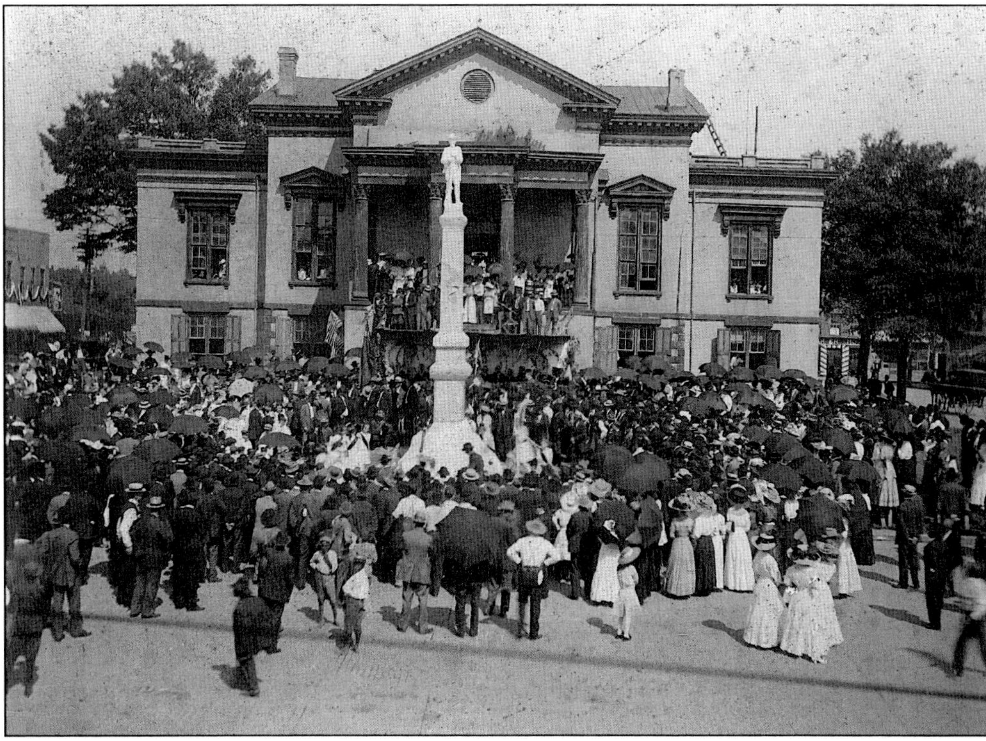

UNVEILING OF THE CONFEDERATE MONUMENT. On September 28, 1910, a large crowd convened on the south side of the Laurens Courthouse for the unveiling of the Confederate Monument, under the auspices of the J.B. Kershaw Chapter United Daughters of the Confederacy. Note the front of the Courthouse before remodeling occurred. (Courtesy of Mrs. Beatrice Babb Bradley.)

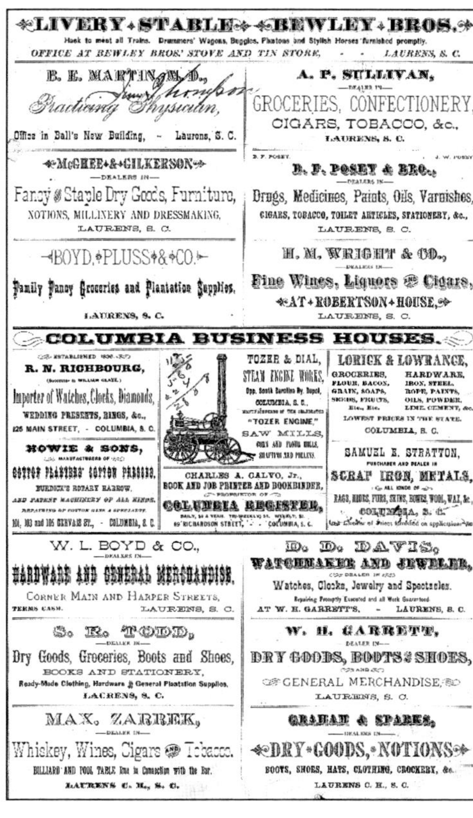

ADVERTISEMENT. An 1884 advertisement from Laurens Courthouse lists, along with other specialties, dry goods, jewelry, boots, whiskey, billiards, hardware, scrap iron, groceries, medicines, furniture, tobacco, and millinery. Also interesting is "Bewley Bros. Livery Stable, Hacks to meet all trains, Drummers' Wagons, Buggies, Phaetons and Stylish Horses furnished promptly." (Courtesy of the Rhodes collection.)

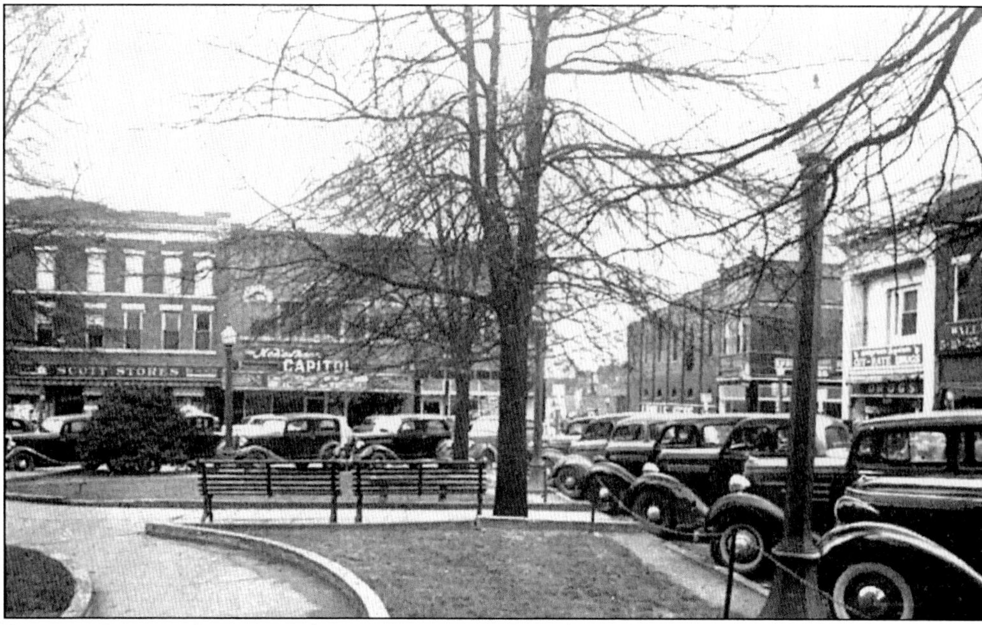

PARKING SPACES. As Laurens business concerns flourished, the Square became a busy shopping center for town residents as well as citizens from all areas of the county. Parking spaces were added to the Square and at times, especially if court was in session, it became impossible to find a "parking place." (Courtesy of the Rhodes collection.)

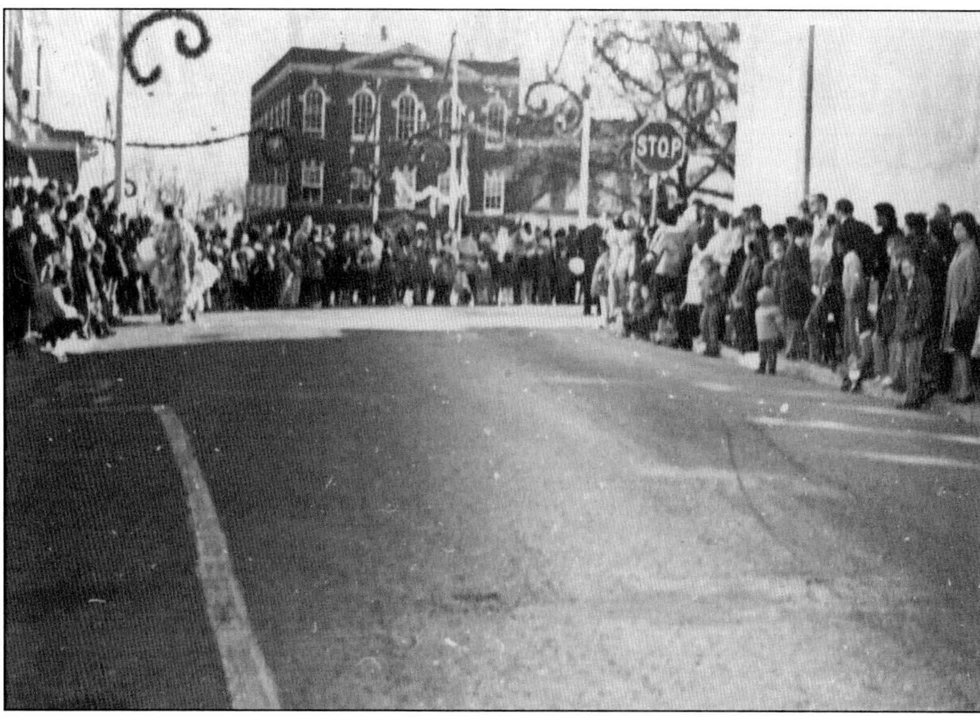

PARADE DOWN LAURENS STREET. Residents line the street to watch the parade advance down Laurens Street. Laurens City Hall is seen in the background. (Courtesy of *Laurens County Advertiser* files.)

Two

Friends, Neighbors, and Their Homes

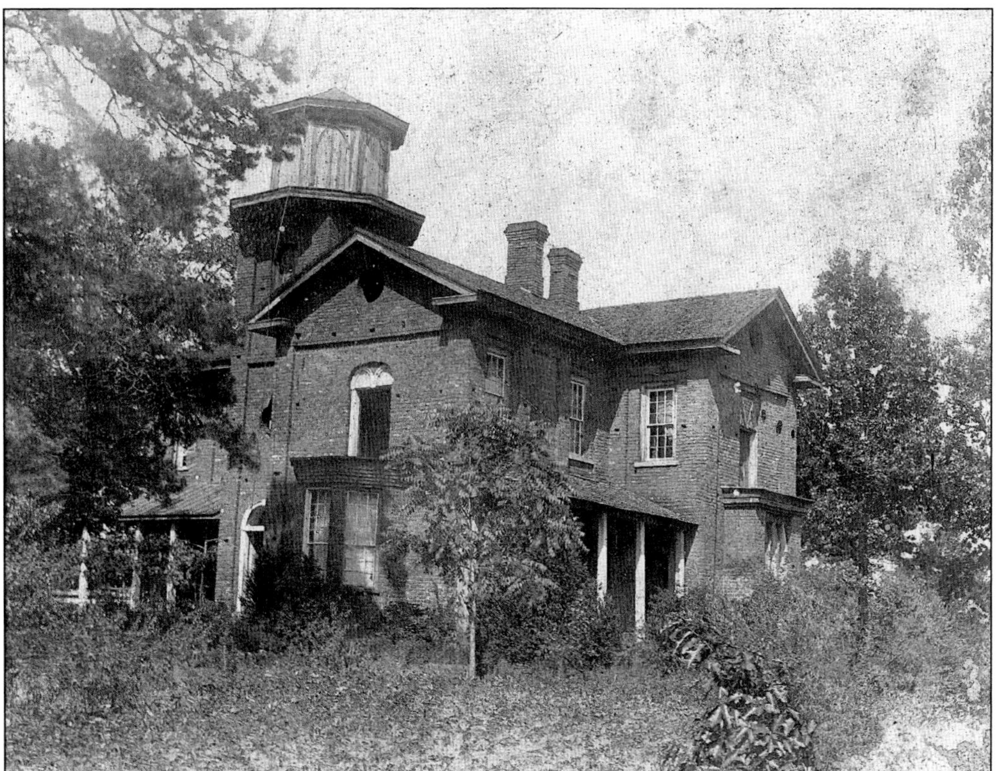

Cupola Removed. Located on the east side of Laurens, the Creswell Garlington House was constructed in 1858. A cupola originally sat atop the house but was removed as a safety precaution after the Charleston earthquake in 1886. The house was constructed of brick by workers on the Garlington Plantation and later covered with stucco. Following Garlington's death, grandson John Wells Todd Jr. and his wife, Kitty Richards Todd, became owners of the home. (Courtesy of John Wells Todd IV.)

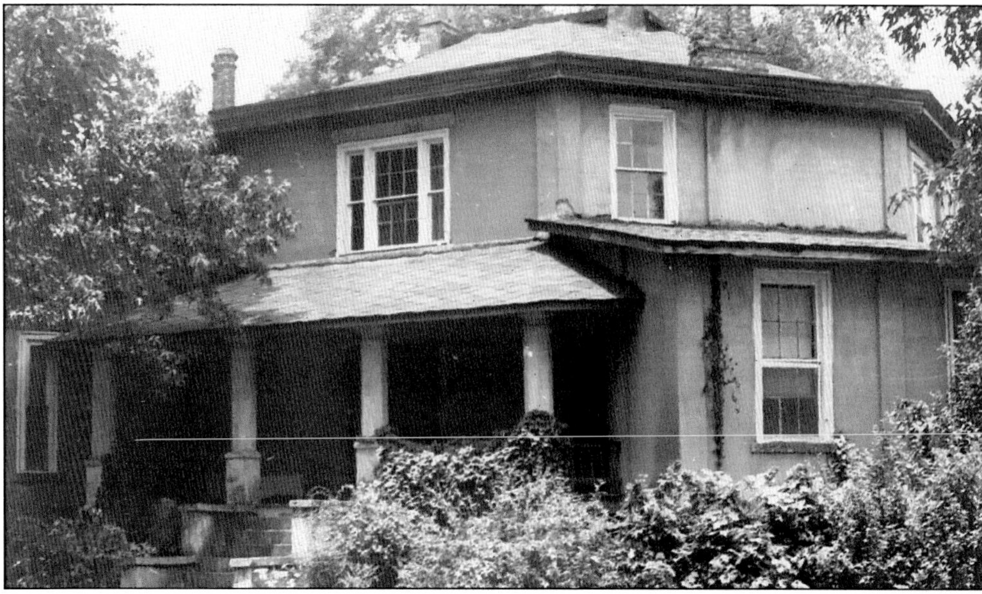

Octagon House. Zelotes Holmes, a Presbyterian minister and educator, was elected professor of the Laurensville Female College in 1859. At that time, he moved to Laurens and constructed the large, 12-room, concrete house on East Main Street. It was one of the first concrete houses in South Carolina. (Courtesy of the Rhodes collection.)

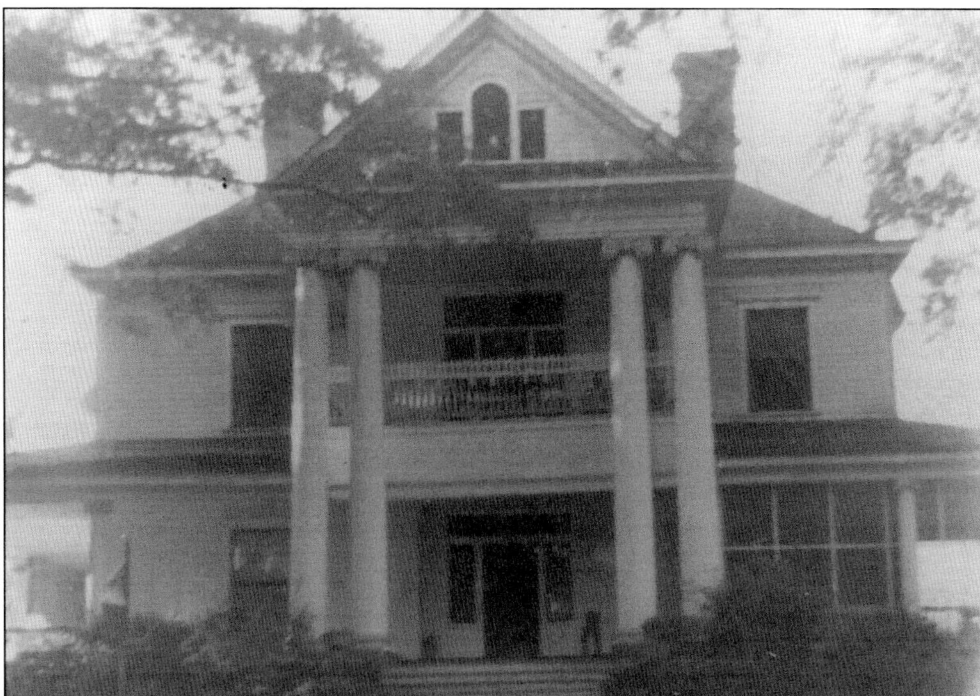

J. Dunklin Watts House. Once located on West Main Street, this residence belonged to J. Dunklin Watts, a farmer and cotton buyer and the son of William Dendy Watts and Sara Cannon Watts. He was married to the former Hattie Frierson, daughter of First Presbyterian Church minister E.O. Frierson. (Courtesy of Laurens County Library.)

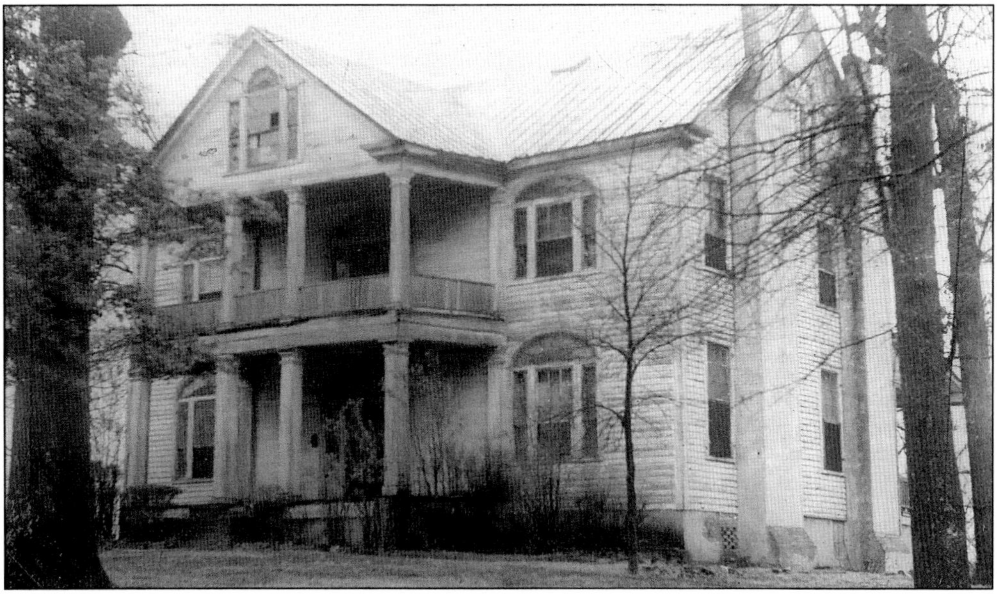

JOHN GARLINGTON HOUSE. In1840 John Garlington constructed a Georgian-style mansion on North Harper Street. It is said that Garlington brought four skilled laborers from Boston to construct the house and that they settled in Laurens and became "good Democrats." After Garlington's death, his son, Stobo, and wife, Mary Young Garlington, inherited the house. In later years, the Roper family resided in the historic home. The house was torn down and replaced by the Laurens Post Office. (Courtesy of the Rhodes collection.)

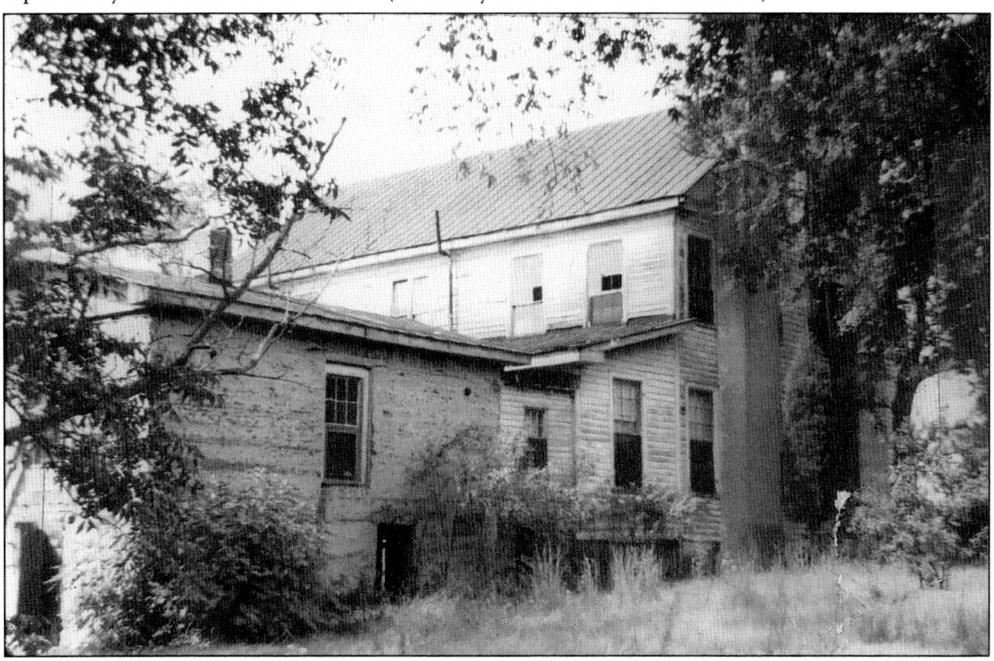

BRICK KITCHEN. A brick kitchen stood behind the John Garlington House on North Harper Street. The structure leaned slightly for many years due to damage from tremors felt in Laurens from the Charleston earthquake of 1886, and the kitchen remained so until it was torn down in the 1960s. (Courtesy of the Rhodes collection.)

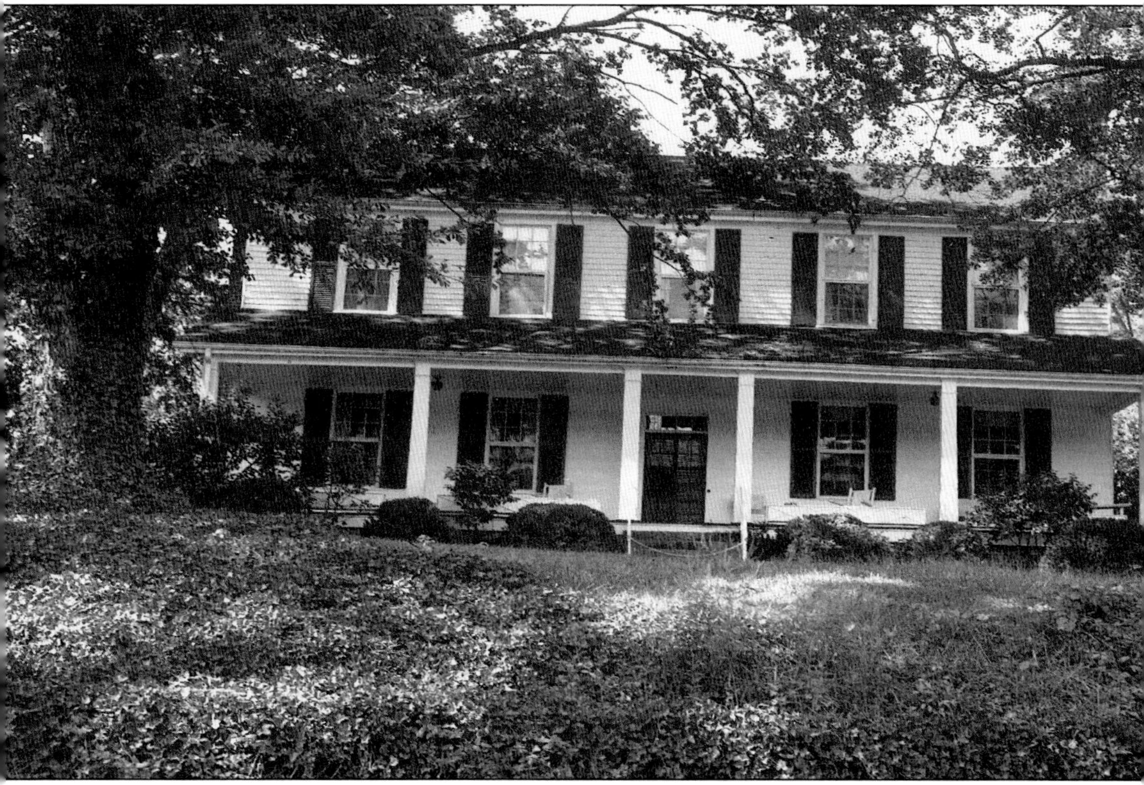

NINETEENTH-CENTURY VERNACULAR STYLE. The house was constructed *c.* 1812 by Washington Williams as a wedding gift to his daughter, Nancy, who married James Watts. Following Watts's death, his widow sold the property to Samuel Todd in 1843 and it remained in the Todd family until the early 1930s. H.E. Timmons was the next owner, followed by James G. Dunklin. The two-story, clapboard house is a classic example of an Upcountry farmhouse. (Courtesy of Laurens County Library.)

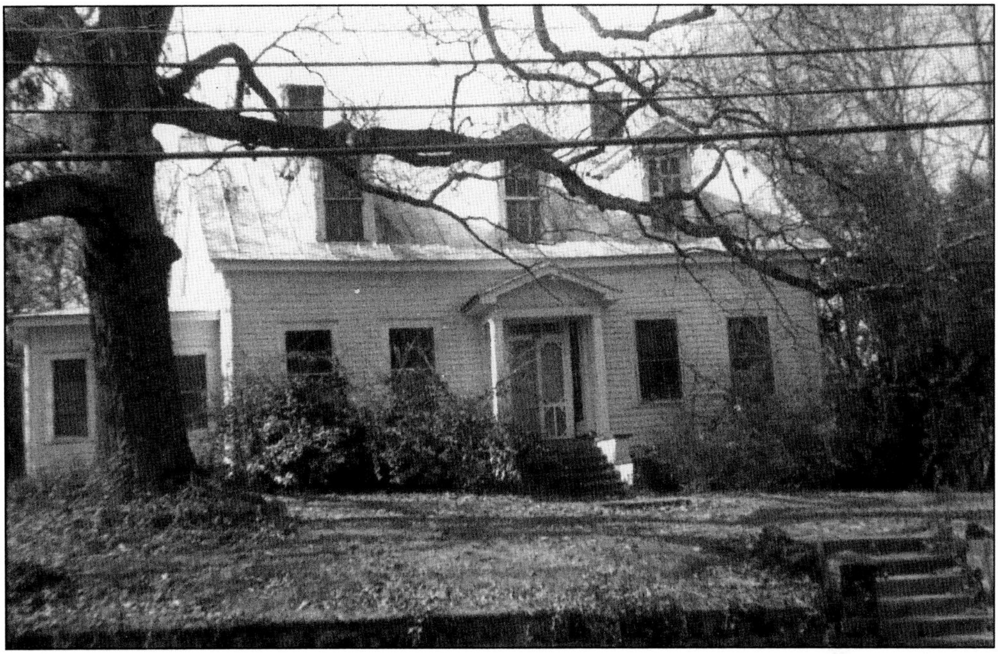

CURVED STAIRCASE. After leaving Virginia and settling in Union, Jesse Scott Hix arrived in the village of Laurens c. 1850. He constructed a house with three dormer windows on South Harper Street. The curved staircase was a special feature of the house. Jesse Hix and his brother Edward operated a furniture factory and gristmill on Hix Creek. Persons traveling on South Harper and Sullivan Streets forded the stream to enter the village of Laurens. Homer Blackwell, a Laurens attorney, later purchased the residence. (Courtesy of the Rhodes collection.)

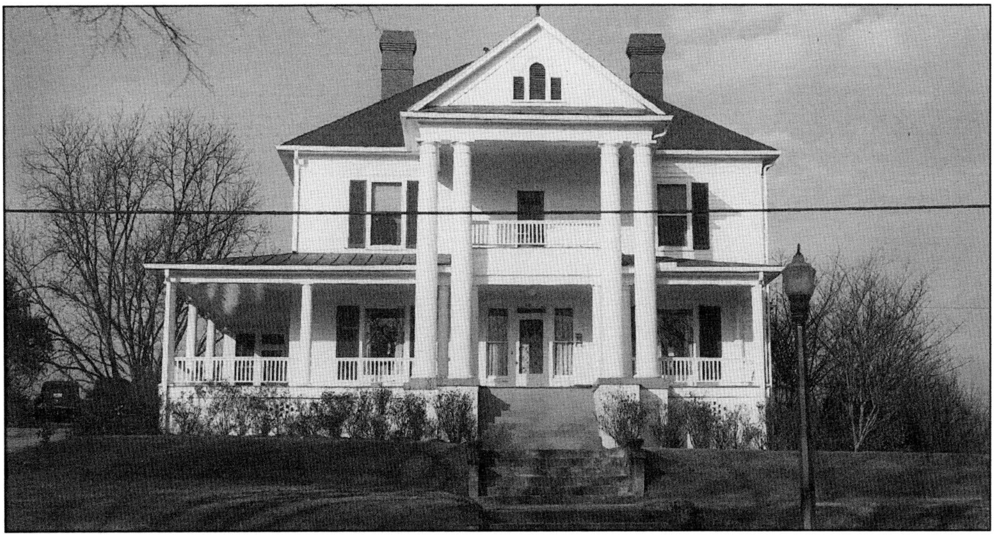

H. DOUGLAS GRAY RESIDENCE. H. Douglas Gray, son of Hugh E. and Susie Sullivan Gray, was married to Lucille Martin, daughter of Ambrose and Harriett Rook Martin of the Chestnut Ridge section of Laurens County in 1909. The Grays constructed a white-columned, two-story house on South Harper Street. They were members of the First Methodist Church and were ardent supporters of many local civic and religious enterprises. (Courtesy of Mrs. Harriet Gray Hunter.)

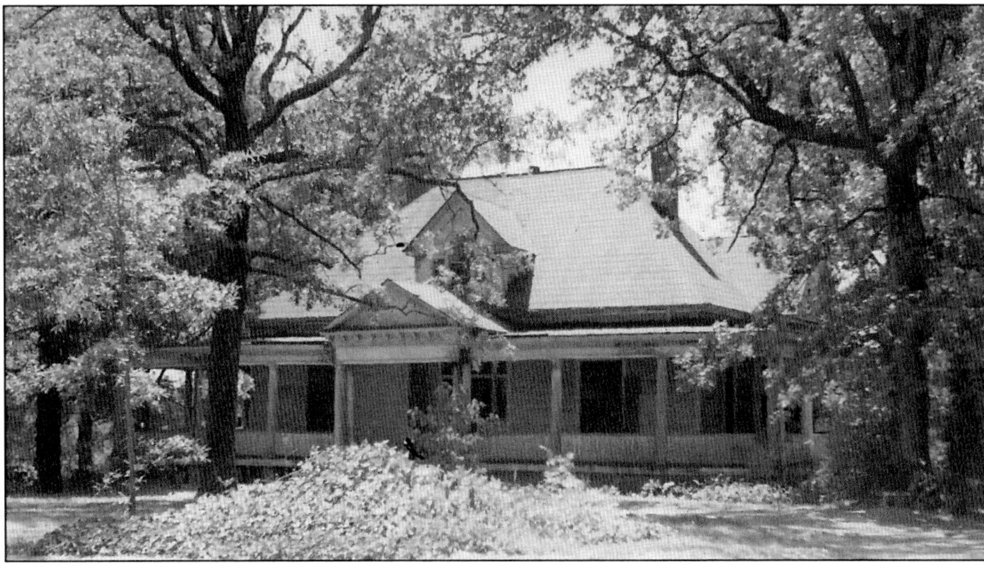

BOBO HOUSE. A native of Cross Anchor, Charles Bobo moved to Laurens in 1882. He was married to Mattie Barksdale of the Gray Court section of the county. In 1887 Bobo and J.C. Owings opened a firm that was for many years one of the largest operations in the Upcountry, dealing in all lines of farm supplies. A member of the First Baptist Church, Bobo was widely known throughout Baptist circles across the South. Charles Bobo built this West Main Street house and lived there with his wife until his death in 1944. (Courtesy of the Rhodes collection.)

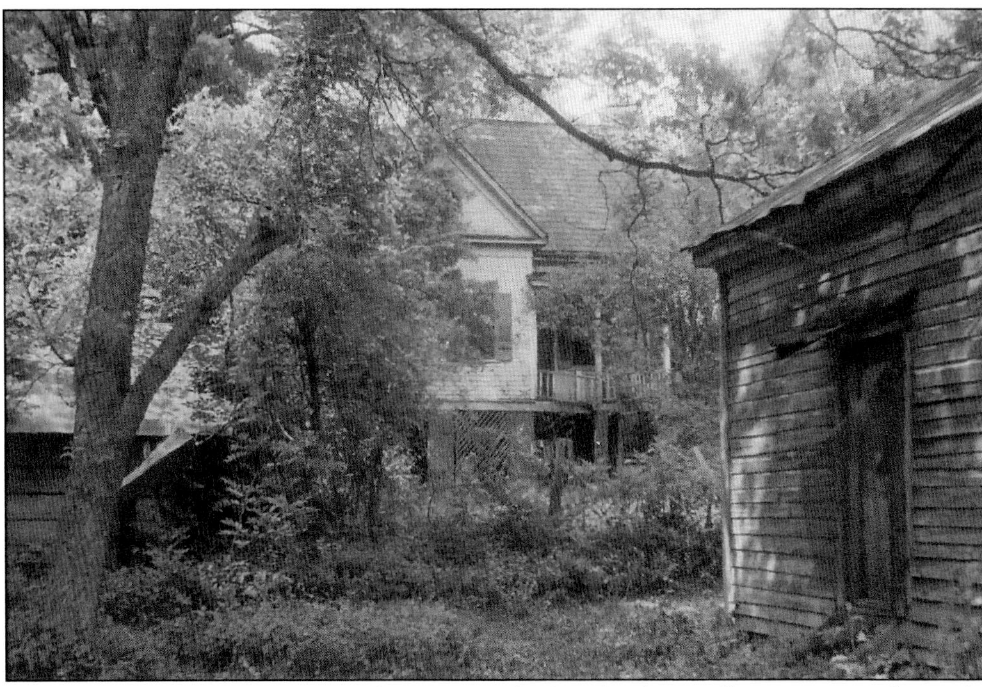

SERVANT'S HOUSE. As in many other Laurens backyards, the small cottage was the cook's house and was located behind the home of Mr. and Mrs. Charles Bobo on West Main Street. (Courtesy of the Rhodes collection.)

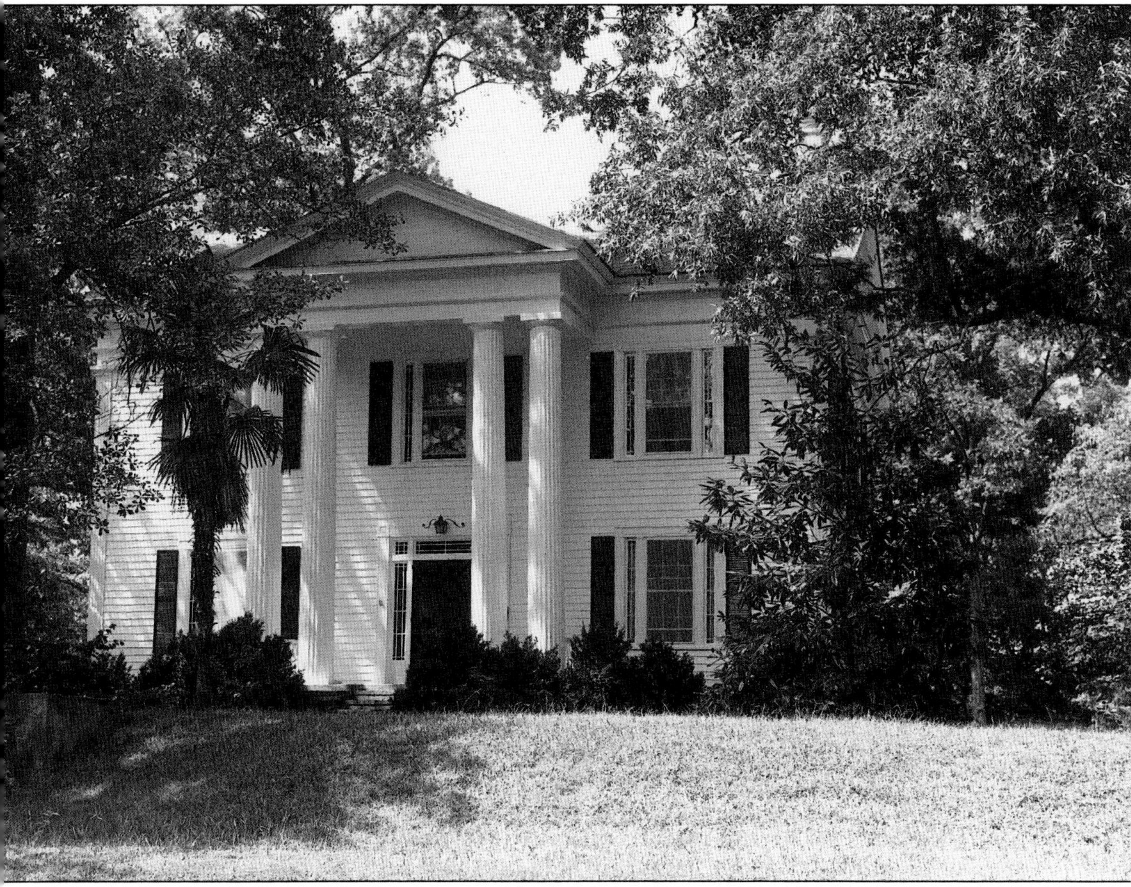

GOVERNOR SIMPSON HOUSE. Christopher Garlington constructed this Greek Revival dwelling in 1839. Upon his death, son Ernest Garlington inherited the house and its spacious gardens and orchards. Major Adam Eichelberger became the next owner of the colonial mansion. Local legend states that the first apricots grown in South Carolina were found in his garden. William D. Simpson, son of Dr. John Wells Simpson, purchased the house and later became governor of South Carolina. Mason T. and Louise Holmes Motes acquired the West Main Street house in 1939. (Courtesy of Ken Eargle.)

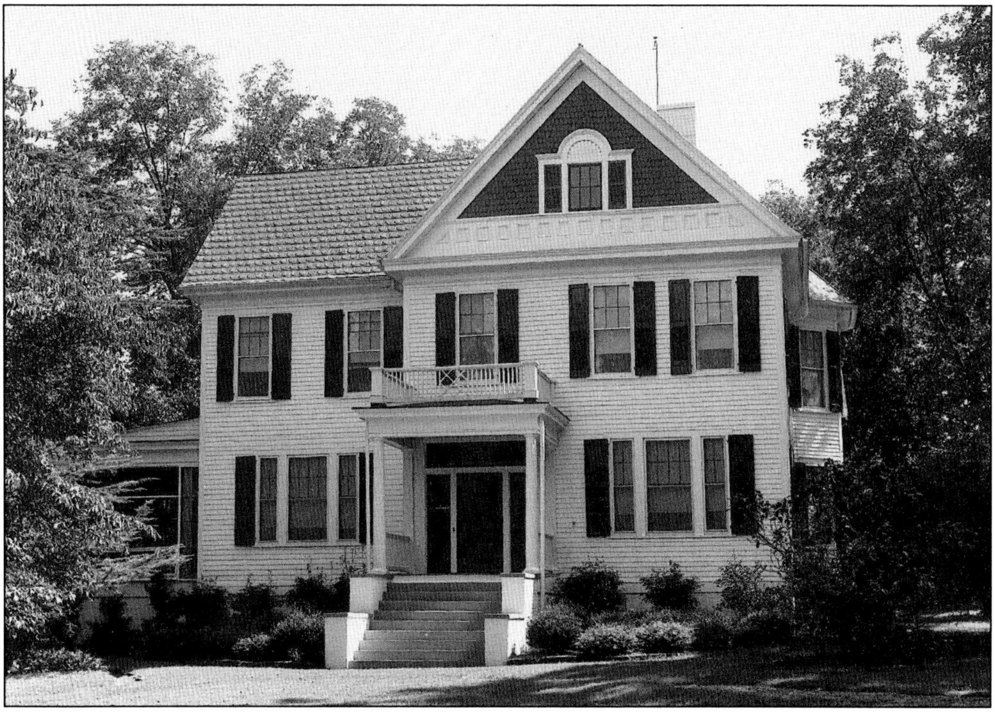

Barksdale House. This tall, stately house on West Main Street was built in 1892 for John Augustus Barksdale, son of Dr. John Allen Barksdale. John Augustus Barksdale helped to found the First National Bank of Laurens in 1896 and served as cashier of the institution. In 1941 the house became the home of Dwight F. and Mary Smith Patterson. Patterson was the president of Palmetto Bank. (Courtesy of Ken Eargle.)

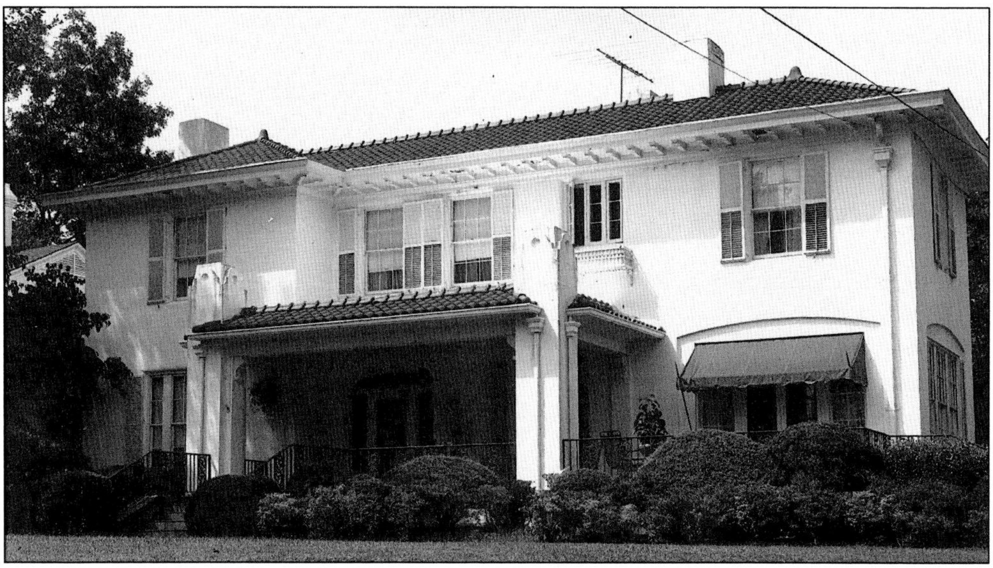

Easterby House. The Spanish-style house located on West Main Street was built by George Wright, a textile executive of Laurens Mills. The house, however, became the home of Ernest D. and Estelle Gregory Easterby. Easterby was a longtime president and chairman of the board of Laurens Glass. (Courtesy of Ken Eargle.)

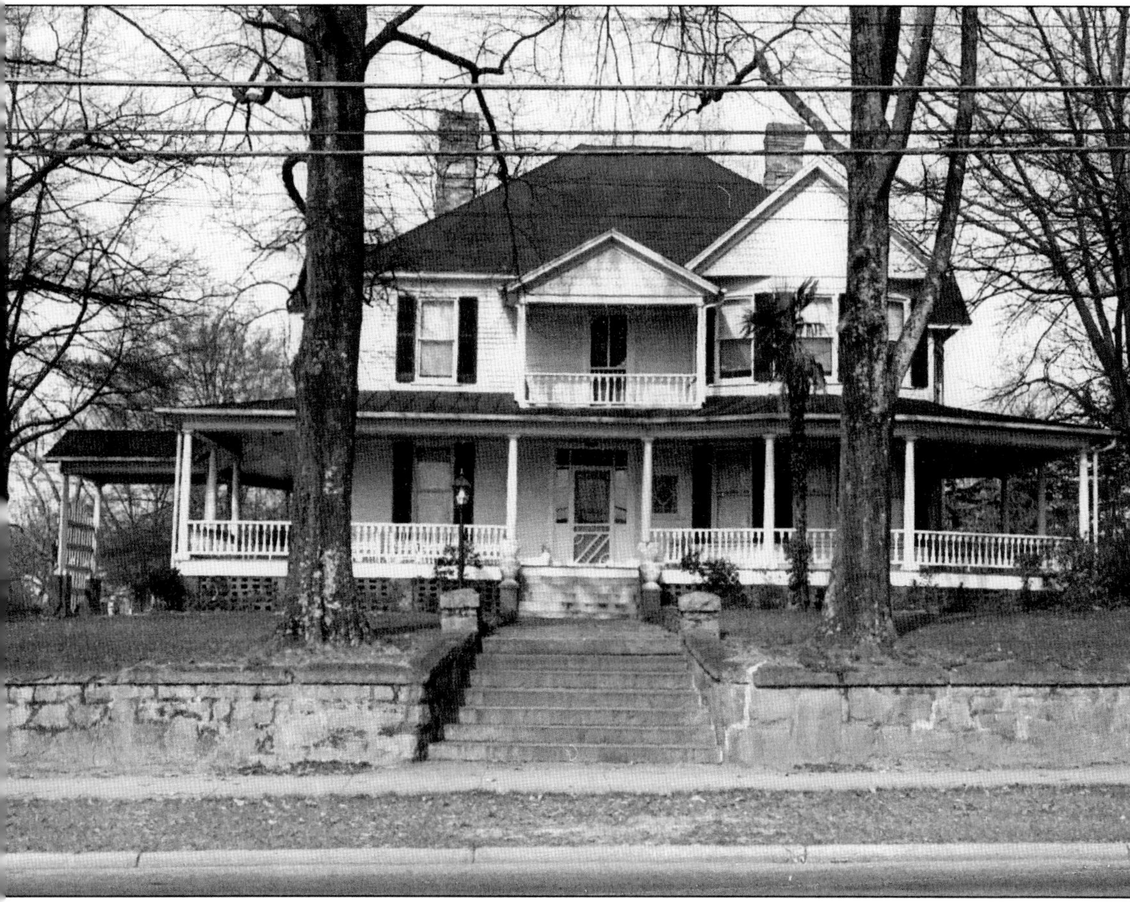

GOVERNOR'S HOME. Standing on South Harper Street is the house once occupied by South Carolina governor Robert Cooper. Before becoming governor in 1918, Cooper served as a magistrate for Laurens, as a solicitor, and as a member of the State House of Representatives. In his younger years, Cooper practiced law with U.S. Senator J.L.M. Irby of Laurens. Cooper died in 1953 and is buried in the Laurens City Cemetery. (Courtesy of the Rhodes collection.)

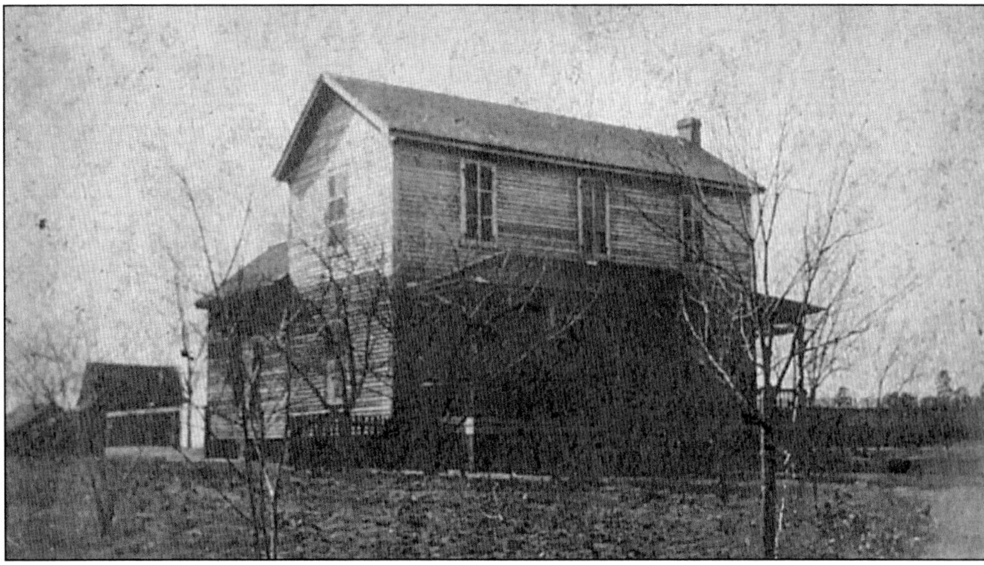

MESSAR BABB HOUSE. Located on Farley Avenue, the two-story frame house was the home of Messar Babb and his wife, Laura Hellams Babb. Messar, the youngest son of Sampson Babb Jr., moved to Laurens from the Babbtown section of the county when he was elected county treasurer. Laura, from Dial's Township, was the daughter of Squire John Hellams. The six children of the family became valuable additions to the civic, political, Masonic, religious, and educational leadership of Laurens. (Courtesy of Mrs. Beatrice Babb Bradley.)

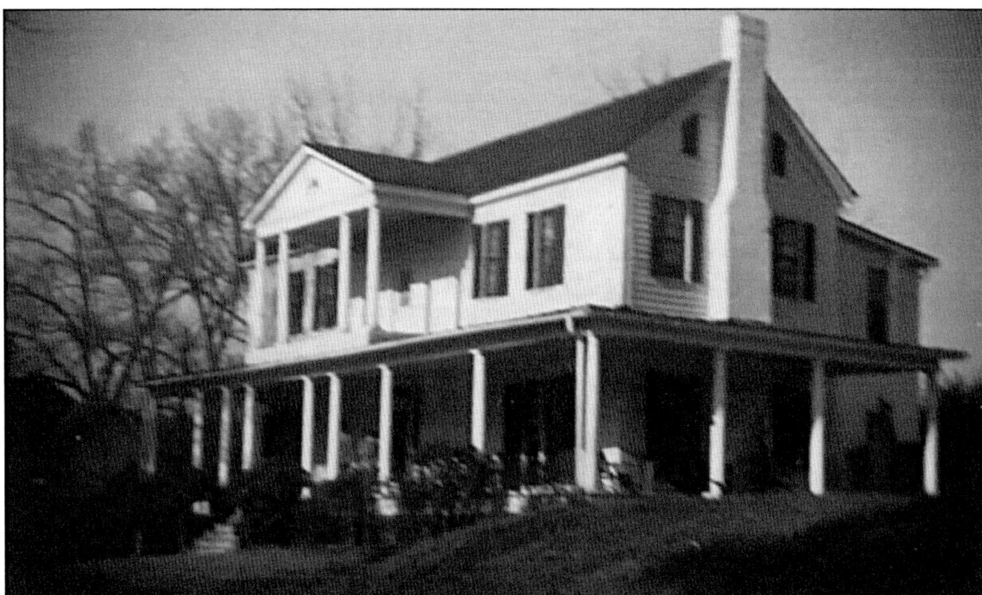

HOUSE MOVED. A valued citizen of Laurens, Dr. John Wells Simpson moved from Belfast, the family plantation, and constructed this house c. 1824 on Laurens Street. Dr. John A. Barksdale purchased the Simpson home, and later, John Warren Bolt, farmer and livestock dealer, bought the house c. 1900. Logs were used to roll the house down the hill to face Church Street. The Laurens Graded School was constructed on the home site. Years later the Commission of Public Works replaced the house. (Courtesy of Laurens County Library.)

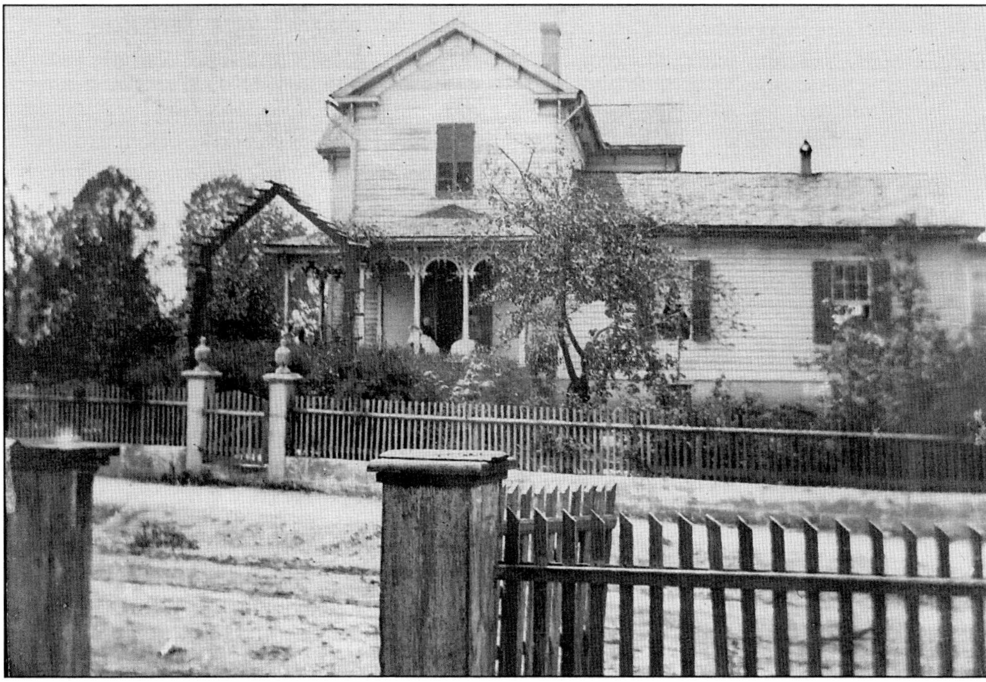

MARTIN DIAL HOUSE. A native of Laurens County, Colonel Williamson Henry Martin and his wife, Anna Sitgreaves Martin, lived in this two-story residence on West Main Street. In his early years, Martin was a merchant, and later in life, he studied law in the office of Colonel R.P. Todd and formed a partnership. He was considered one of the leading civil lawyers in Upstate Carolina. (Courtesy of Mrs. Barbara Dial McAlister.)

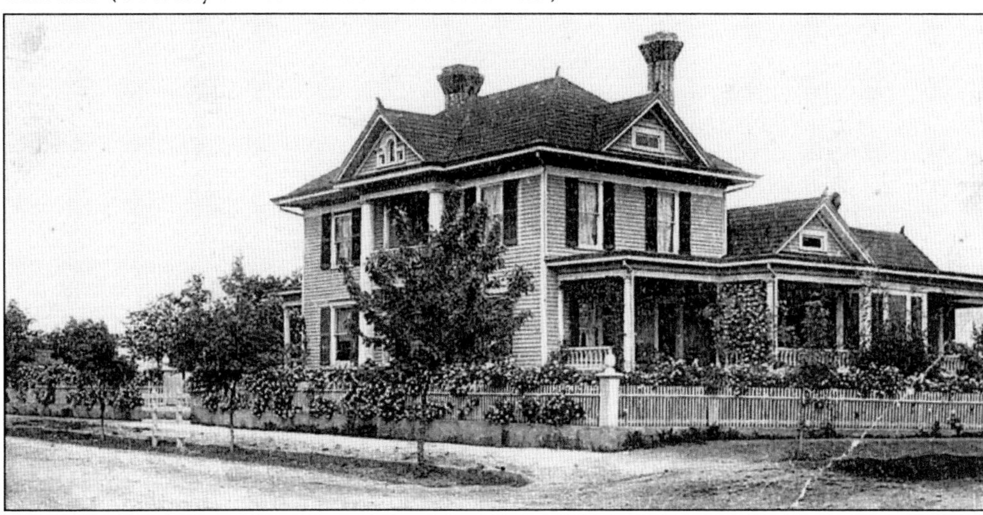

MISS LUCY'S HOUSE. Colonel Henry Williamson and his wife, the former Anna Sitgreaves, lived in this West Main Street residence. Later, Lucy and Albert Dial purchased and moved into the dwelling. It is interesting to note that Anna Sitgreaves was Lucy Sitgreaves Dial's aunt. After the death of Albert Dial, Lucy continued to live in the charming two-story residence, and thus it came to be known as "Miss Lucy's" House. The photograph, taken from West Main Street, shows a front and side view of the residence. (Courtesy of Laurens County Library.)

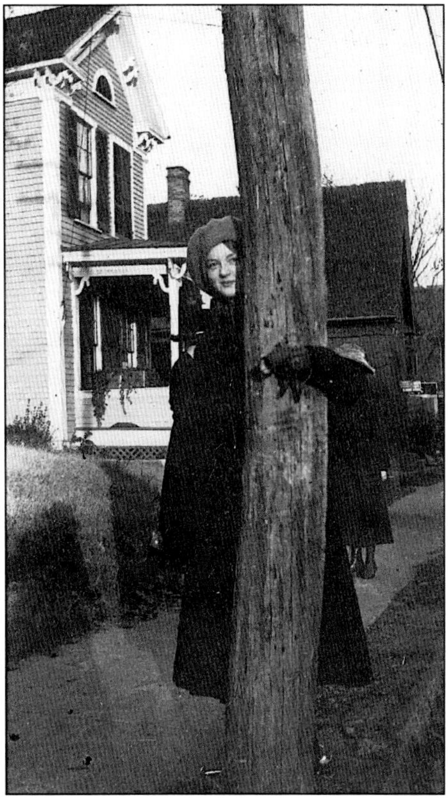

MISS EMMIE'S HOUSE. Emma Lou Washington stands in front of Miss Emmie's House on West Main Street. Emily Meng Jones, "Miss Emmie," was married to Barney Jones. She taught hundreds of elementary schoolchildren during her long career as a teacher in Laurens and was admired and loved by both parents and children. (Courtesy of Mrs. Beatrice Babb Bradley.)

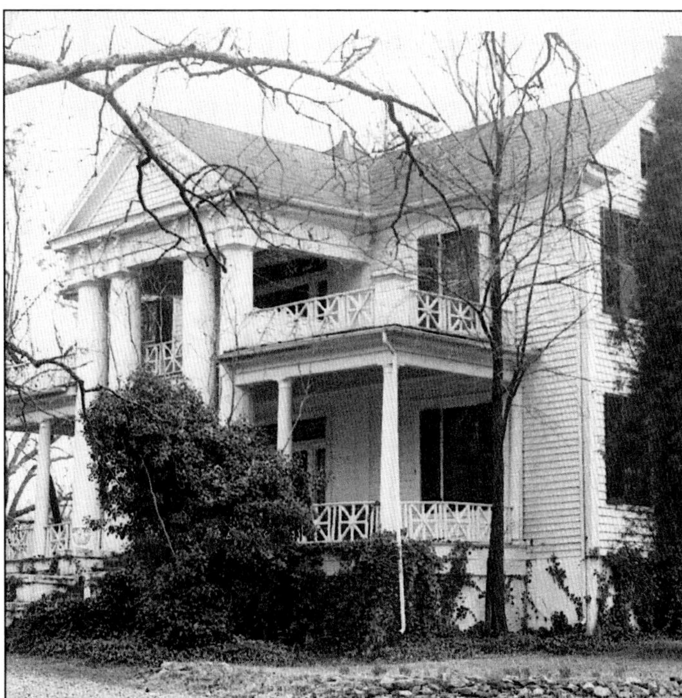

IRBY, HENDERSON, TODD, MCDANIEL HOUSE. James H. Irby built the house *c.* 1838, and it was enlarged by William Henderson *c.* 1855. The residence was enlarged once again by Rutherford P. Todd *c.* 1880. During Todd's ownership, a landscape architect from New York designed the grounds and planted an avenue of oaks leading to the Todd Avenue house. Colonel Todd's son, Samuel, came into possession of the house and moved there in 1905. Robert McDaniel purchased the property in 1921. (Courtesy of Laurens County Library.)

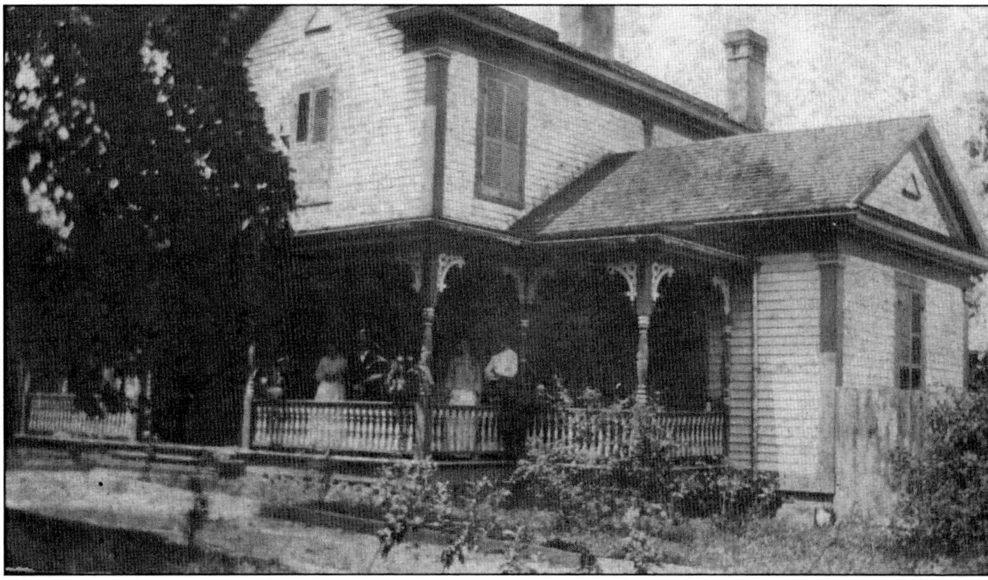

BALLE HOUSE. The Lipman G. Balle house was constructed *c.* 1880 on the corner of West Main and Downs Streets. Lipman George Balle Sr. and his wife, Mary Ann Hellams Balle, lived in the Main Street residence. The house was later owned by the Sitgreaves family and was destroyed by fire in 1927. (Courtesy of Miss Mary Balle.)

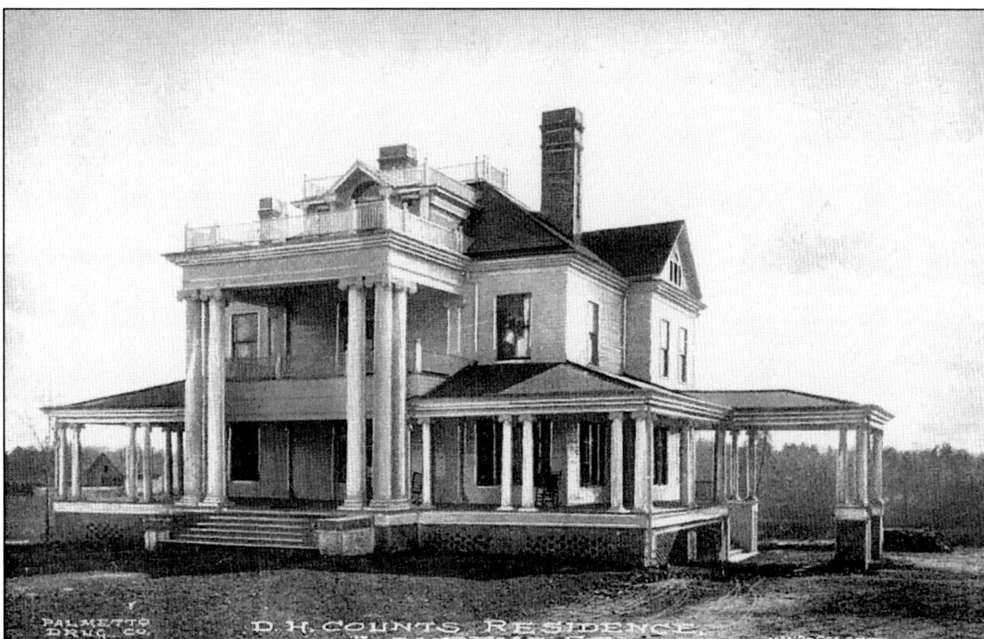

DAVID HENRY COUNTS RESIDENCE. Coming from Bamberg County to Laurens as a young man, D.H. Counts became a prominent livestock dealer. He was held in high esteem for his honesty and fair dealings. Counts and his wife, the former Bessie Hartzog of Greenwood, resided in the West Main house. Later the house was purchased by Dr. and Mrs. Graves L. Knight, and Dr. Knight served as the president of Anderson College. Eventually torn down, the house was replaced by an apartment complex. (Courtesy of Mrs. Katherine Weathers Johnson.)

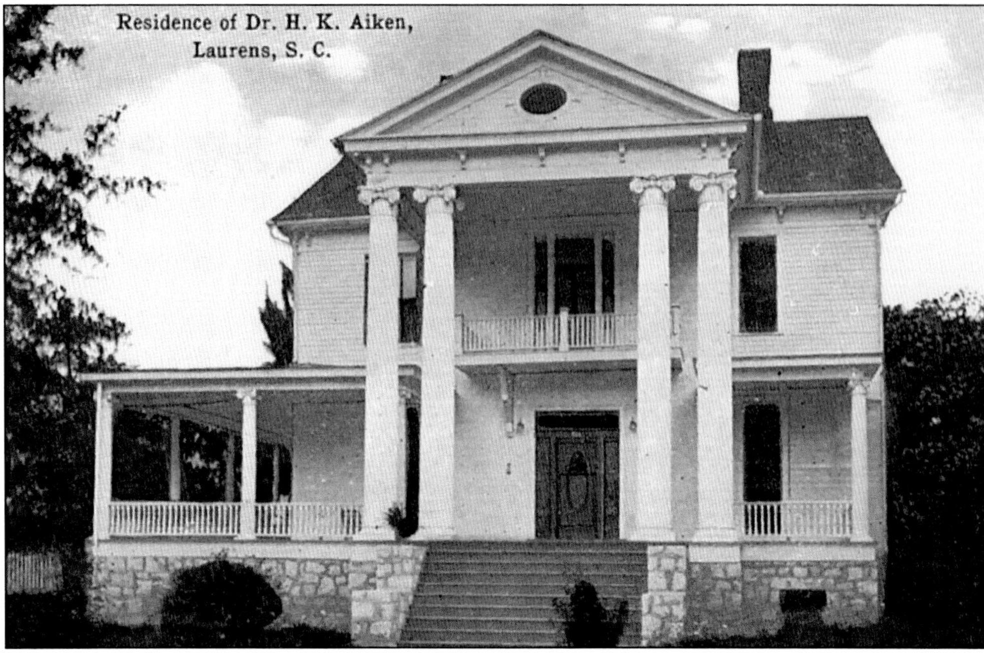

DR. AIKEN HOUSE. Located on West Main Street, Dr. John D. Pitts began construction of this Greek Revival house in the late 1860s, and it was completed *c.* 1870. Dr. Aiken, a doctor, pharmacist, and later a banker, purchased the house in the 1930s. (Courtesy of Laurens County Library.)

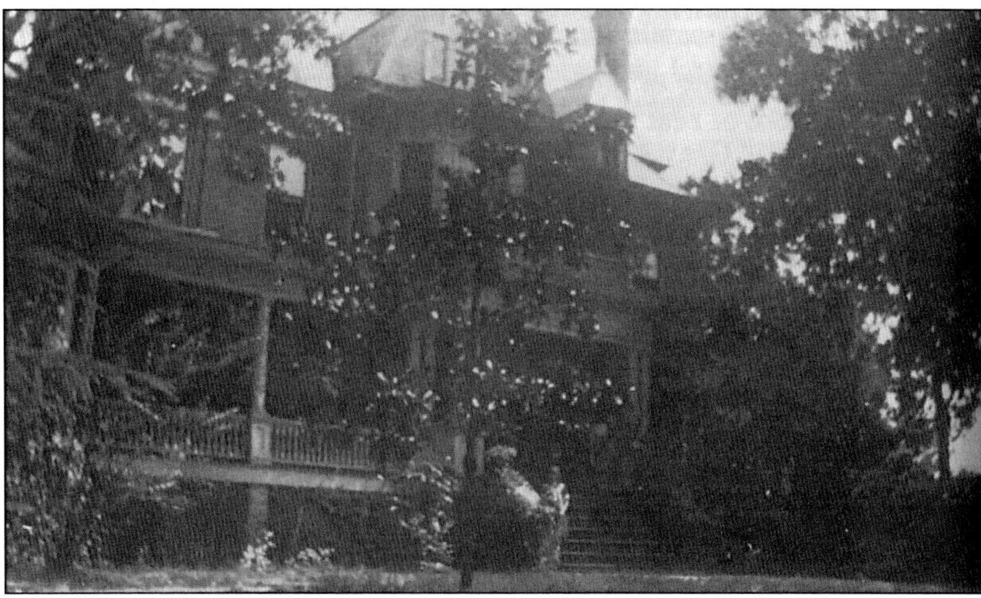

ROMANCE NEXT DOOR. Nathaniel Dial became a widower at the age of 44. From this West Main Street house, he met and fell in love with his neighbor, Josephine Minter. He slipped notes, flowers, and fruits through the gate adjoining the properties. Due to her stepmother's recent death, "Josie" wished to have little fanfare but found it difficult not to flash Nat's gift, a diamond sunburst. It was said that Nat enjoyed a courtship without publicity but not without romance. (Courtesy of the late Rebecca Dial.)

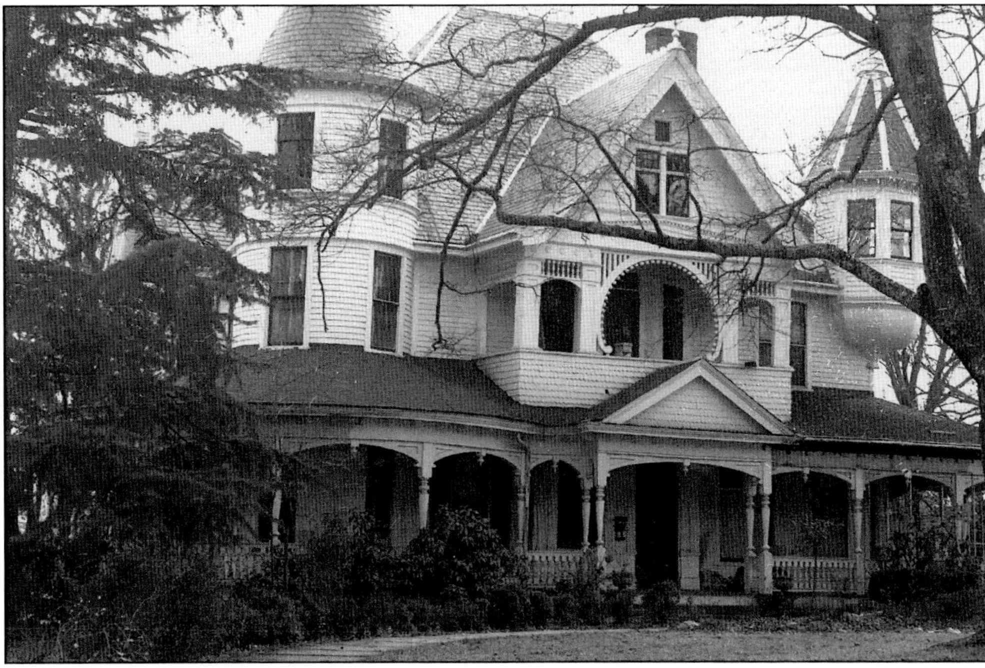

James Calvin Owings House. Built *c.* 1896, the Owings house is an example of Victorian (Queen Anne) architecture. Owings, builder of this West Main Street dwelling, devoted his life to good deeds and the welfare of the Laurens community. He was a member of the First Baptist Church, a member of the Owings & Bobo Firm, a trustee for the Laurens City School District, and served as the mayor. Born in Dial's Township, Owings came to Laurens as a young man. He was married to the former Elizabeth Bruce Hughes of Fountain Inn. (Courtesy of Ken Eargle.)

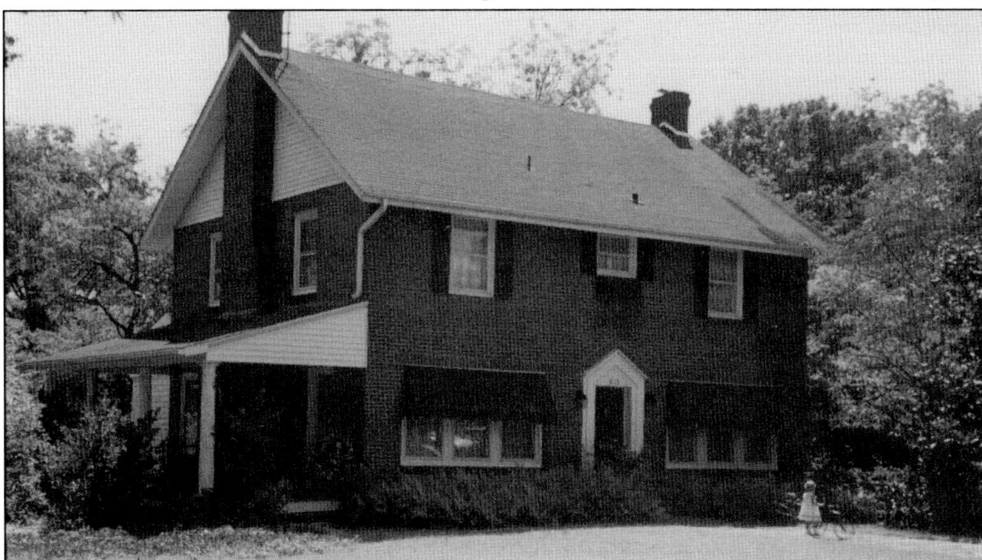

Blakely House. Built in the mid-1930s by George Hunter and Bruce Hughes Owings Blakely, this brick two-story house is located on West Main Street. Blakely, originally from Ora, was a bank employee and worked in several early Laurens banks, including the Palmetto. "Brucie" was the daughter of Laurens businessman J.C. Owings. (Courtesy of the Rhodes collection.)

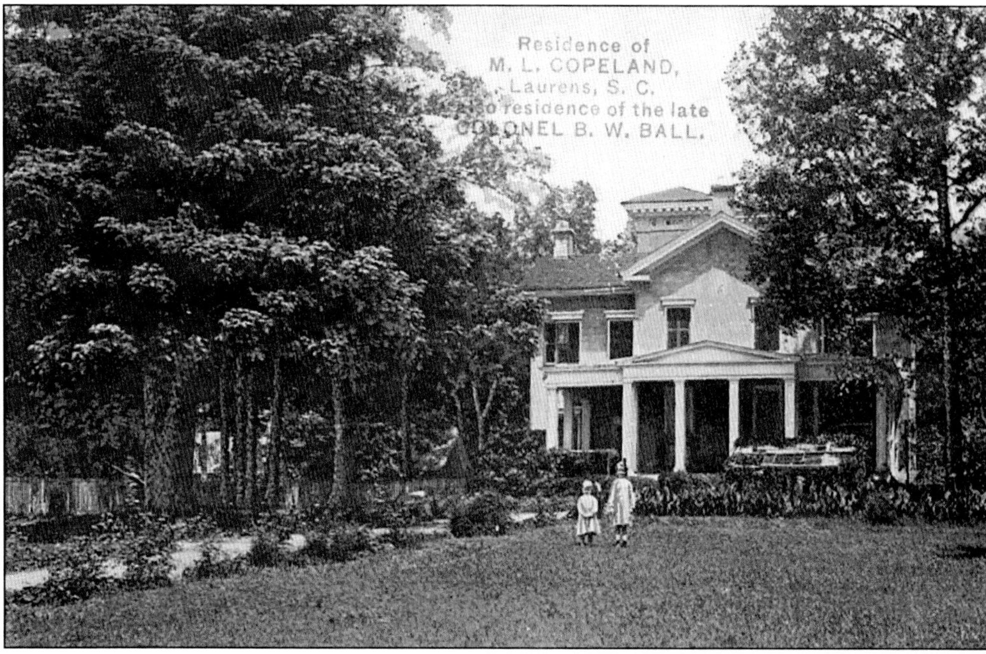

The Villa. Colonel John Drayton Williams began construction on an Italian villa house in 1859. He continued to live at White Plains, his plantation in lower Laurens County. The Civil War interrupted the completion of the home. B.W. Ball purchased the Villa in 1875. Ball is attributed with planting the boxwood walk and completing the interior. Mason L. Copeland, Ball's son-in-law, and his daughter, Sara Ball Copeland, were the next owners of the home. Mrs. Copeland and her daughter, Beaufort, continued to live in the house until it was sold to Clyde Franks. Located on Hampton Street, the Villa is now a part of the Martha Franks Baptist Retirement Center. (Courtesy of Laurens County Library.)

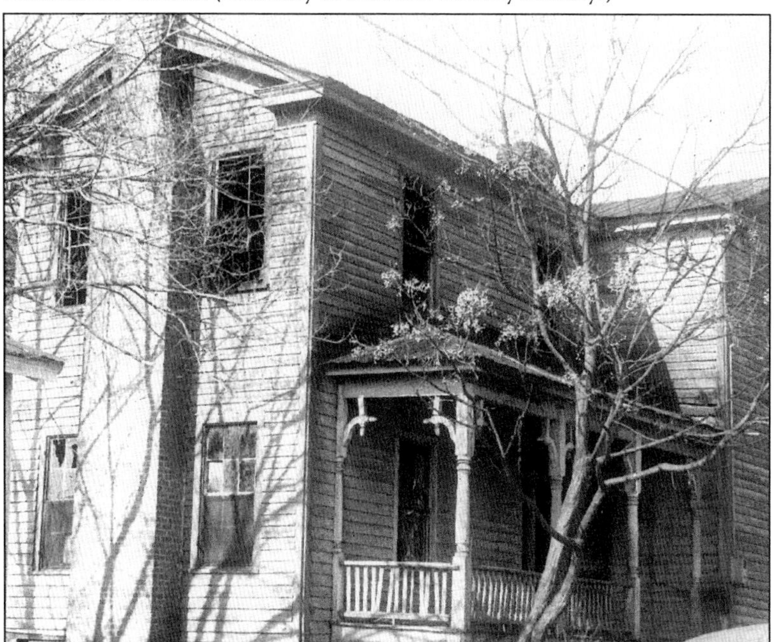

Anderson House. Located on West Main Street and near the Laurens Square, this house, no longer standing, is believed to be the Anderson residence. (Courtesy of the Rhodes collection.)

Three

MEN, WOMEN, AND CHILDREN OF THE TOWN

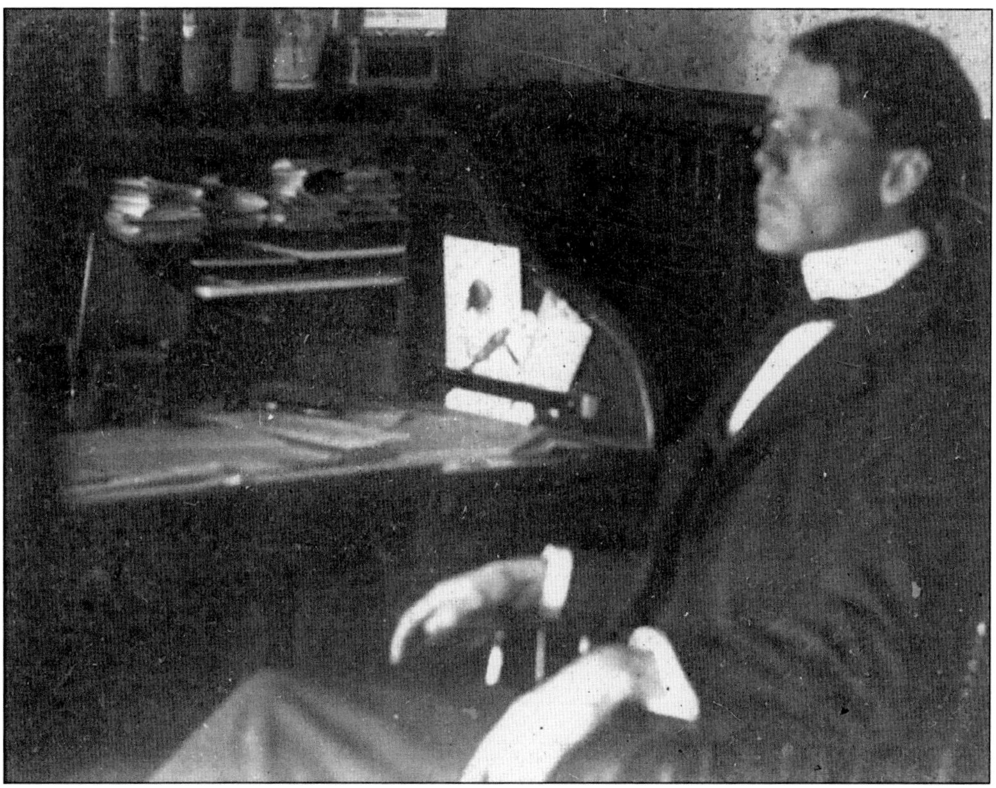

DEAN OF THE LAURENS BAR. Robert E. Babb, son of Messar and Laura Hellams Babb, graduated from The Citadel. He read law in the offices of Colonel J.L.M. Irby and W.R. Richey and was associated with Robert A. Cooper and Colonel Henry Y. Simpson in the firm of Simpson, Cooper and Babb. He was appointed by chief justices to serve as a judge on many occasions and also served as a U.S. commissioner and the city and county attorney. He was married to Donie A. Babb, and the family resided on West Main Street. (Courtesy of Mrs. Beatrice Babb Bradley.)

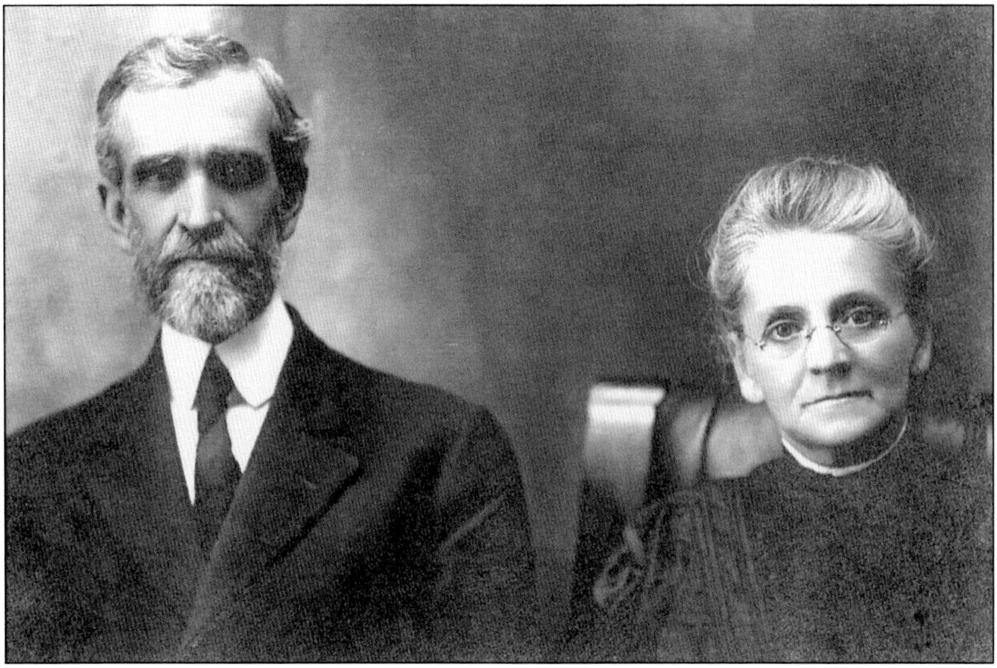

MR. AND MRS. JOHN WELLS TODD. Harriet Susan Garlington, the daughter of Creswell and Elizabeth Fleming Garlington, was born in 1860. She was married in 1879 to John Wells Todd, who was born in 1857 and was the son of Samuel R. and Jane Boyd Todd. Samuel Todd arrived in America in 1816 and settled in Laurens County. John Wells Todd was associated with the People's Loan and Exchange Bank of Laurens and later with Todd, Simpson and Company. (Courtesy of John Wells Todd IV.)

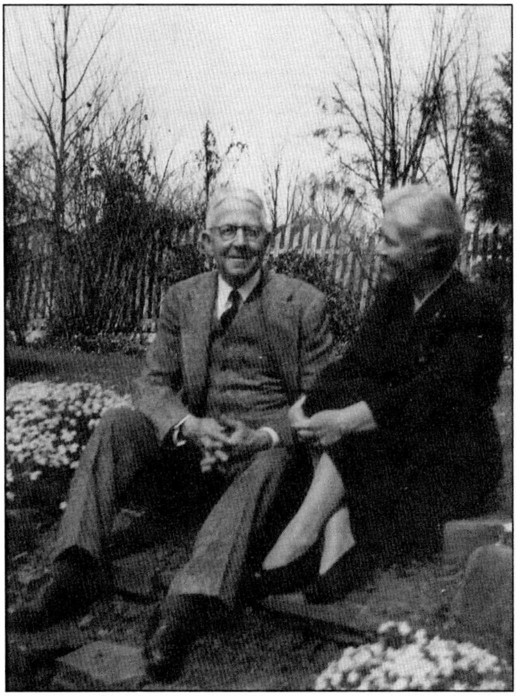

FIRST HARDWARE STORE ON THE SQUARE. James Dunklin, son of Dr. Irby Dunklin and Harriet Montgomery Dunklin, took pride in having the first hardware store on the square. The young merchant started business in a modest store on Sullivan Street before opening Laurens Hardware. He built up a large business during his lifetime. Jim Dunklin was married to Zelene Gray Dunklin, and they were of the Methodist faith. (Courtesy of Mrs. Harriet Gray Hunter.)

LAURENS COUNTY'S LAST CONFEDERATE VETERAN. Major William Augustine Watts was a prominent banker and industrialist. The son of John Watts and Elizabeth Cannon Watts, he moved at the age of 12 with his family to Laurens and established a home on North Harper Street. Watts assisted in promoting the Laurens Cotton Mills and later the Watts Mill, which was located in sight of his home. He was a mill director and board member until his death at the age of 93. (Courtesy of Julian Coats.)

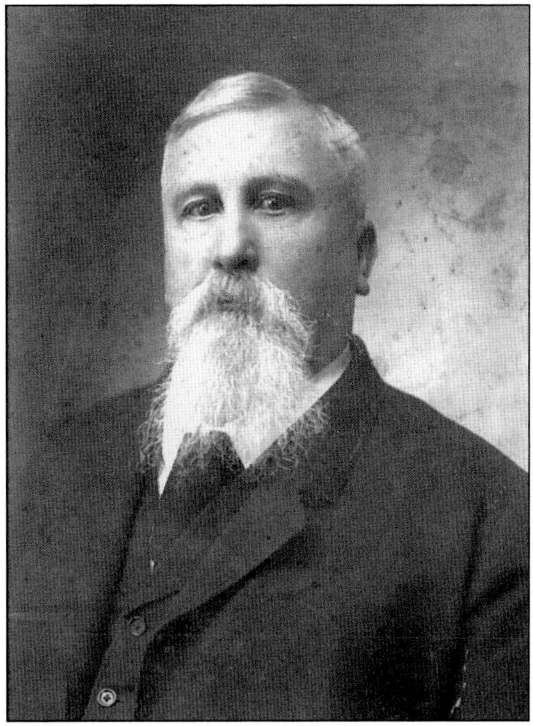

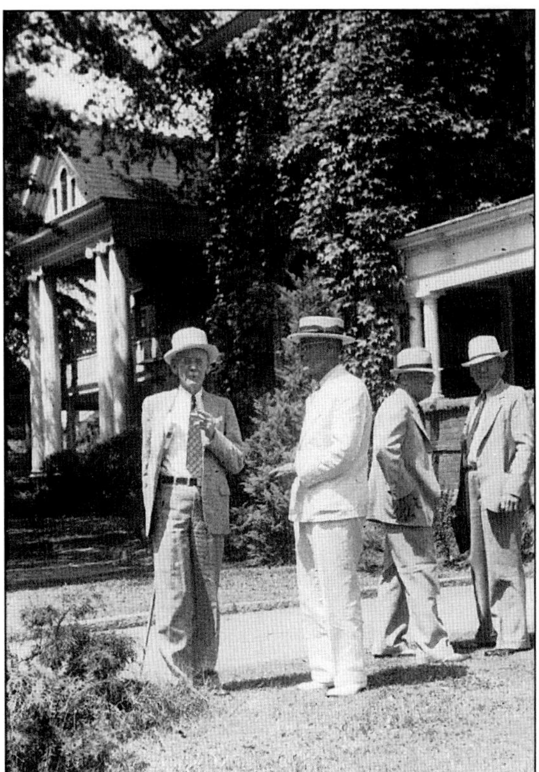

FRIENDS AND NEIGHBORS. From left to right, Robert E. Babb, H. Douglas Gray, and two unidentified men, dressed in summer attire, enjoy a discussion on the front lawn of a West Main Street house. (Courtesy of Mrs. Beatrice Babb Bradley.)

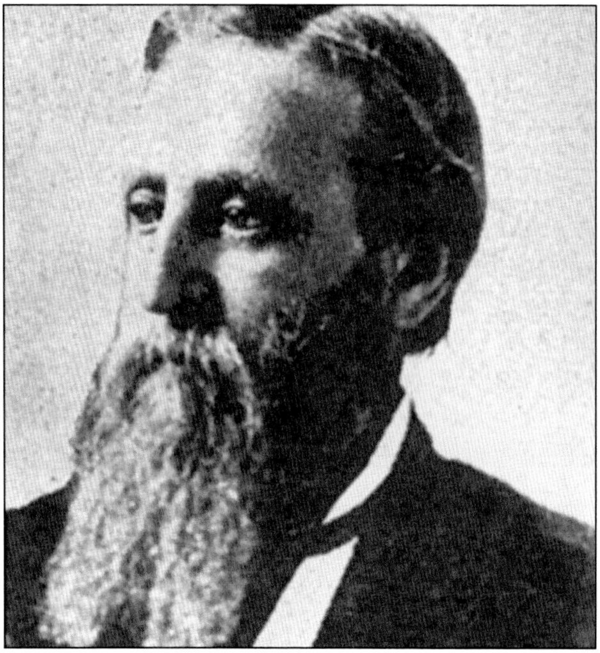

Served in Three Branches of Government. William D. Simpson, a native son of Laurens, served in all three branches of state government: legislative, executive, and judicial, and he had the distinction of achieving the highest positions in two: governor and chief justice of the Supreme Court. The son of Dr. John Wells Simpson and Elizabeth Satterwhite Simpson, he was born in 1823. He married Jane Elizabeth Young, daughter of his law partner, Henry Clinton Young. (Courtesy of Laurens County Library.)

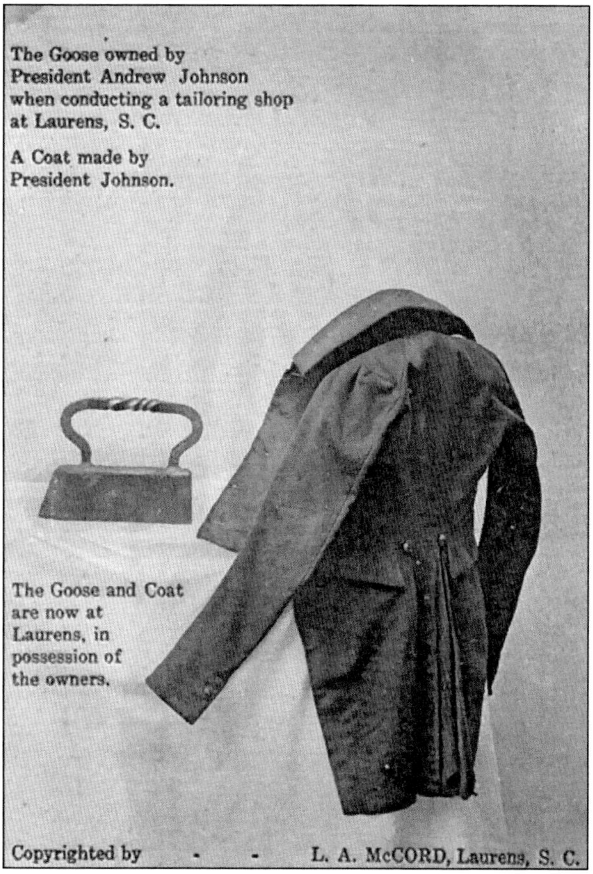

Made by U.S. President Johnson. This is a photograph of a coat that was sewn by President Andrew Johnson when he had a tailoring shop just off the Laurens Square and a "goose" owned by the tailor. The photograph was made and copyrighted on a postal card by Luther A. McCord, a well-known Laurens photographer. (Courtesy of Miss Louise McCord.)

PRESIDENT OF THE UNITED STATES. Andrew Johnson, the 17th President of the United States, once lived and operated a tailor shop on the Laurens Square. While in Laurens, Johnson became engaged to Sarah Word, a young lady of the community. Mrs. Word, a widow, would not permit her daughter to marry a simple tailor. The disappointed Johnson left Laurens immediately. He later settled in Greeneville, Tennessee. (Courtesy of Laurens County Library.)

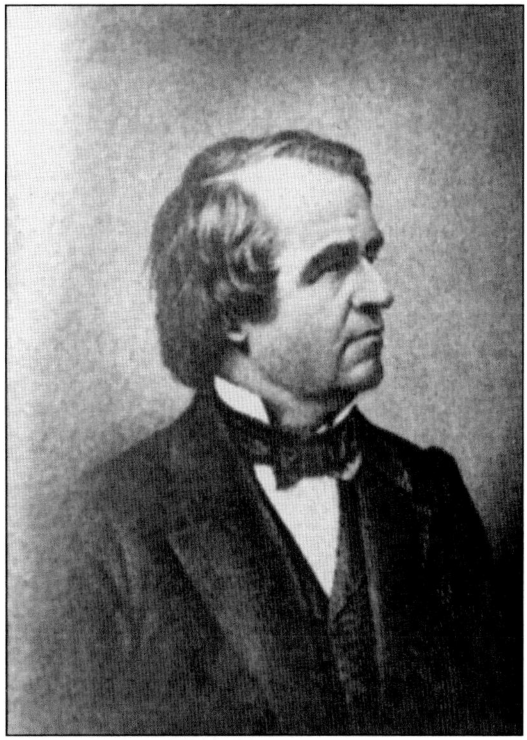

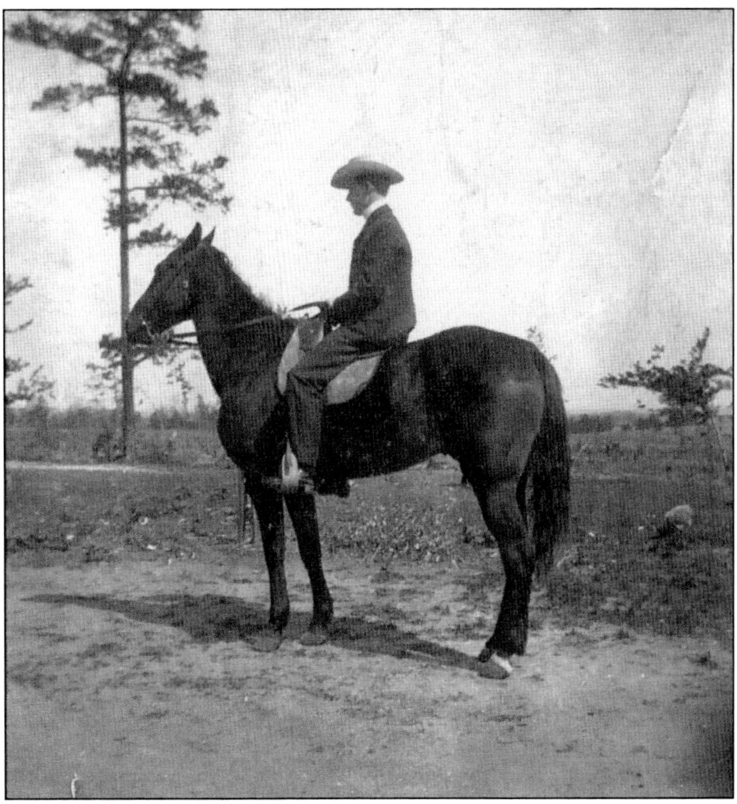

YOUNG EQUESTRIAN. Gus Babb, son of Messar and Laura Hellams Babb, is pictured with his horse in the yard of the Babb home on Farley Avenue. (Courtesy of Mrs. Beatrice Babb Bradley.)

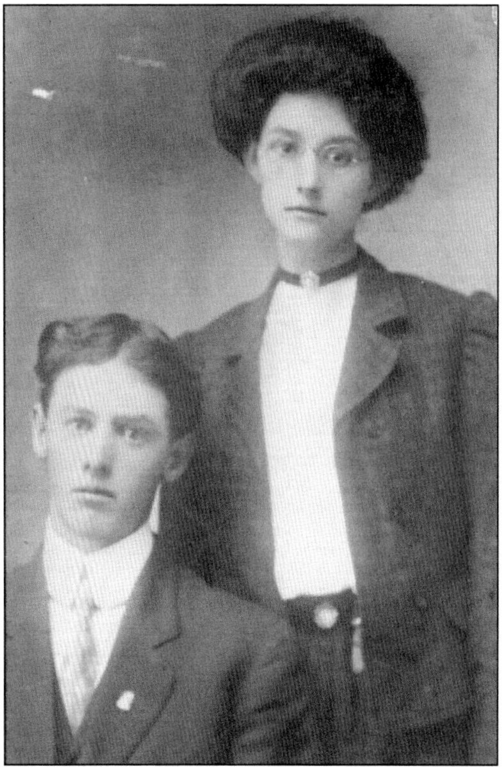

Store Founder and Contractor. James Robert Brownlee was one of the founders of Motes and Brownlee General Merchandise Establishment in Watts Mill. He later was engaged in the contracting business and was a leading Laurens contractor. Brownlee is shown with his wife, the former Nora Bobo. (Courtesy of Mrs. Agnes Brownlee Sherer.)

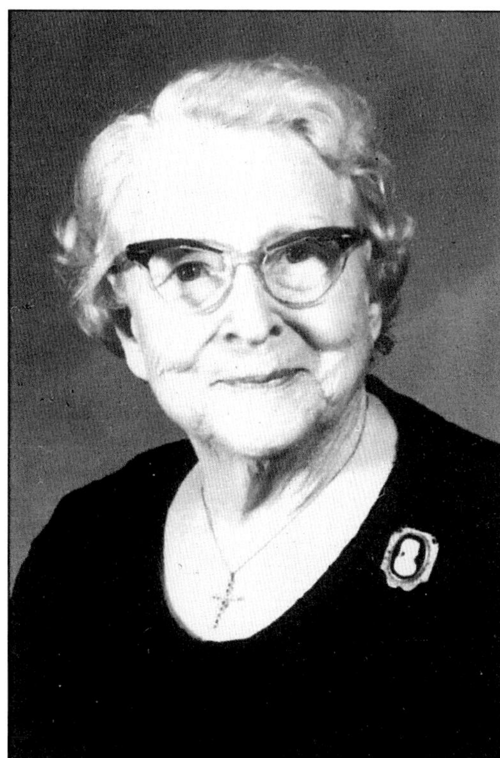

Educator. Wil Lou Gray, daughter of William Lafayette and Sarah Lou Dial Gray, lived on West Main Street. A graduate of Columbia College, she completed graduate work at Winthrop, Vanderbilt, and Columbia University. Her teaching career began at Jones School in 1903 and then at Wallace Lodge, or Young's School. She began an experimental adult education program at the rural Laurens School in 1915 while serving as supervisor of rural schools. Gray was the founder of the South Carolina Opportunity School in Columbia. (Courtesy of Laurens County Library.)

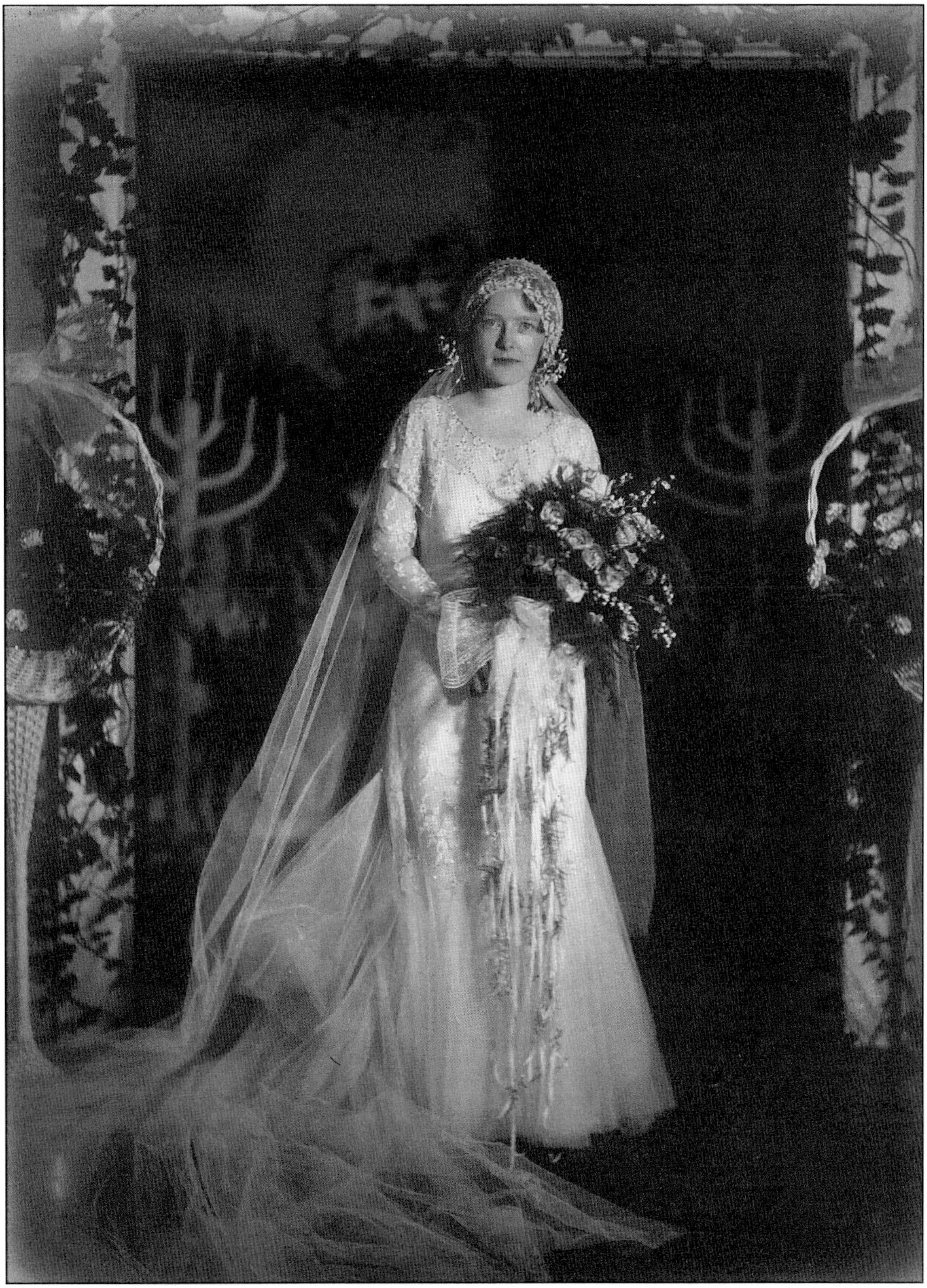

Wedding on West Main. Beatrice Babb, daughter of Mr. and Mrs. R.E. Babb, was married to Moore Bradley in the 1900s at the home of her parents on West Main Street. (Courtesy of Mrs. Beatrice Babb Bradley.)

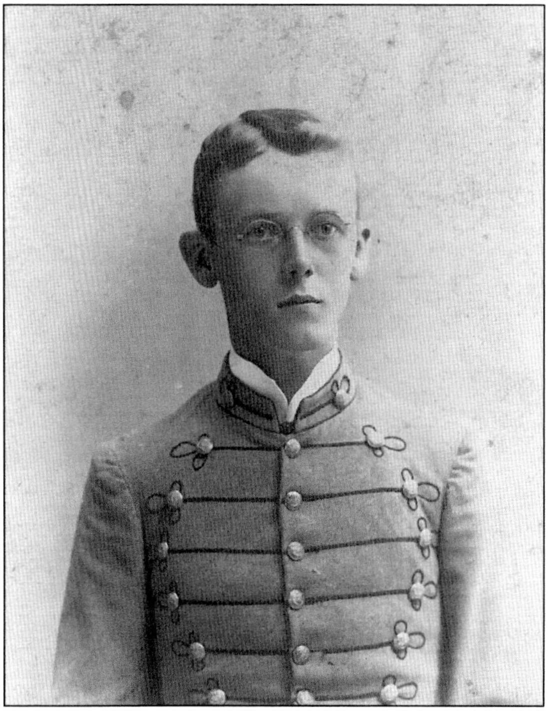

CITADEL CADET. Robert E. Babb is shown in uniform while a student at The Citadel. Babb was the son of Messar and Laura Hellams Babb and lived on Farley Avenue. Later in his life, Babb became a respected attorney and judge. He was often billed as "the Dean of Laurens Bar." (Courtesy of Mrs. Beatrice Babb Bradley.)

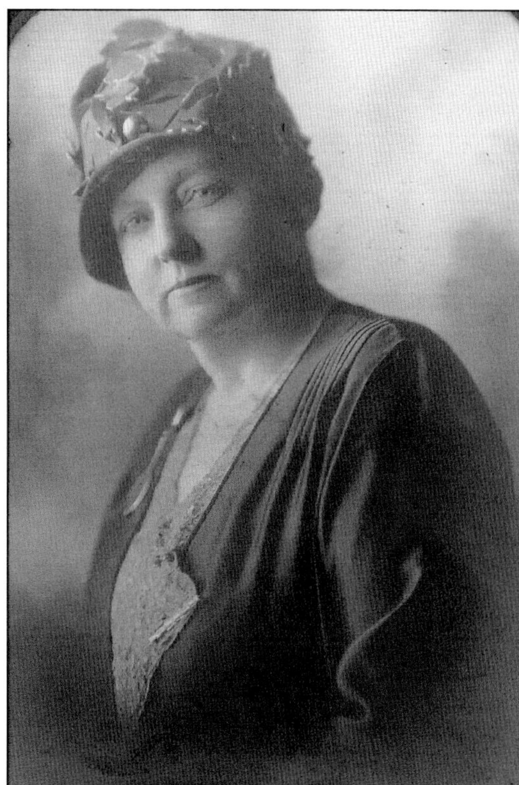

WIFE OF ROBERT A. BABB. Mrs. Donie Babb was the wife of prominent Laurens attorney Robert Edgar Babb. The Babbs made their home on West Main Street and were active members of the Laurens First Methodist Church. (Courtesy of Mrs. Beatrice Babb Bradley.)

Mary Hammond Sullivan Davis. Mary was the daughter of Cornelia Herndon Sullivan Jones and Arthur Pickney Sullivan. This photograph was taken in 1913 prior to her marriage to James Robert Davis. Mr. and Mrs. Davis made their home on South Harper Street and were members of the First Presbyterian Church. (Courtesy of Mrs. Mary Herndon Davis Todd.)

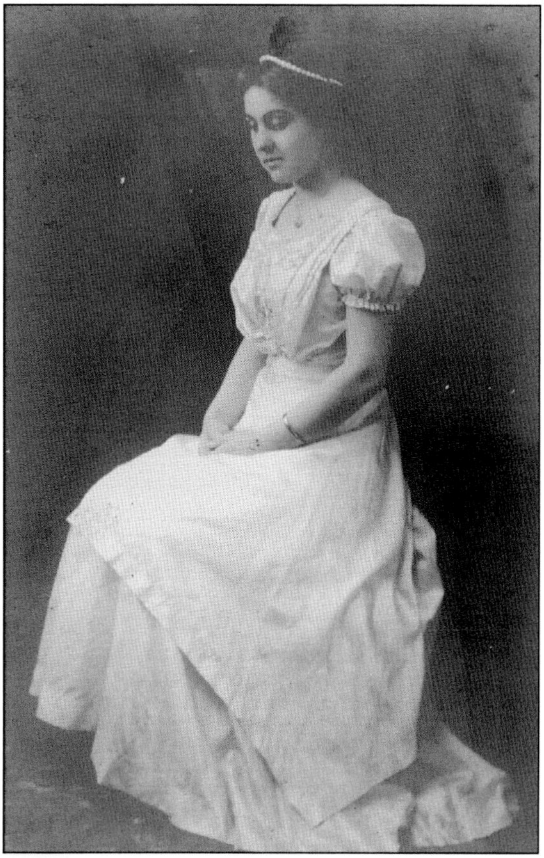

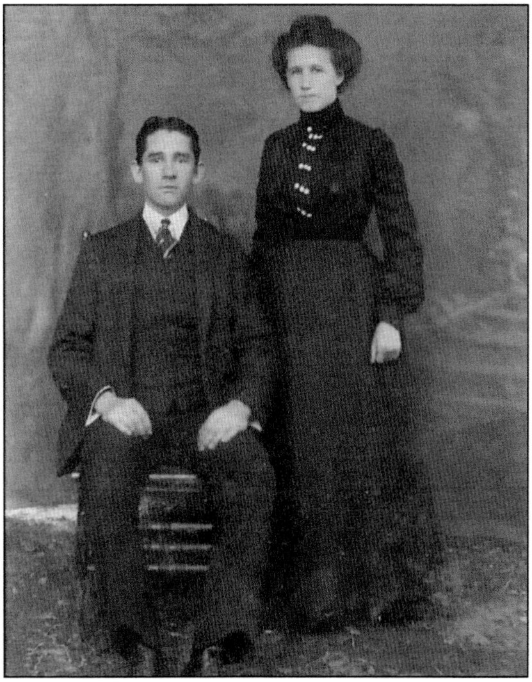

North Harper Street Couple. Mace Langston Motes and his wife, Nancy Jane Blakely Motes, lived on North Harper Street. As a young man, Motes was associated with the Motes and Brownlee General Mercantile Store and later became manager of the People's Cooperative Store. He was involved in the general mercantile business in Watts Mill for 40 years. Motes was one of the founders and a longtime board member of the Laurens Hospital System. (Courtesy of Mason C. Motes II.)

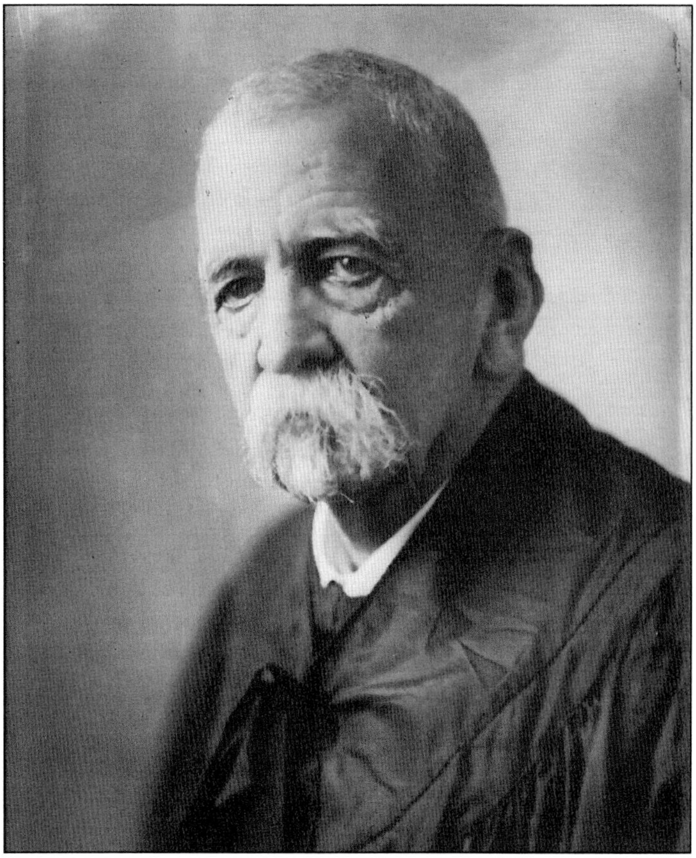

NATIVE SON. Born March 15, 1853, at the Watts plantation in the old Chestnut Ridge community, Richard Cannon Watts was the son of John Watts and Elizabeth Carwile Watts. One of Laurens County's most distinguished and honored native sons, he was also one of South Carolina's most eminent jurists for 38 years. (Courtesy of Laurens County Library.)

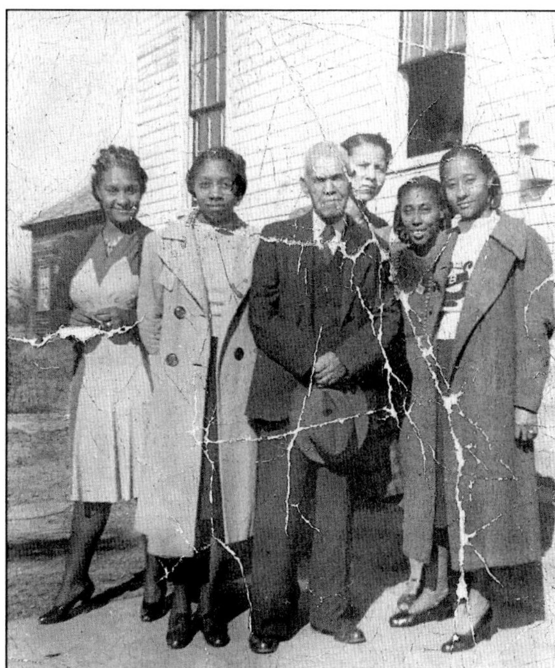

PROFESSOR SANDERS AND TEACHERS. Thomas Sanders, Laurens educator and founder of the Hampton Street School, worked diligently to improve the quality of education for his pupils. Standing outside the school built in 1937 and named in his honor are the "Professor" and Sanders High School teachers; from left to right are Miss Peterson, Miss Blocker, Miss Willie Boyd, Miss Nance, and Mrs. Butler. (Courtesy of the Rhodes collection.)

Alice Brown Coats. Born in Darlington County, Alice Hyler Brown moved with her family to Laurens as a young girl. She was married to James Julian Coats, and they made their home in the Watts Mill community before moving to a farm in the Oak Grove community. (Courtesy of Julian Coats.)

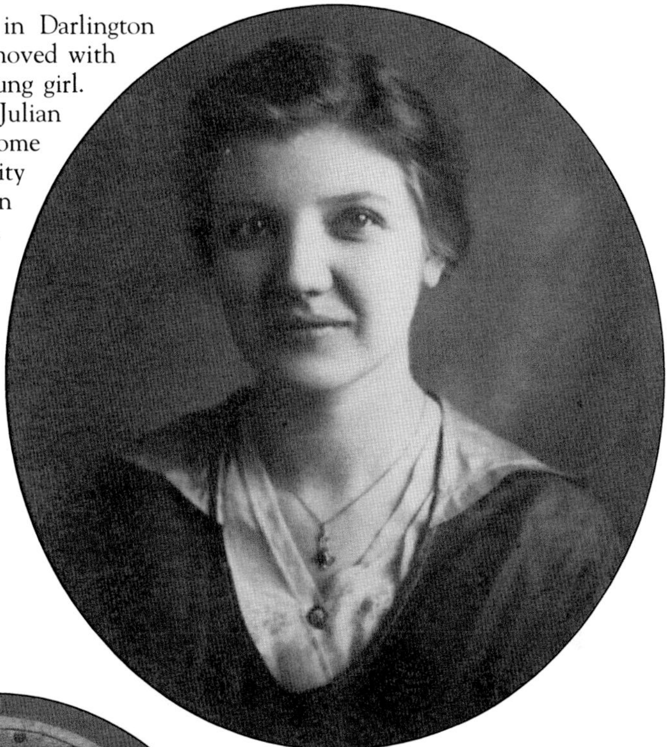

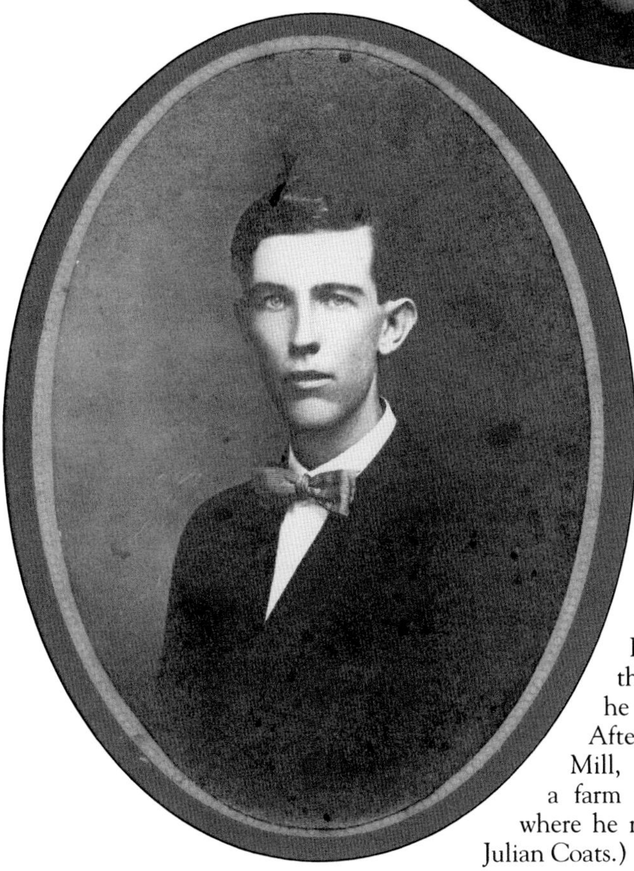

Originally from Cross Hill. James Julian "Duck" Coats Sr. left the farm in Cross Hill as a young man and moved to the Watts Mill community, where he met and married Alice Brown. After working for a time at Watts Mill, Coats and his wife purchased a farm in the Oak Grove community, where he returned to farming. (Courtesy of Julian Coats.)

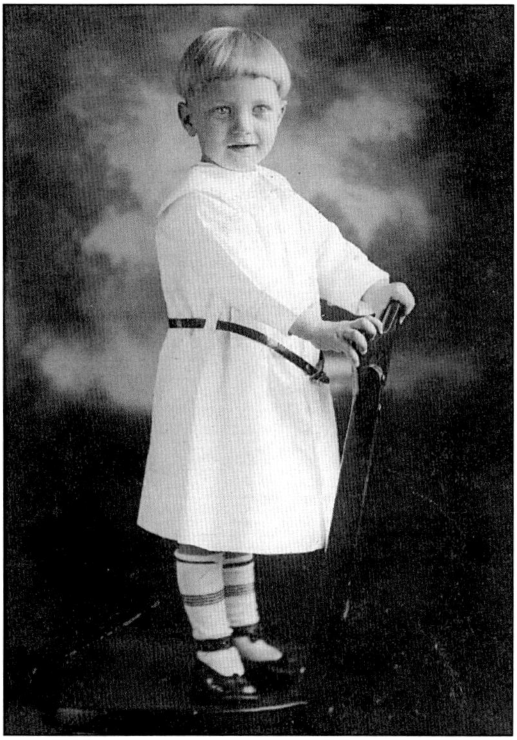

1920 Fashion. Dressed in the fashion of the day—belted dress, stockings, and button shoes—James Julian Coats Jr. posed for the photographer at the popular McCord Studio in Laurens. Julian was the only child of James Julian Sr. and Alice Brown Coats. (Courtesy of Julian Coats.)

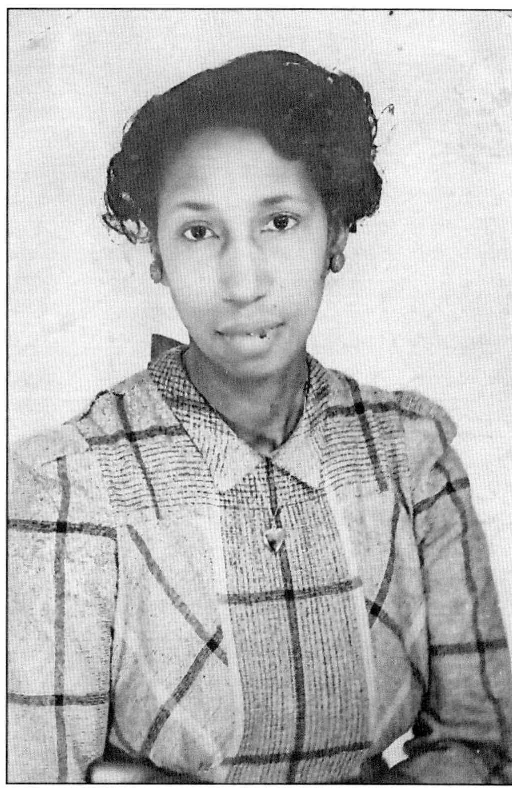

Inspirational Teacher. Born in the Duncan Creek section of Laurens County, Mrs. Elel Finley was the only child of Arzell and Willie Watts. Elel moved to the town of Laurens when she was in fourth grade. She walked past Professor Sanders's house to attend the Hampton Street School. She later graduated from Benedict College and returned to Laurens and was hired by Sanders to teach fourth grade at her alma mater. The Laurens teacher married Albert Finley and continued to live on Hampton Street. (Courtesy of Mrs. Elel Finley.)

A LAURENS GRANDMOTHER. Mrs. Laura Hellams Babb, wife of Messar Babb, farmer and county official, leans on the backyard fence of her home on Farley Avenue and watches her granddaughter at play with a favorite baby doll. (Courtesy of Mrs. Beatrice Babb Bradley.)

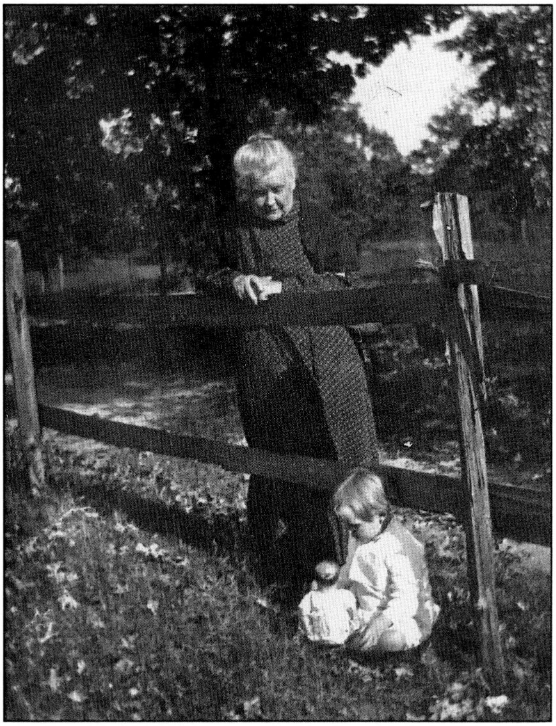

LAURENS FAMILY. Clarence Eugene Kennedy and his brother Hugh S. Kennedy established Kennedy Mortuary in 1885. Clarence was the first professional funeral director in Laurens. He was the son of Captain Nathaniel Kennedy and Frances Meaders Kennedy. Clarence Kennedy is shown with his wife, the former Mittie Henderson, and their sons, F.N. and H. Lawrence Kennedy. (Courtesy of Mrs. Agnes Brownlee Sherer.)

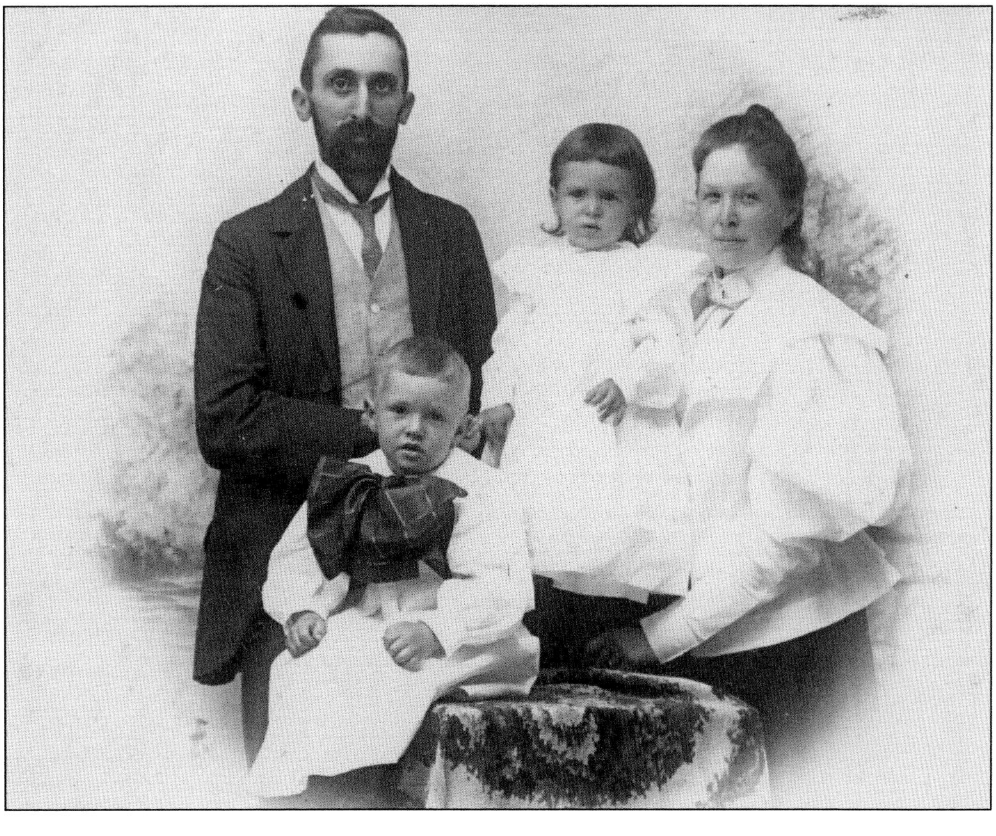

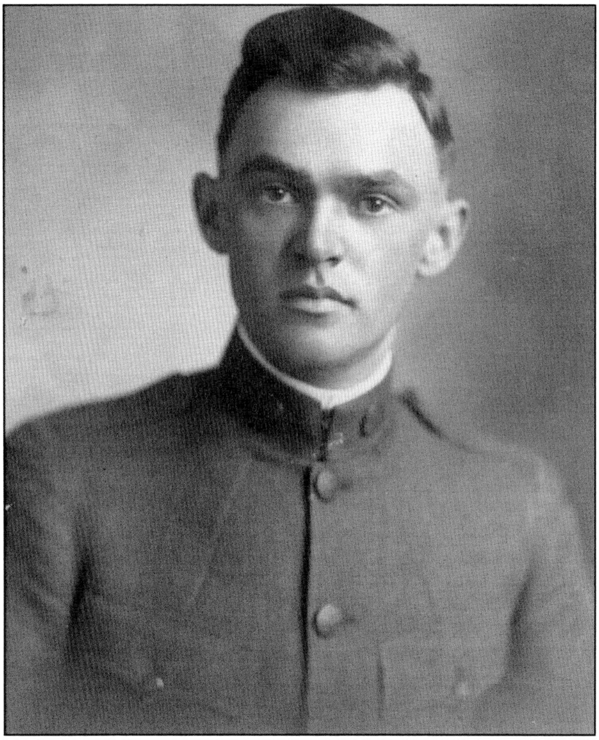

BENGHAM CADET. Frances Nathaniel Kennedy was known to family and friends as "Nat." For many years, he, with his father, operated Kennedy Mortuary. Kennedy was a graduate of Bengham Military School in Mebane, North Carolina, a student at the University of South Carolina, and a graduate of Eastman School of Business Administration in Poughkeepsie, New York. A World War I veteran, Kennedy lived on West Main Street with his wife, Catheryn Padgett Kennedy. (Courtesy of Mrs. Agnes Brownlee Sherer.)

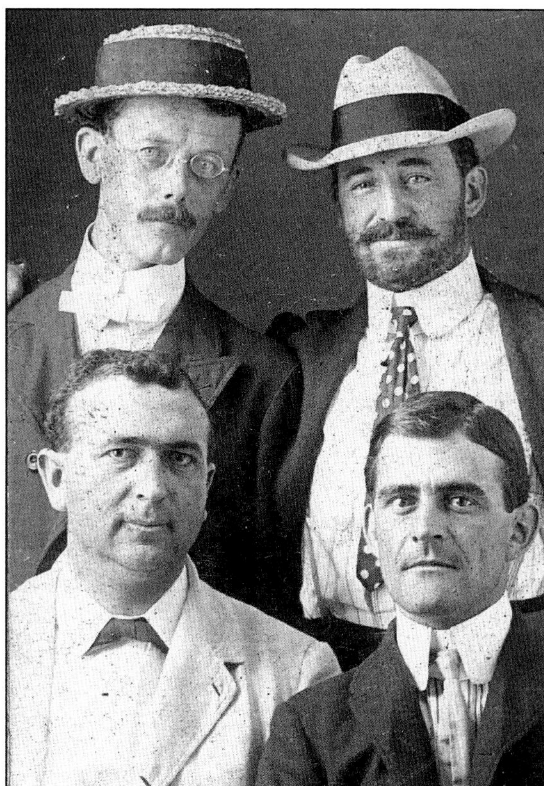

LAURENS GENTS. These four gentlemen were friends as well as business associates and were known all about town. They are, from left to right, as follows: (front row) ? Irby and Vance Irby; (back row) R.E. Babb and Dr. Ferguson. (Courtesy of Mrs. Beatrice Babb Bradley.)

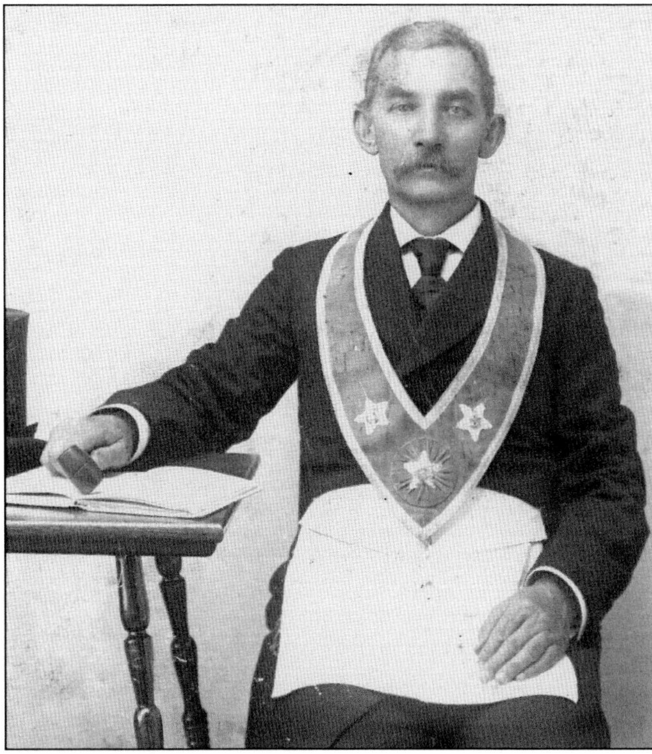

NATIVE OF GERMANY. Lipman G. Balle arrived in the United States at the age of 18. After working in New York for a few years, he headed south and settled in Laurens and operated a tailoring business until the Civil War broke out in 1861. Balle at once enlisted in the Army of the South, joined James's Battalion and fought throughout the war. Following the war, Balle engaged in farming and business. He was elected city clerk in 1890 and served until 1906. (Courtesy of Miss Mary Balle.)

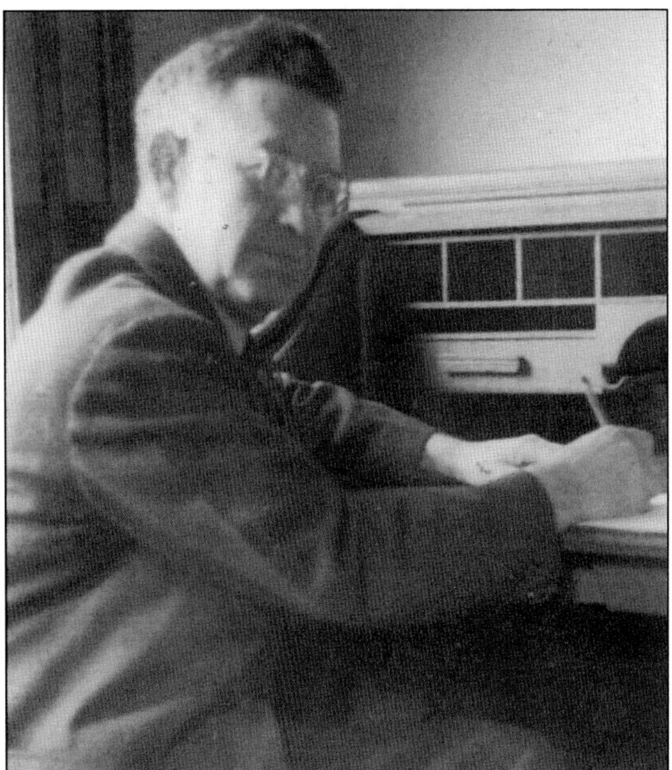

BANK PRESIDENT. Son of L.G. and Mary Ann Hellams Balle, George began his career at the Enterprise Bank. In 1915 he accepted a position as cashier of Palmetto Bank, then located on the west side of the Square. Upon the death of Palmetto president R.B. Terry, Balle stepped into that position in 1936. The bank relocated to the corner of South Harper and Main and then to the north side of the Square. Balle later became chairman of the board of the Palmetto Bank. (Courtesy of Miss Mary Balle.)

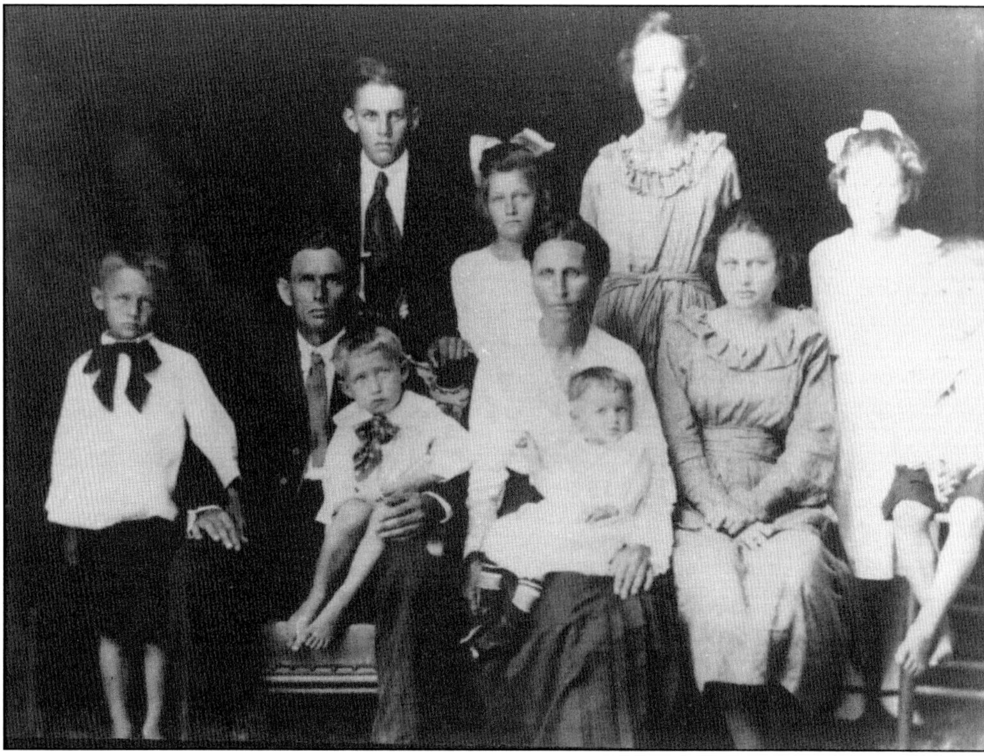

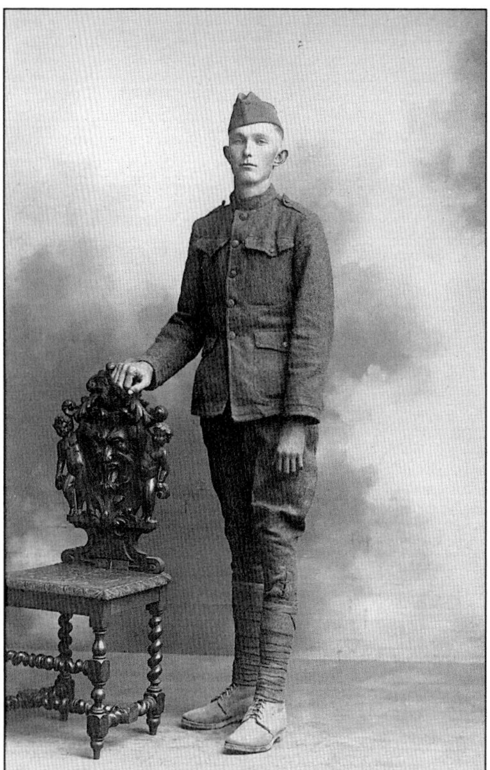

Twelve Children. Will and Rosa Rhodes moved to the Watts Mill community after leaving the farm in Gray Court. They were the parents of 12 children, some of which are shown in this photograph. Two sons, Allen and Robert, were killed in World War II, and the Laurens Gold Star Chapter, an organization for mothers of lost sons, was named in Mrs. Rhodes's honor—the Rosa Rhodes Chapter. (Courtesy of the Rhodes collection.)

World War I Veteran. Robert Herbert "Hub" Coats left the farm in Cross Hill and, as a young man, moved to Watts Mill, where he married the former Ruby Monroe. He delivered ice in the Watts Mill community. R.H. Coats served in France during World War I. (Courtesy of Julian Coats.)

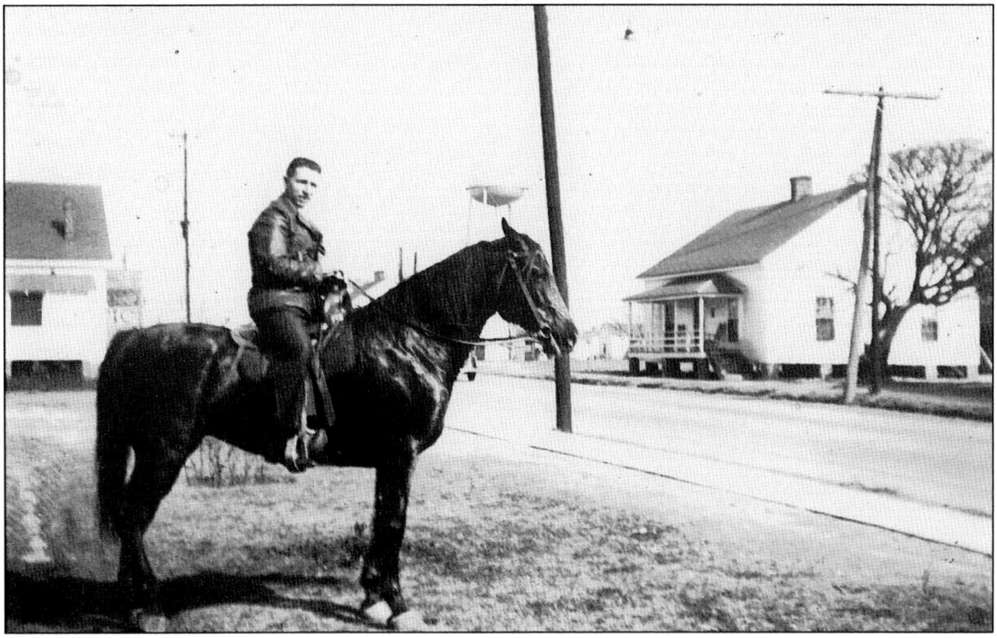

VIEW OF LUCAS AVENUE. Sitting astride a horse, young Thomas H. Bramlett has a view of Lucas Avenue in Watts Mill. Bramlett was a Laurens policeman in later years. He was the son of John and Carrie Brown Bramlett. (Courtesy of Julian Coats.)

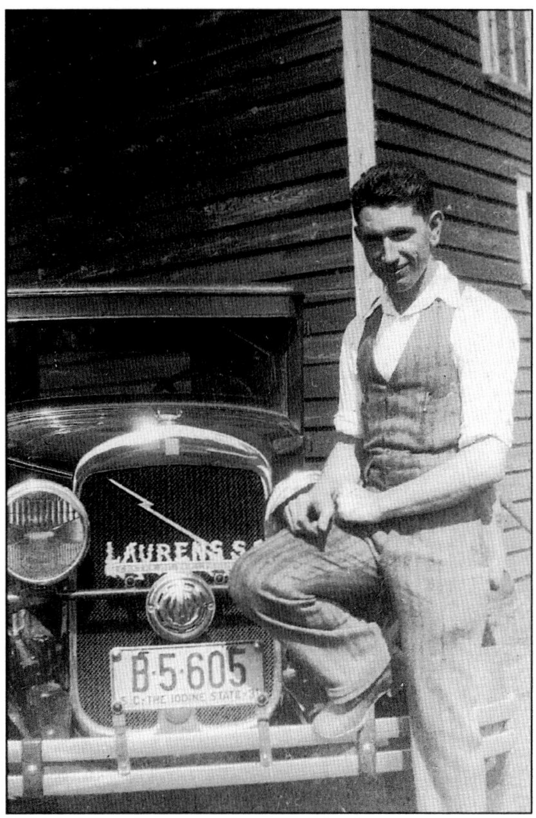

PARKED ALONGSIDE THE BOARDING HOUSE. T.H. Bramlett first posed with a horse and later with an automobile parked alongside the Watts Mill Boarding House. The car's chrome ornament appropriately reads, "Laurens." (Courtesy of Julian Coats.)

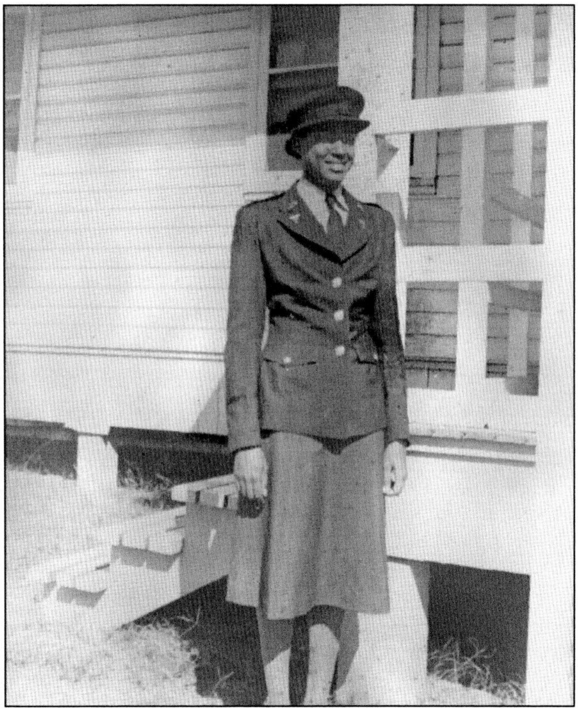

World War II Nurse. Lieutenant Sammie Mae Rice joined 29 nurses and 9 doctors for an assignment to Liberia in West Africa. She was the only nurse from South Carolina and was a member of the first contingent of African-American personnel ever given overseas duty. Following the war she returned to Laurens and taught at Sanders High School. She later taught at Paine College in Augusta, Georgia, before retiring in Laurens. (Courtesy of Miss Sammie Mae Rice.)

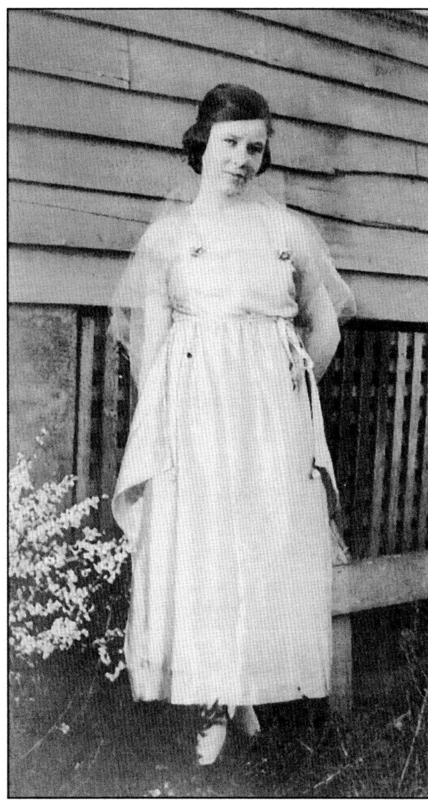

Young Lady of Laurens. Rosa Lee Sullivan, a young lady of Laurens in the early 1900s, is dressed in the fashion of the day. (Courtesy of Mrs. Beatrice Babb Bradley.)

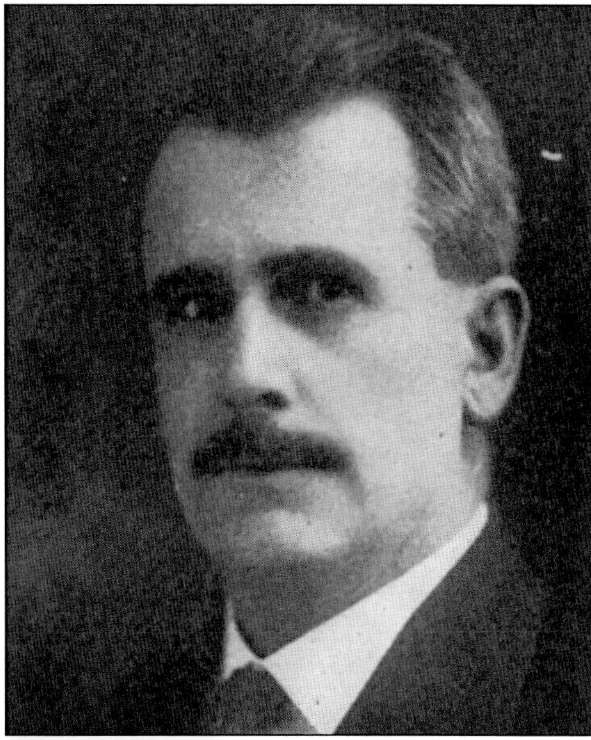

GOVERNOR OF SOUTH CAROLINA. Robert A. Cooper of Laurens stepped into the governorship when Manning's administration came to a close. A noteworthy piece of legislation that passed while Cooper was in the governor's office was the Budget Commission Act (now the Budget and Control Board). Governor Cooper's administration pleased the people and he was popular in all section's of the state. He was attractive physically and his gracious manner won many friends for him. (Courtesy of Thomas A. Babb.)

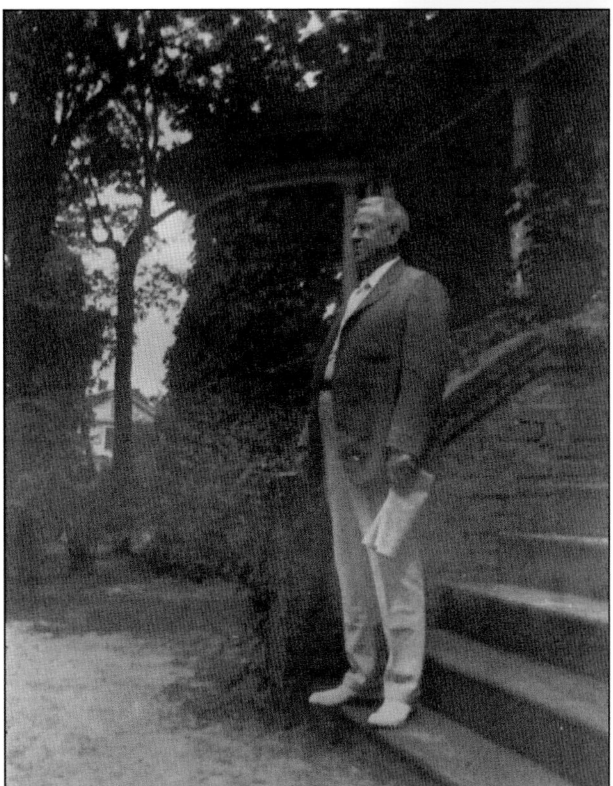

"NAT" DIAL. The son of Colonel Albert and Rebecca Barksdale Dial, Nathaniel Dial was born in the Trinity Ridge section of Laurens County. He attended Richmond College, Vanderbilt University, and Law School at the University of Virginia. He was a retired banker, industrialist, and United States senator. Dial was twice married: first to Ruth Mitchell of Batesburg, and upon her death to Josephine "Josie" Minter, daughter of Captain J.R. Minter of Laurens. The Dial home was located on West Main Street. (Courtesy of the late Rebecca Dial.)

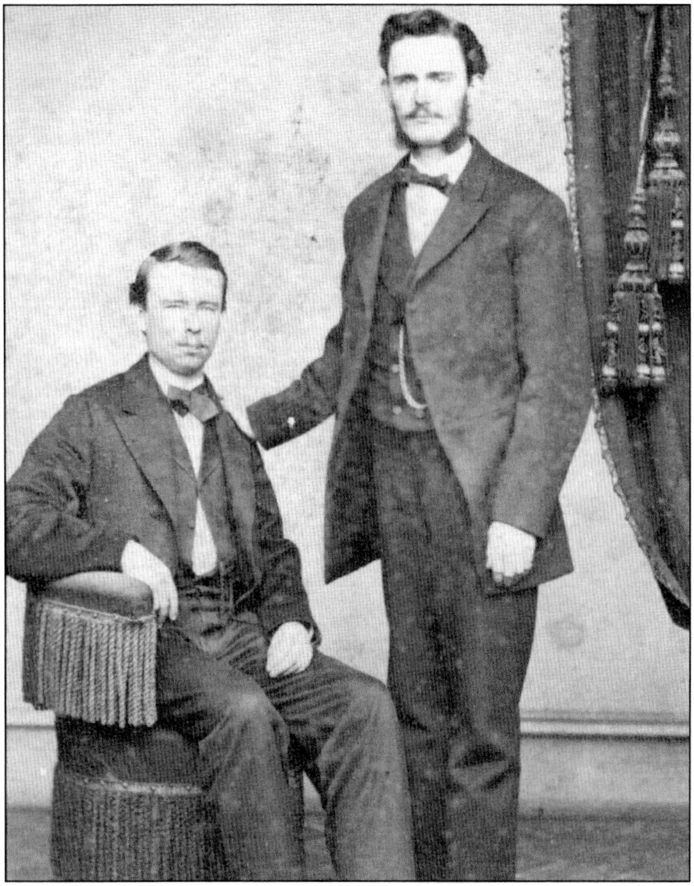

LAURENS PHYSICIANS. Dr. J. Pattillo Simpson (seated) and Dr. William C. Irby attended Jefferson Medical College in Philadelphia. Simpson practiced in Laurens and lived with his wife, Anna Knox Simpson, on East Main Street. Irby practiced medicine in Clinton before moving to Irby Avenue in Laurens. The son of Laurens attorney Colonel James Irby, Dr. Irby was married in 1872 to Laura Vance, the daughter of Nancy Farrow and Robert Vance of Clinton. (Courtesy of Mrs. Mary Herndon Davis Todd.)

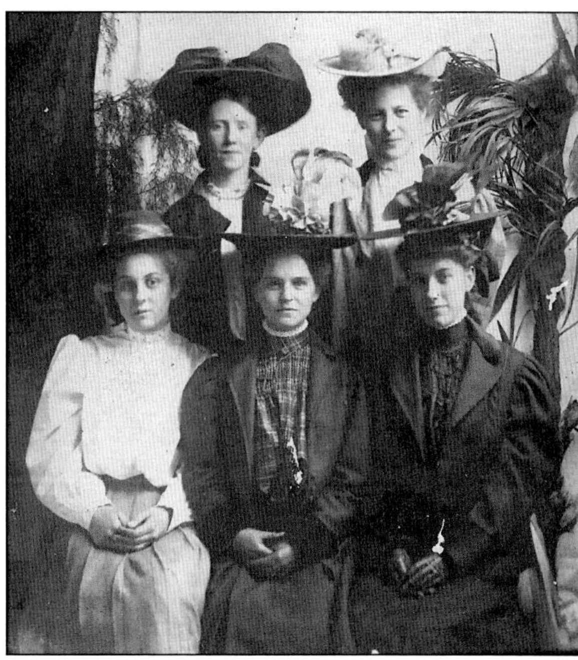

YOUNG FRIENDS. Sara Babb, daughter of Messar and Laura Hellams Babb, poses with a group of school friends. "Miss Sara" is wearing the large hat (left) on the back row. The other girls are unidentified as well as the date and location. (Courtesy of Mrs. Beatrice Babb Bradley.)

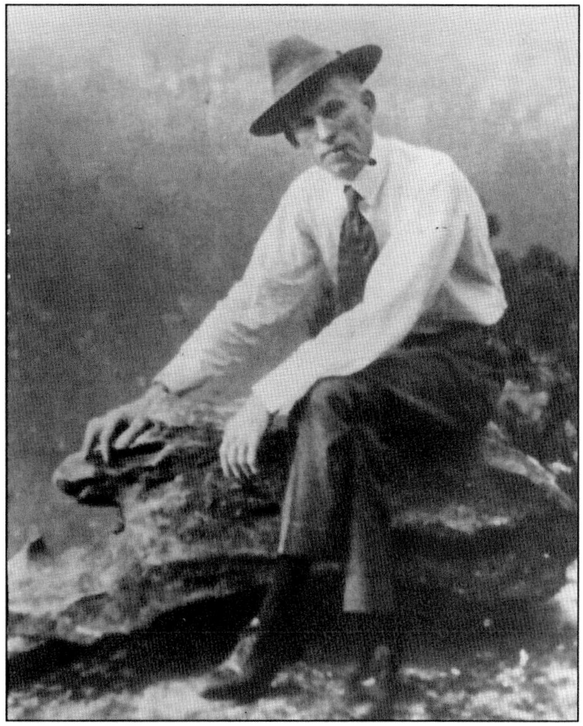

BUSINESSMAN. Albert Dial was the son of Dr. W.H. Dial and Lalla Moore Dial and the husband of Lucy Sitgreaves Dial. He was the president of Laurens Glass, and his principal business achievement was putting Laurens Glass on a sound basis. He took hold of a plant when it was a weakling industry, nursed it through the early stages, and made it one of Laurens's most substantial enterprises. A member of the city council, he was one of the most popular men in the community, both as a public spirited citizen and as a friend. (Courtesy of Mrs. Barbara Dial McAlister.)

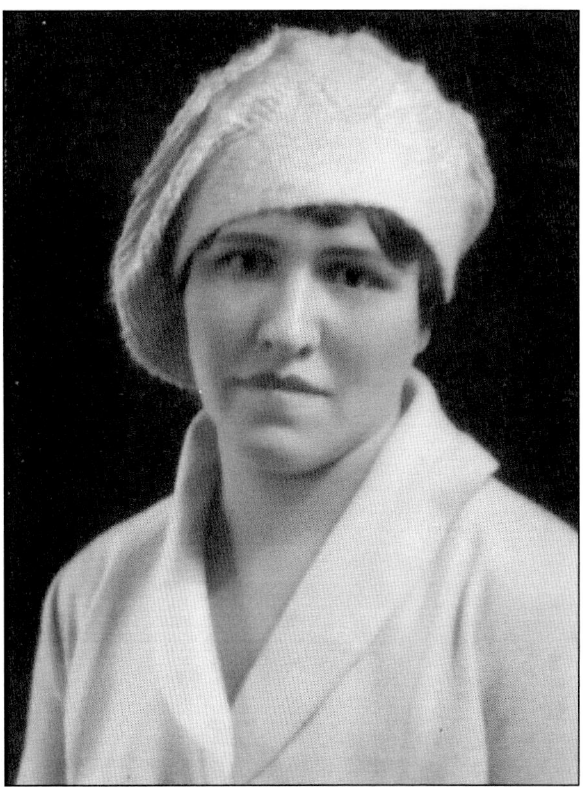

ADMIRED LAURENS LADY. Lucy Sitgreaves Dial was born in Bristol, Virginia, to Catherine and Oceolia Sitgreaves. In 1915, she married Albert Dial, president of Laurens Glass. After her husband's death, she became the secretary of Laurens Glass. She was remarried in 1943 to Dr. LeRoy Habencht, a retired chemist. Affectionately known as "Miss Lucy," she was a member of the Episcopal Church and a strong supporter of individual, community, and church causes until her death at the age of 100. (Courtesy of Mrs. Barbara Dial McAlister.)

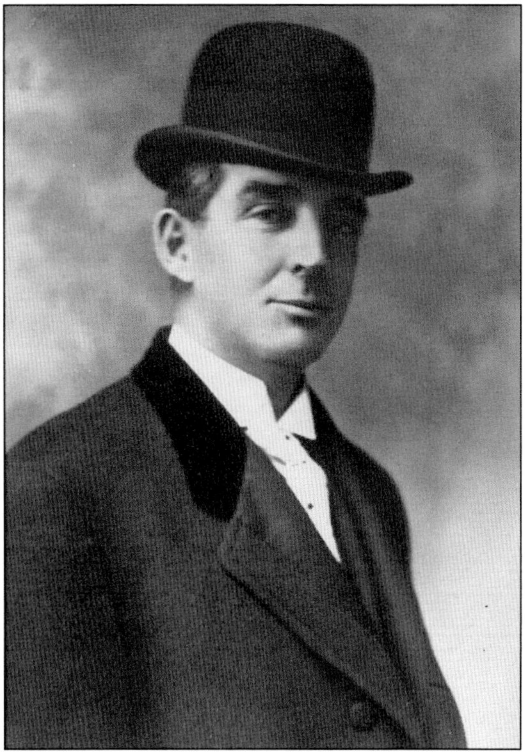

Colonel Thomas Deane Darlington. Originally from Allendale County, Colonel Darlington was a salesman and traveled over a wide area before settling in Laurens in 1902. He became prominently identified with business interests of the city. Extensively engaged in the sale of fertilizer, he maintained offices in Savannah, Charleston, and Laurens. Darlington was married to Lyde Irby, daughter of Dr. W.C. Irby, and resided with his family on Irby Avenue. (Courtesy of Dr. James C. Todd III.)

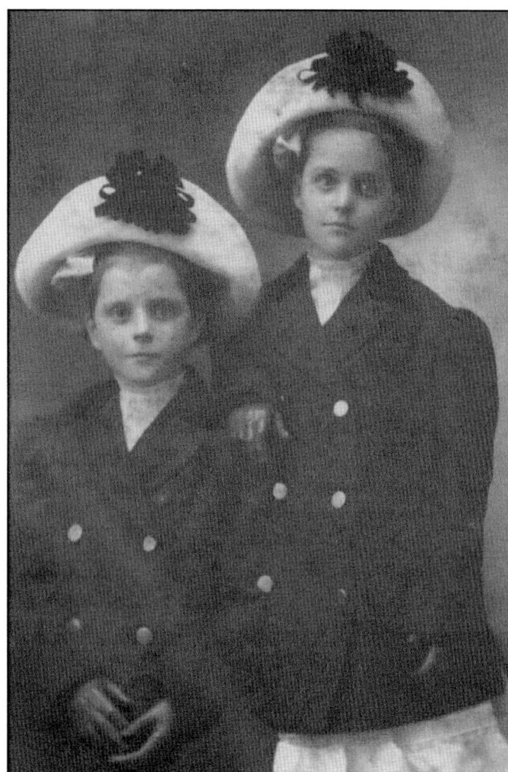

Sisters. Lucy Vance (right) and Claudia Irby Darlington, daughters of Colonel Thomas D. and Lyde Irby Darlington, lived with their parents in a large Victorian home on Irby Avenue. This photograph shows the sisters in 1908. Claudia Irby Darlington became the wife of James C. Todd Sr. of Laurens and Lucy Vance became the wife of Edward McCrady of Greenville. (Courtesy of Mrs. Mary Herndon Davis Todd.)

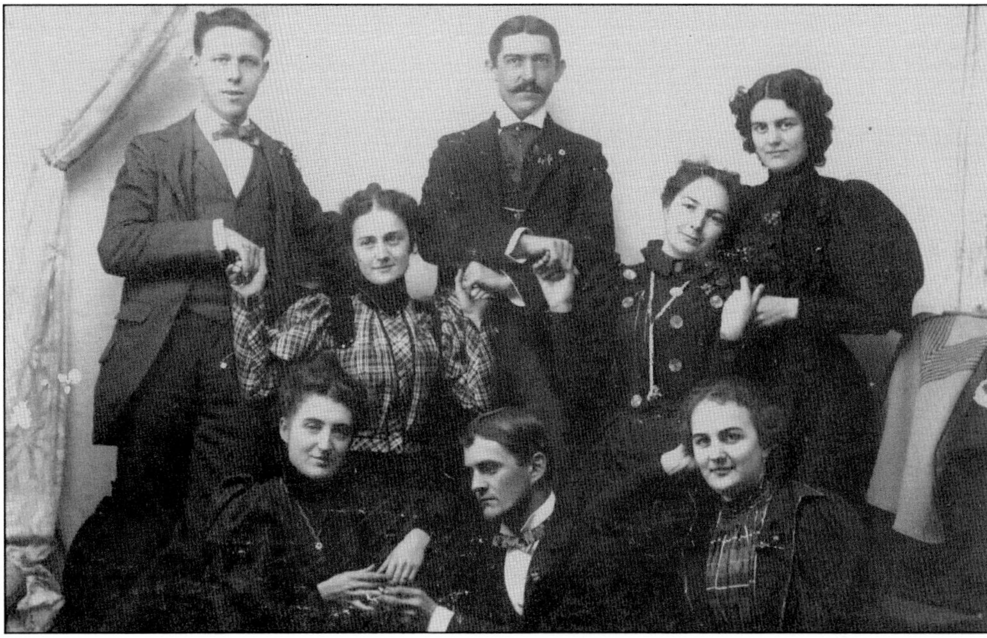

IRBY FAMILY. Members of the Irby family posed for Luther McCord, a popular photographer, in his Laurens Studio. Shown, from left to right, are the following: (front row) unidentified, Vance Irby, and Laura Vance Irby Jones; (middle row) Lyde Irby Darlington and unidentified; (back row) unidentified, unidentified, and Claude Irby Ferguson. A street in Laurens was named for the Irby family. (Courtesy of Dr. James C. Todd III.)

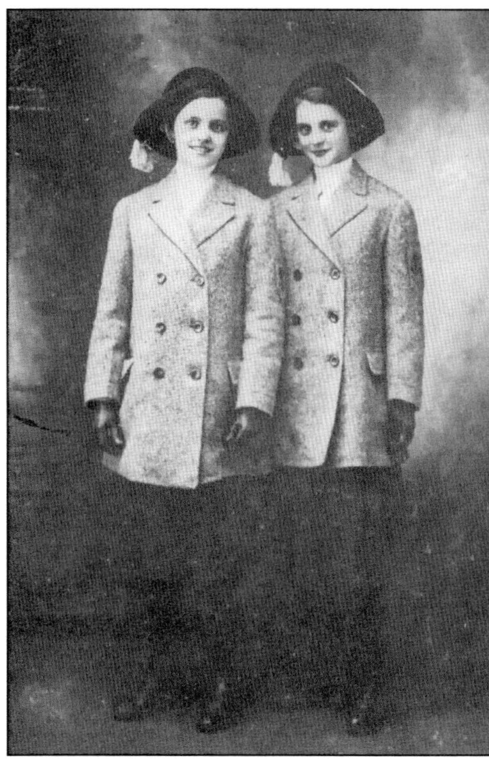

DAUGHTERS OF COLONEL DARLINGTON. Even though they were not twins, the daughters of Colonel Thomas and Lyde Irby Darlington often dressed in identical clothes. The girls, only a year apart in age, acquired the nicknames Claudia Irby "Toots" and Lucy Vance "Dan," which remained with them throughout their lives. Their father was a distinguished Laurens businessman and served on the military staff of Governor Duncan C. Heyward. (Courtesy of Mrs. Mary Herndon Davis Todd.)

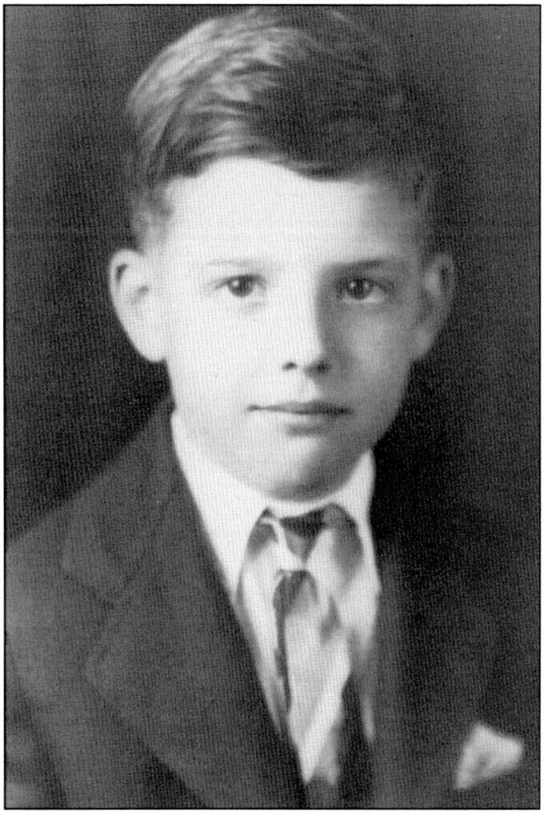

A Laurens Lad. James Conway Todd Jr. was the son of James C. and Claudia Darlington Todd. He lived with his parents and younger brother, Tommy, on West Main Street. Upon reaching adulthood, "Jim" married Mary Herndon Davis, also of Laurens. Like his father before him, he became one of the proprietors of Spratt Grocery, a wholesale grocery business. (Courtesy of Mrs. Mary Herndon Davis Todd.)

Todd Family. Mr. and Mrs. James Conway Todd pose in the yard of their West Main home with their youngest son, Thomas Darlington "Tommy" Todd. (Courtesy of Mrs. Mary Herndon Davis Todd.)

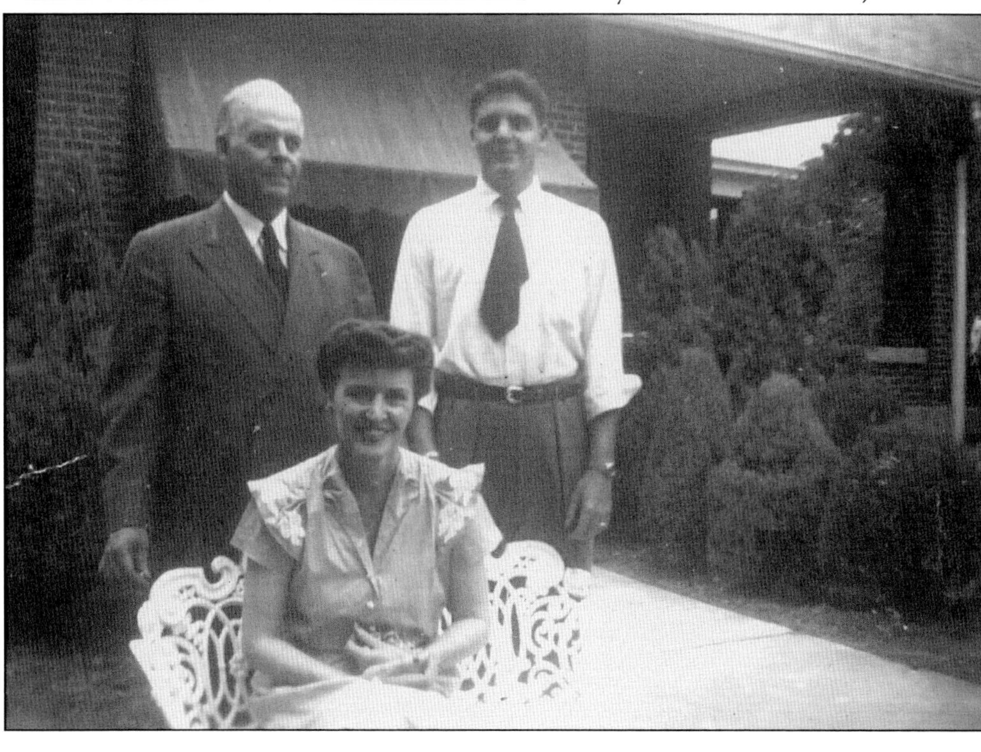

Patriotic, Public-Spirited Gentleman. Messar Babb entered the Confederate service as a private at the age of 16 in 1861 and served throughout the war. A soldier in Company A, 6th C. Calvary, Butler's Brigade, Army of Northern Virginia, Babb was wounded on two occasions, had lost three horses, and was later imprisoned. Following the war, Babb engaged in farming and merchandising. He served as Laurens County treasurer for two terms and later occupied several clerical positions in the Courthouse. (Courtesy of Mrs. Beatrice Babb Bradley.)

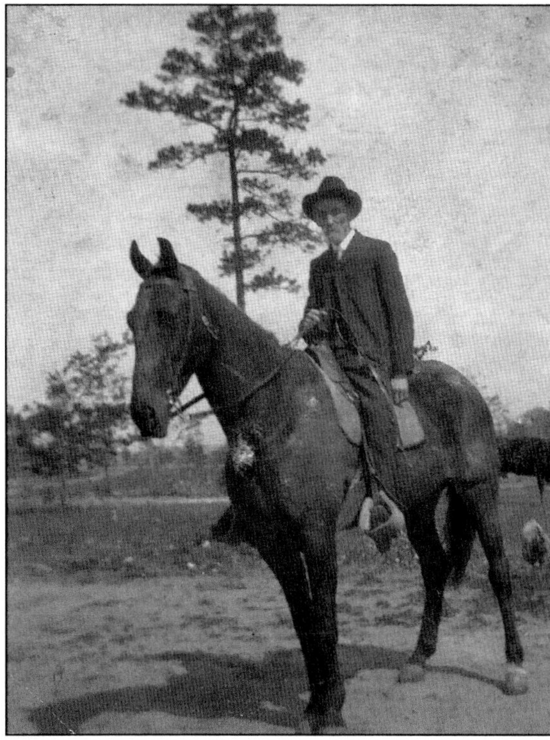

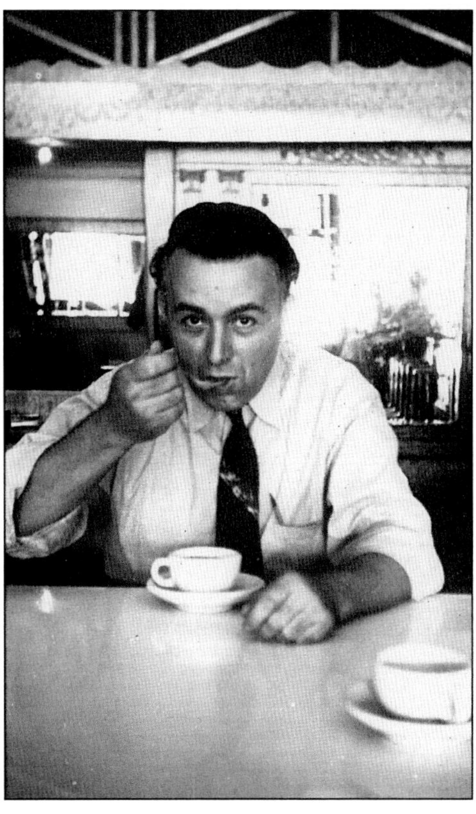

The Palace of Sweets. A native of Sparta, Greece, Peter Arthur Mitchell came to Laurens in 1910 to open a candy store, the Palace of Sweets. He later owned the Laurens Cafe on the east side of the Square and became known for cakes and candies, which were widely distributed at Christmas. He served on the city council and was noted for his humanitarian deeds, patriotic zeal, and interest in good government. He was affectionately called "Pete" by his associates and the hundreds of people he befriended. (Courtesy of Mrs. Beatrice Babb Bradley.)

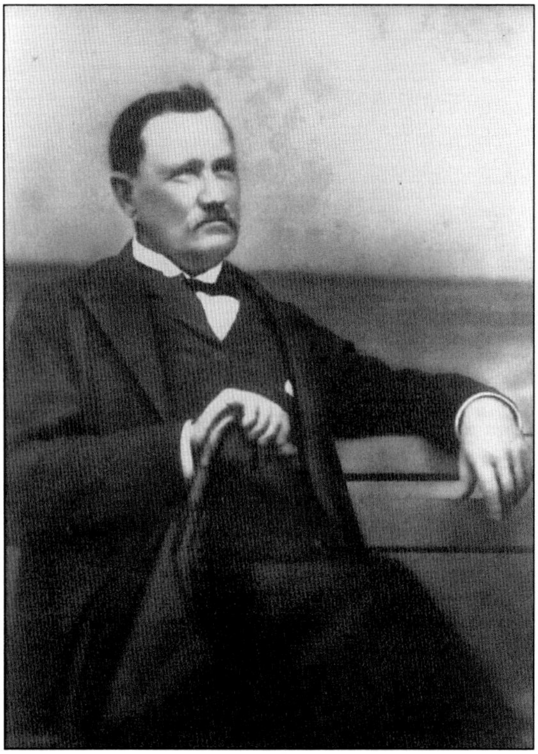

PROMINENT FIGURE. At the age of 14, Robert Henry Hudgens went to the front with the Confederate Army. After the war, he became a successful farmer and later bought an iron foundry and machine works and a ginnery. Hudgens built the Laurens Bonded Warehouse and was manager of Southern Cotton Oil Company. He was married to the former Nannie Barksdale and lived on Sullivan Street. (Courtesy of Robert H. Roper III.)

HUSBAND AND WIFE. H. Douglas and Lucille Martin Gray are shown in the parlor of their South Harper Street home. A large formal garden graced the back lawn of the Gray home. Along with Albert Dial and Ernest Easterby, Gray was one of the founders of Laurens Glass. (Courtesy of Mrs. Harriet Gray Hunter.)

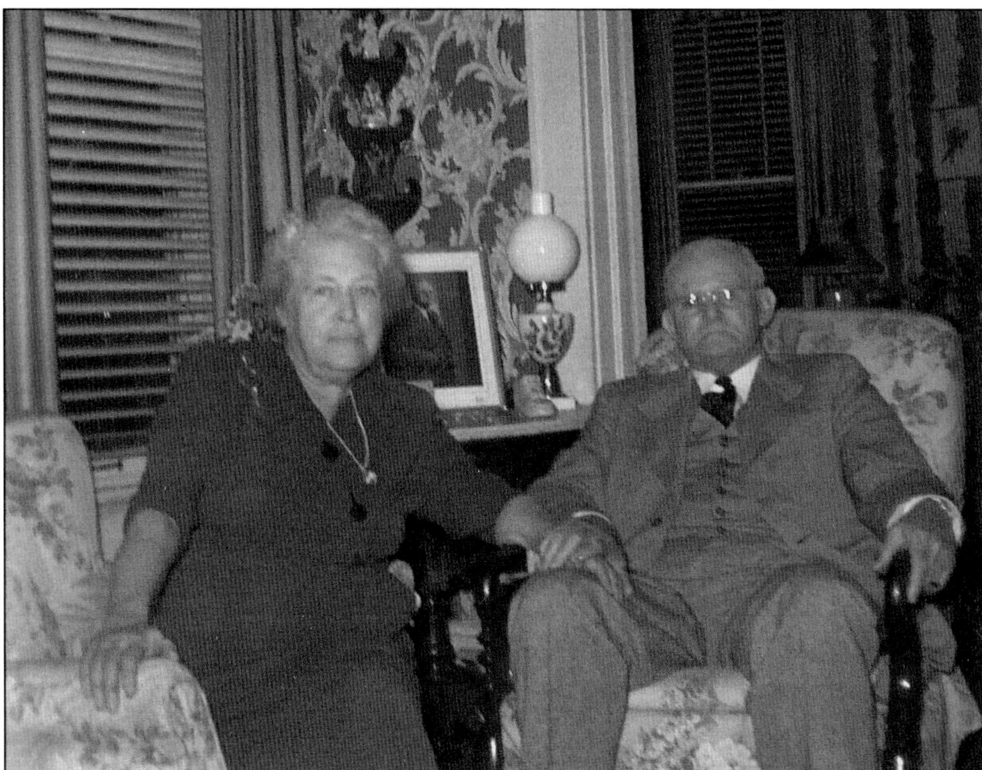

COMMUNITY MINDED. Ernest Douglas Easterby was the chairman of the board for Laurens Glass and remained so until his death. Easterby, Albert Dial, and Douglas Gray purchased a broken-down plant and did what they were told couldn't be done: make glass. Easterby was a charitable and community-minded man, and he contributed generously to worthwhile causes, many of which were never made public. He was an active member of the First Baptist Church. Ernest and his wife, Estelle Gregory Easterby, lived on West Main Street. (Courtesy of Mrs. Harriet Easterby Faris.)

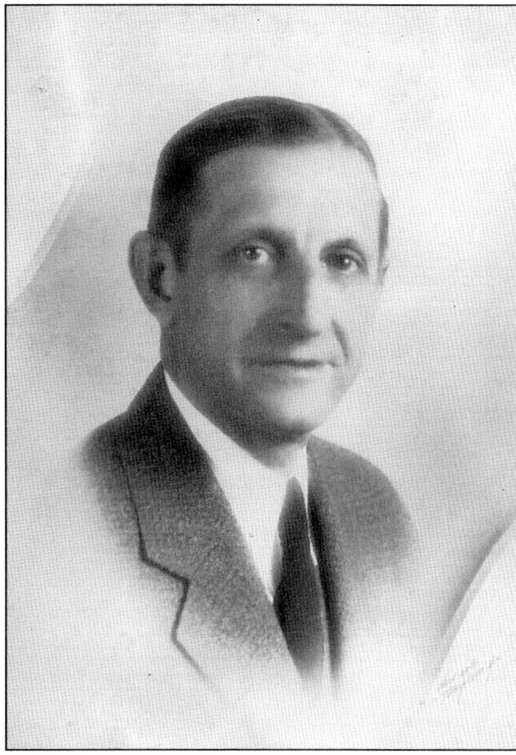

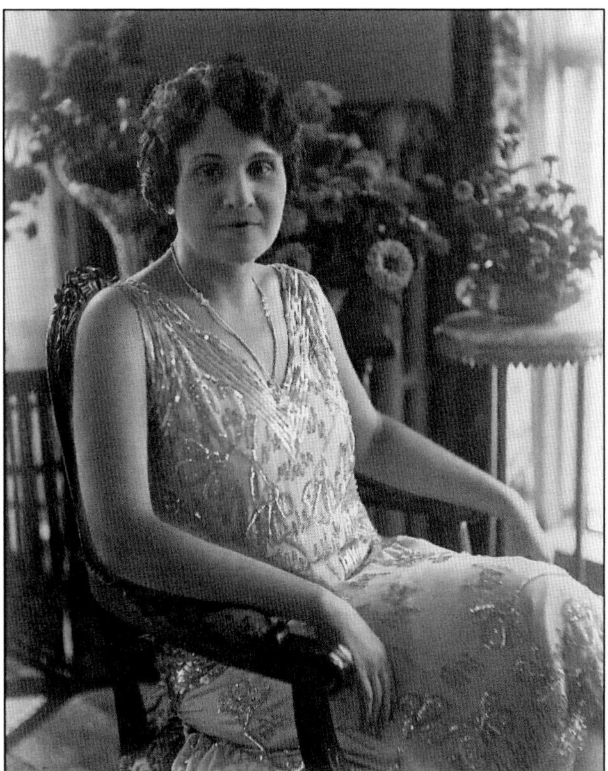

ACCREDITED FLOWER SHOW JUDGE. Wife of Ernest Easterby, the former Estelle Gregory was born in Lancaster to Howell Jackson and Hattie Jordan Gregory. Estelle graduated from Furman University and taught in the Laurens School System. She was a member of the Cora Cox Lucas Music Club, the Green Thumb Garden Club, the Wednesday Club, and Laurens First Baptist. Mrs. Easterby was a national accredited flower show judge and author of *Home Book of Flower Arrangements*. (Courtesy of Mrs. Harriett Easterby Faris.)

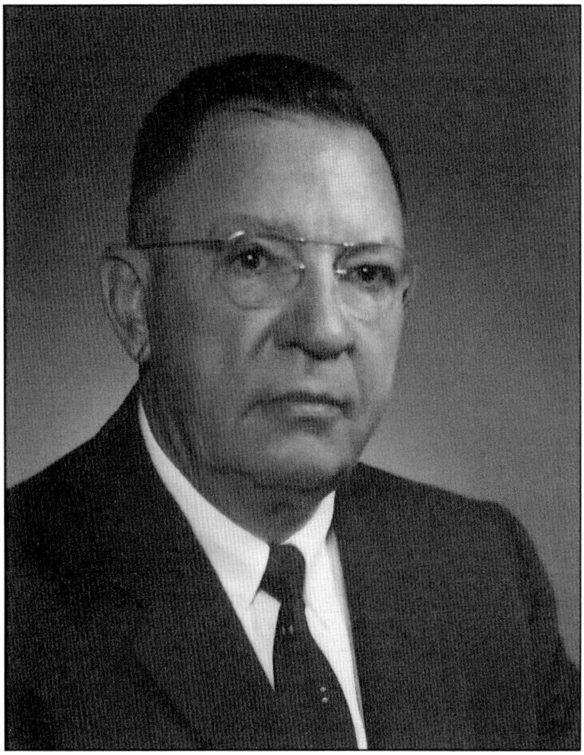

CIVIC, CHURCH, AND INDUSTRIAL LEADER. Robert Hudgens Roper, executive vice president of Laurens Glass, was a lifelong resident of Laurens and the son of Charles and Eula Hudgens Roper. One of the pioneers in the soft-drink industry, he was known for devoting his life to the betterment of his church, community, and business. He and his wife, the former Ruth Altman, lived on West Main Street. (Courtesy of Robert H. Roper III.)

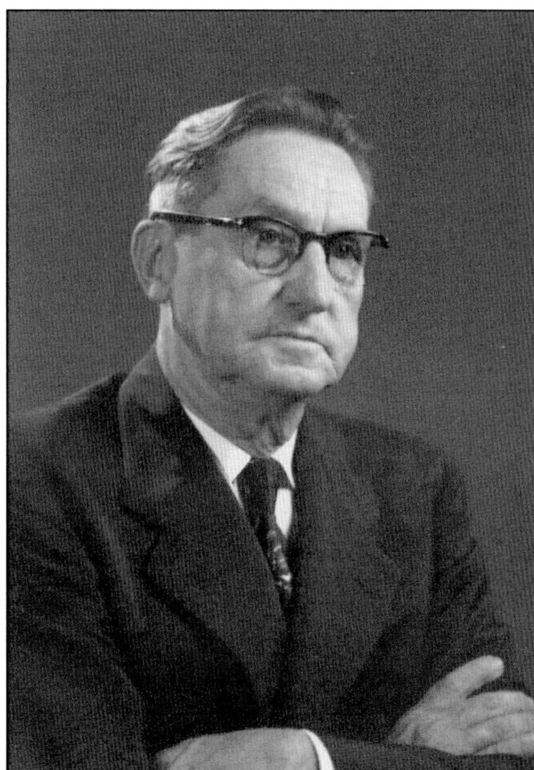

COUNTY AND CITY ATTORNEY. Ralph Traywick Wilson, an attorney and public official, was a member of the Blackwell, Sullivan and Wilson Law Firm. He served one term as superintendent of education and at different times in his career served as county and city attorney. Wilson was a state senator from 1948 to 1956. He was twice married, first to the former Clara Woods and later to former Inez Franks Wood. (Courtesy of Ralph T. Wilson III.)

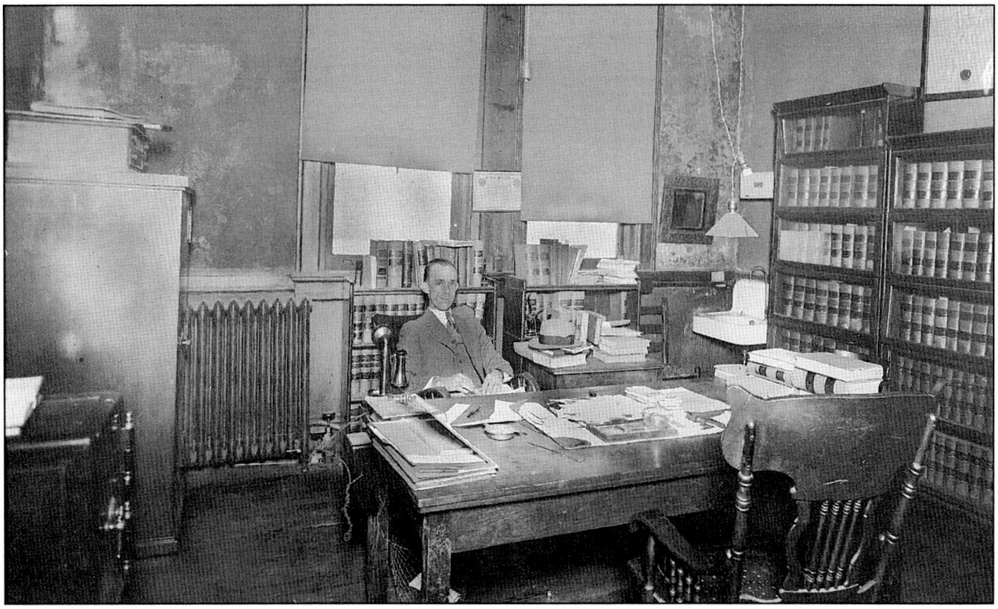

State Senator. Attorney Otto Langdon Long, pictured in his law office, was one of Laurens's most distinguished citizens. This Citadel graduate was a mayor of Laurens and also a state senator. Long served as a school trustee and was a member of the First Methodist Church. Langdon and his wife, Sarah Dwight Long, lived on South Harper Street. (Courtesy of Mrs. Saralise Long Kennedy.)

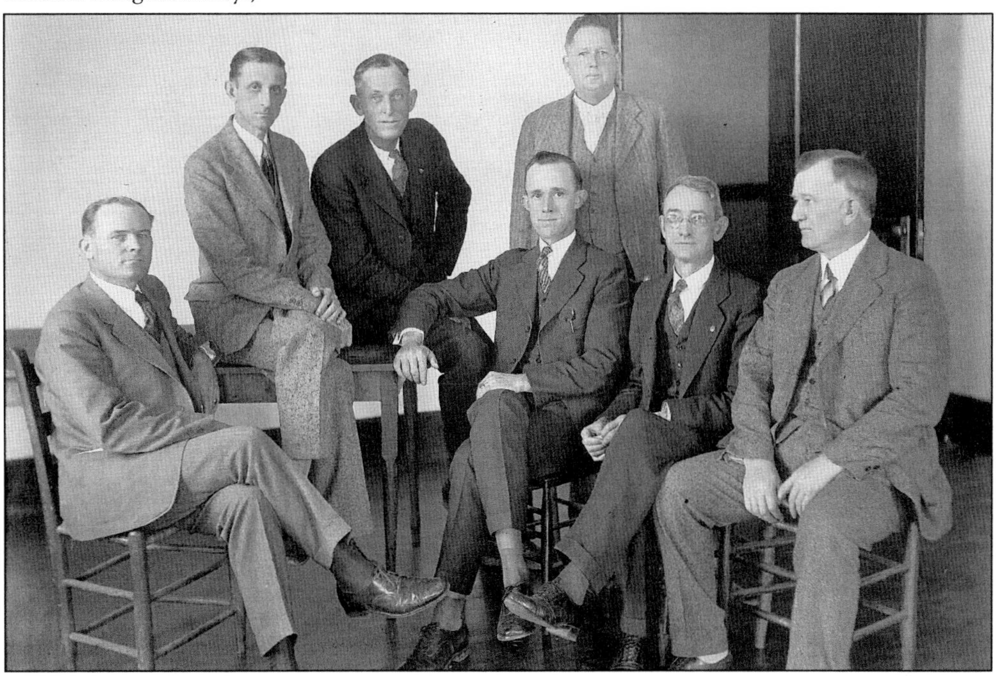

Laurens City Council. The 1928–1930 Laurens City Council and the mayor were responsible for the construction of a new city hall. Pictured, from left to right, are H.D. Gray, E.D. Easterby, J.F. Montgomery, Mayor O.L. Long, E.R. Blakely, L.B. Blackwell, and J. McD. Moore. (Courtesy of Mrs. Saralise Long Kennedy.)

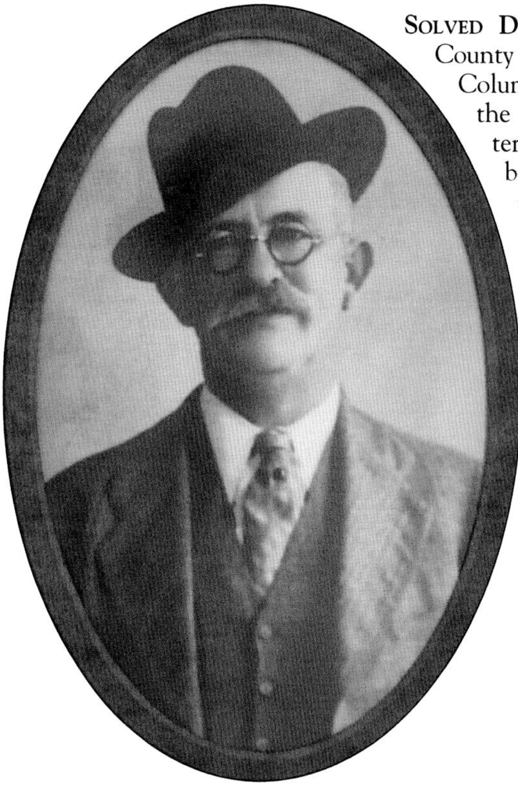

SOLVED DIFFICULT CASES. Elected sheriff of Laurens County in 1924 and re-elected in 1928 and in 1932, Columbus Owens broke a century-old precedent: the custom for the sheriff to serve only two terms. Generally regarded as one of the best sheriffs in the state, Owens showed an expertise in several outstanding cases, and his detective ability allowed him to solve some of the most baffling and difficult cases that occurred in Laurens County. (Courtesy of Mrs. Katherine Owens Waldrep.)

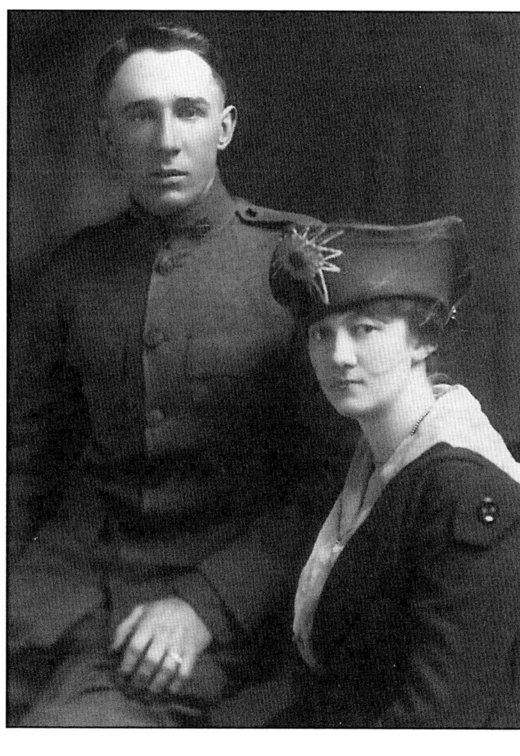

SHERIFF FOR 20 YEARS. Before becoming Laurens County sheriff in 1936 and serving in that capacity for 20 years, Caldwell W. Wier was the assistant police chief for the town of Clinton. After serving as sheriff, Wier was elected to the Laurens City Council. A veteran of World War I, he was married to Elizabeth Copeland, a nurse. The Wiers were members of the First Presbyterian Church. (Courtesy of Robert H. Roper III.)

CHIEF CREWS. James T. "Chief" Crews began his career in 1882 as chief of the Laurens Fire Department, and in 1914, he became chief of police. He carried a walking stick and referred to it as "My Winchester." The Laurens Business League presented him a loving cup for more than 50 years of loyalty, faithfulness, and efficiency. As a lad, Crews worked in the print shop for his father, Colonel Thomas B. Crews, publisher of the *Laurensville Herald* and also for the town's other newspaper, the *Laurens Advertiser*. (Courtesy of Laurens County Library.)

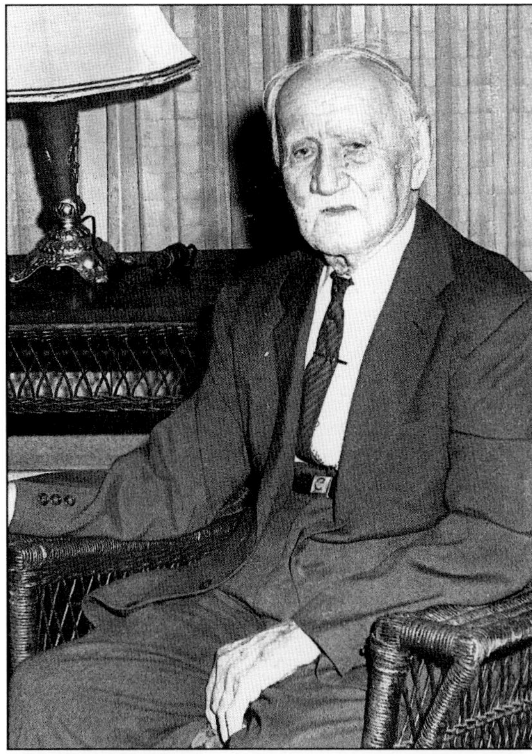

HANDING OVER THE OFFICE. Longtime Laurens County sheriff Caldwell Wier (left) turns over the office of sheriff to R. Eugene Johnson. Laurens County deputy Leroy "Bud" Keeble looks on as the outstanding law enforcement officials shake hands. (Courtesy of Robert H. Roper III.)

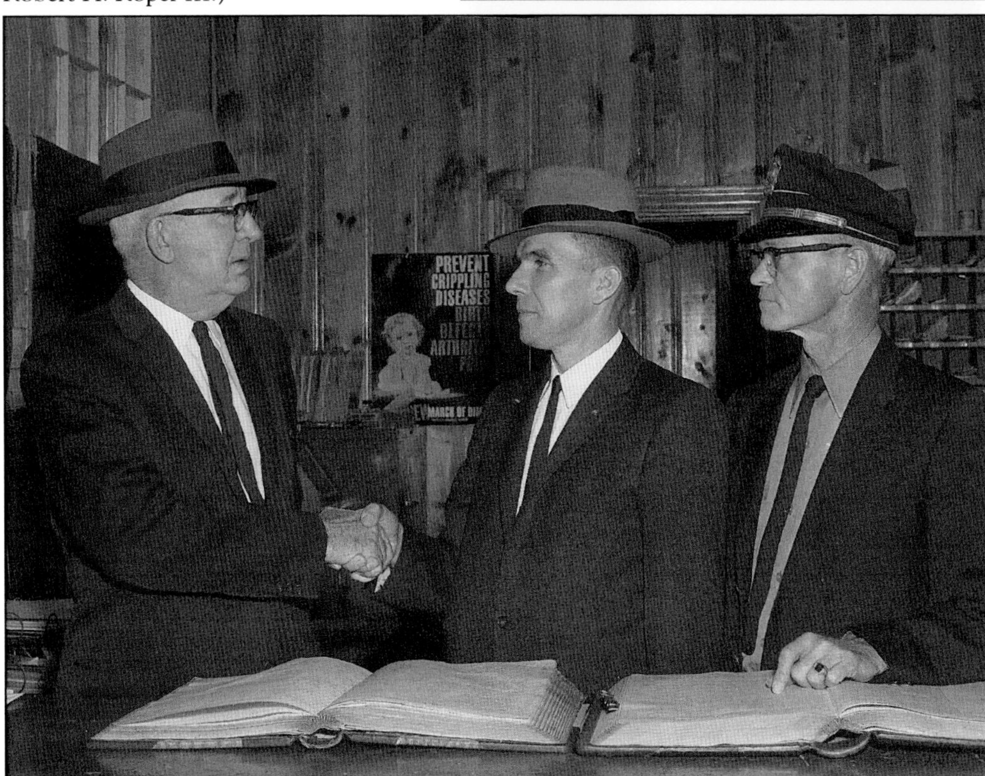

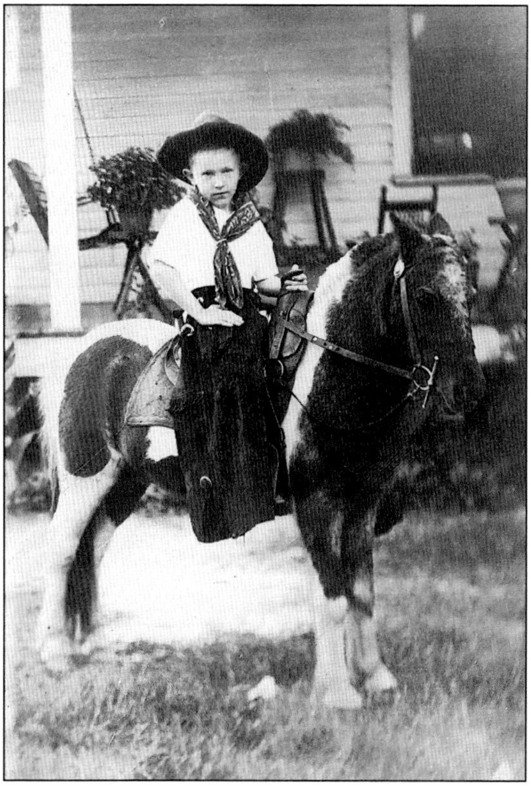

Traveling Photographer. Complete with pony, saddle, bridle, chaps, hat, and camera, traveling photographers went door to door and enticed mothers into having their children's pictures made. The thrilled child posed for the camera and then awaited the arrival of his "cowboy picture" in the mail. Durrand G. Coats, son of Robert H. and Ruby Monroe Coats, was one of many lads that had a brief moment on the painted pony. (Courtesy of Julian Coats.)

Tailor. Claude Martin was probably the last known tailor in Laurens. For many years, he fitted garments for Laurens gentlemen from his shop on the east side of the Square. Martin (with visor) measures a sleeve for an unidentified young man while another unidentified fellow writes down the measurements. (Courtesy of *Laurens County Advertiser* files.)

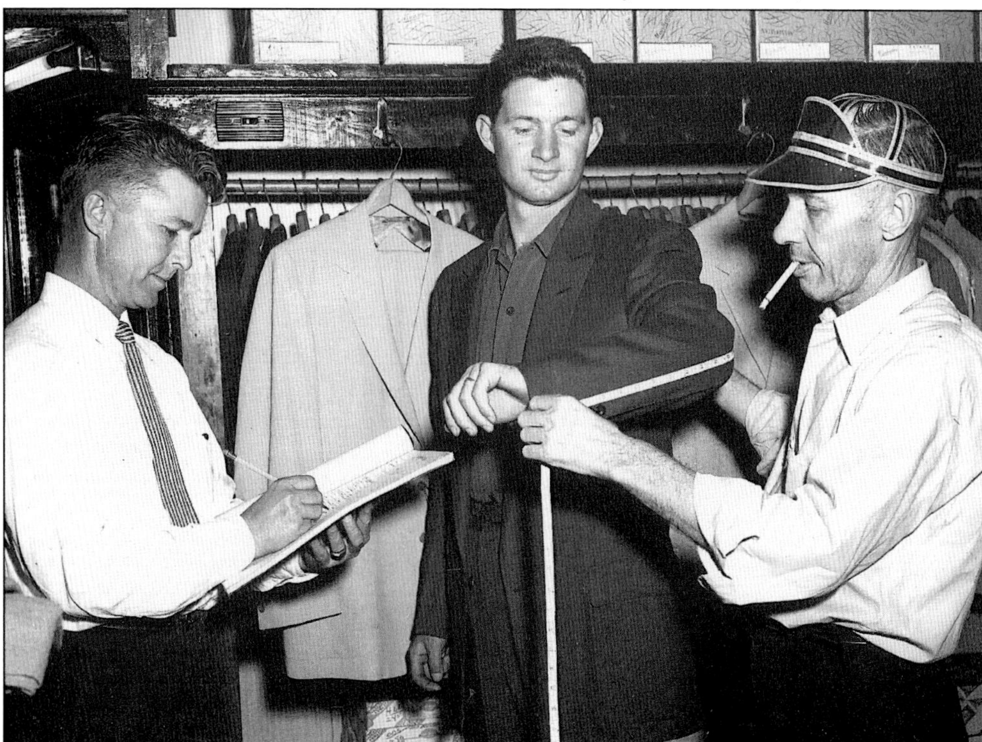

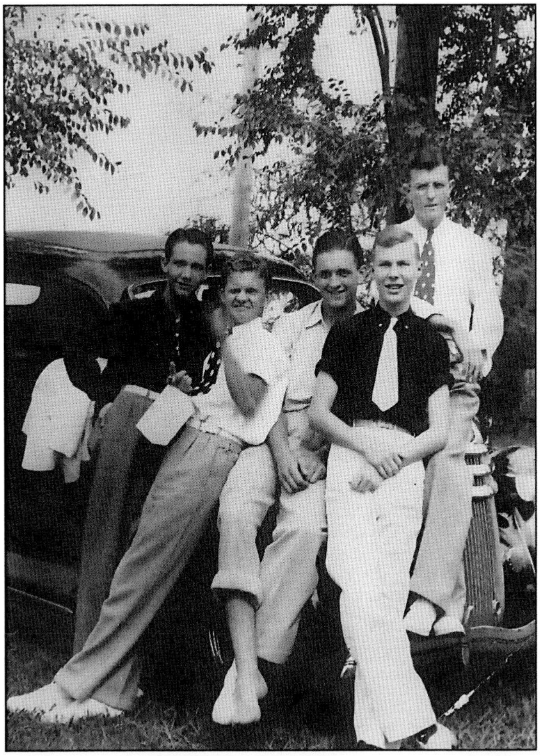

In the Forties. Prior to WW II, a group of Laurens friends clown for a photographer. Shown, from left to right, are the following: unidentified, James Owings, Lang Long, unidentified, and Dan Sherer (behind). (Courtesy of Mrs. Harriett Easterby Faris.)

Laurens Leaders. Possibly at a chamber of commerce function, Laurens gentlemen, from left to right, are listed as follows: (front row) ? Carr, Scotts Five & Dime Store; Dr. Martin Teague, Laurens physician; and Robert "Bob" Erwin, Laurens Glass; (back row) Skip Brightwell, Coca-Cola Bottling; J.R. Derrick, Laurens High School Principal; and J.E. "Red" Hunt, Studebaker Dealership. (Courtesy of *Laurens County Advertiser* files.)

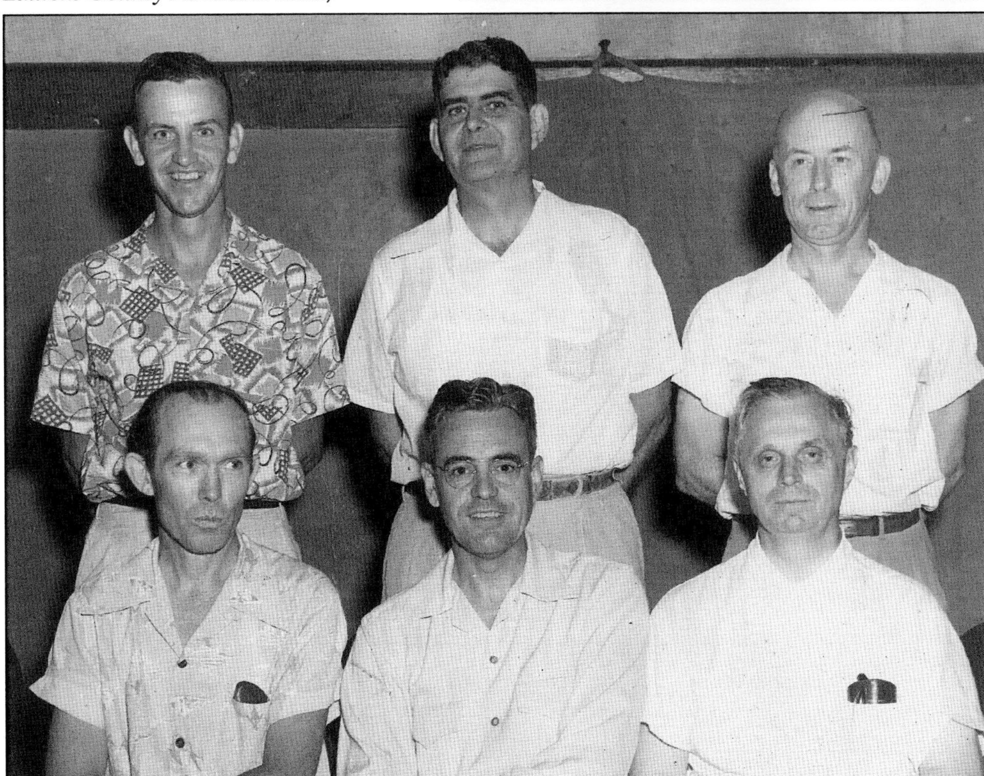

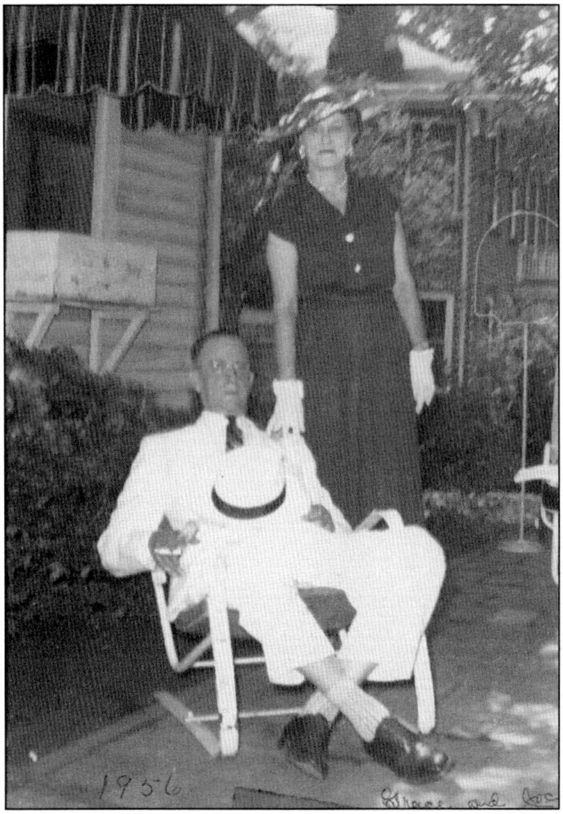

LAURENS PHYSICIAN. Dr. Robert Paul McGowan and his wife, Grace Cannon McGowan, are shown in the yard of their South Harper home. Dr. McGowan practiced medicine in Laurens and his office was located upstairs in a building on the south side of the Public Square. Mrs. McGowan was the former Grace Cannon of Fountain Inn. (Courtesy of Caldwell Wier III.)

TAUGHT FOR 40 YEARS. Mrs. Carrie D. Edmunds (first row, second from left) was born in the Waterloo section of Laurens County. She received an education at Brewer, a Presbyterian school in Greenwood, and at Allen University. After teaching in several locations throughout the Upstate and at numerous rural schools in the county, she settled in Laurens, became the principal of the Hampton Street School, and later taught at Sanders High School. (Courtesy of Mrs. Carrie D. Edmunds.)

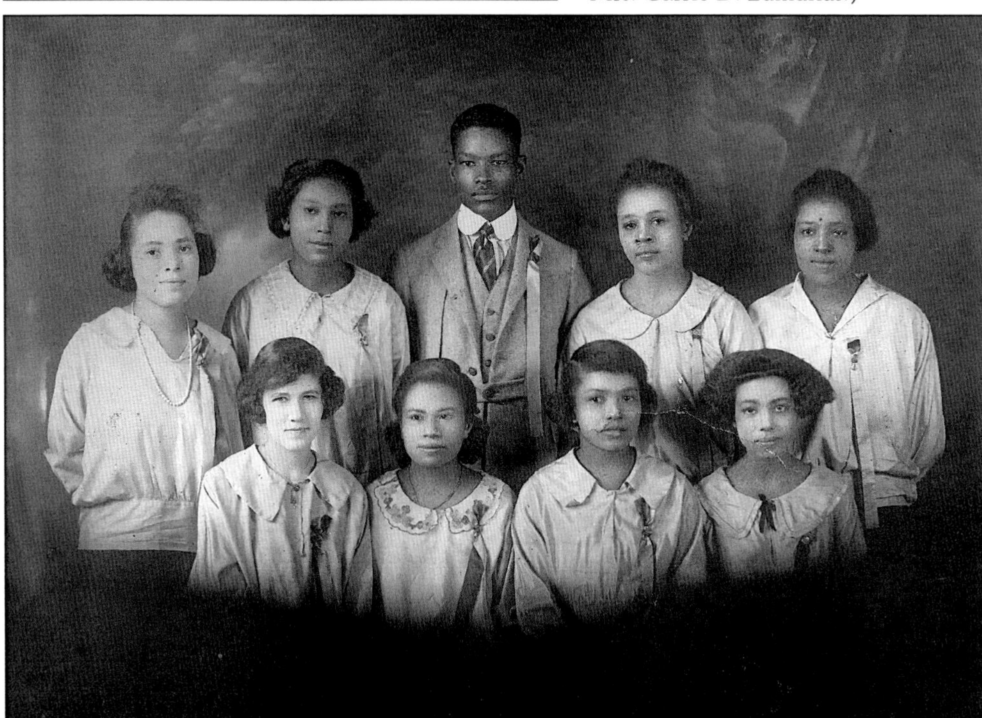

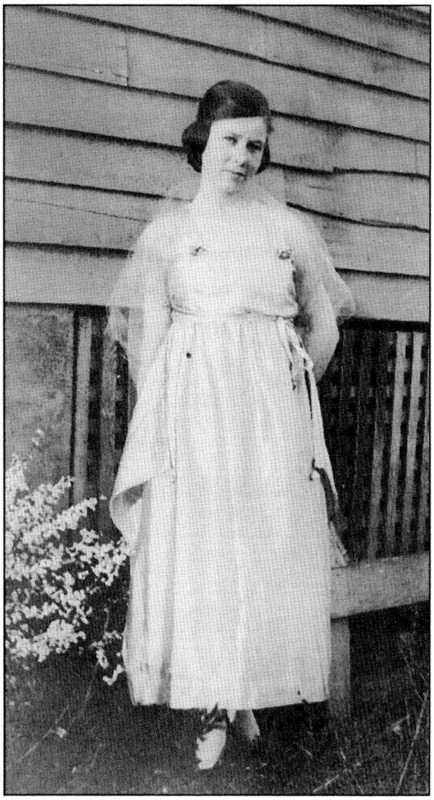

YOUNG LADY OF LAURENS. Rosa Lee Sullivan, a young lady of Laurens in the early 1900s, is dressed in the fashion of the day. (Courtesy of Mrs. Beatrice Babb Bradley.)

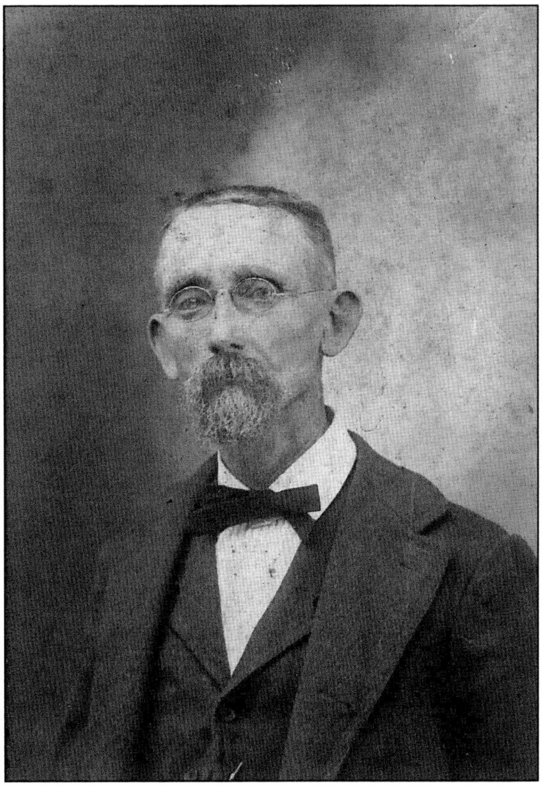

NATIVE OF BABBTOWN. The son of Sampson Babb, Messar Babb left his rural Babbtown home and moved with his family to Laurens. He became a respected Laurens official, serving as county treasurer as well as in other capacities. (Courtesy of Mrs. Beatrice Babb Bradley.)

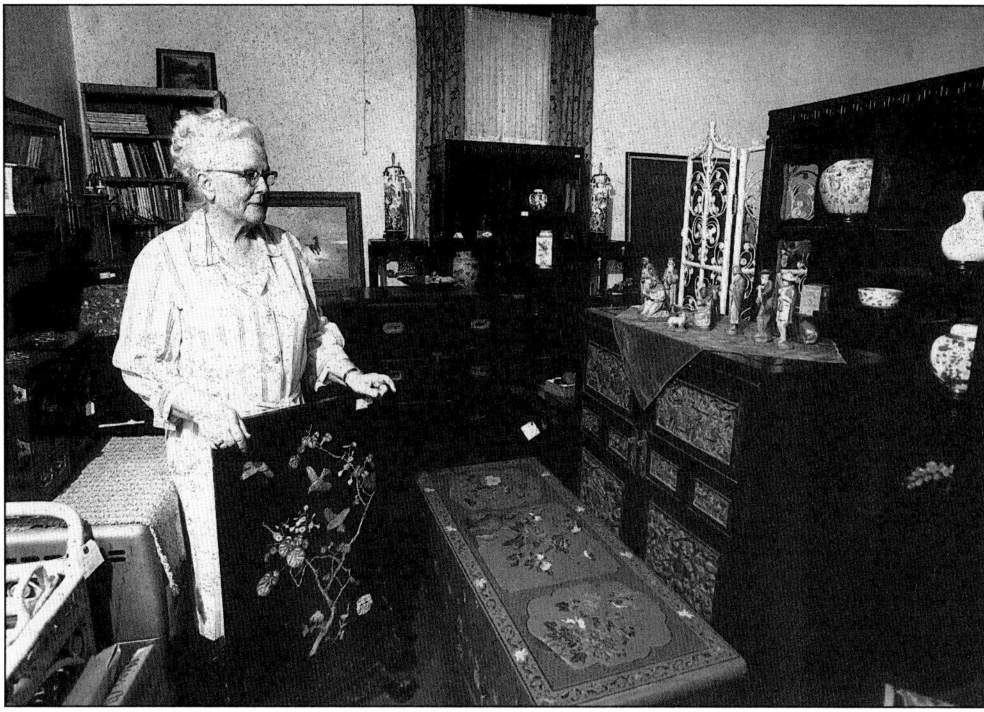

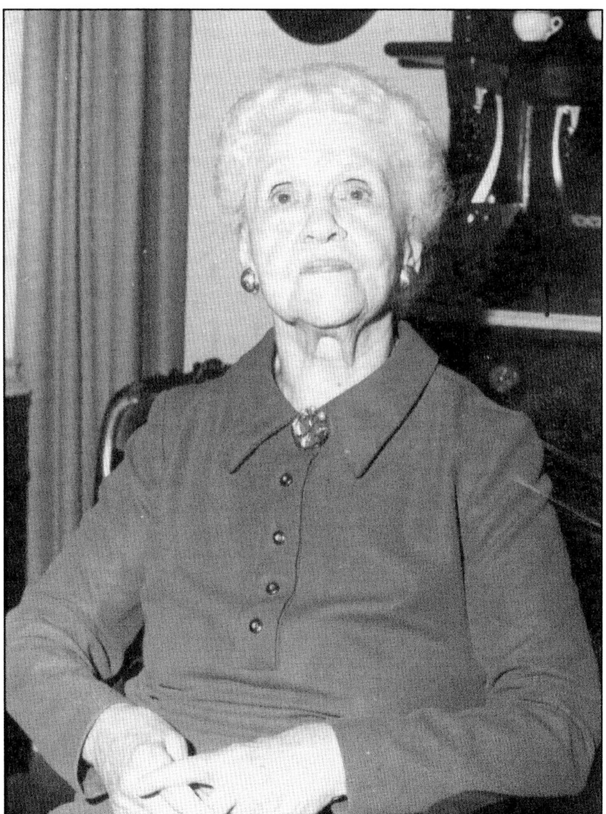

BELOVED MISSIONARY. Martha Linda Franks was born in the family home on South Harper Street to John and Sallie Franks. She graduated from Winthrop College and the Southern Baptist Seminary in Louisville, Kentucky. She served as a missionary to China and later Taiwan. Upon retirement and after returning to Laurens, "Miss Martha" established a Christian Retirement Center on property donated by her brother, Clyde Franks. The center was named in her honor. (Courtesy of Laurens County Library.)

OLDEST CHURCH MEMBER. Claudia Crews Todd was the daughter of William T. and Elizabeth Wolff Crews and the wife of Samuel R. Todd. At the time of her death, she was the oldest member of the First United Methodist Church of Laurens. (Courtesy of Laurens County Library.)

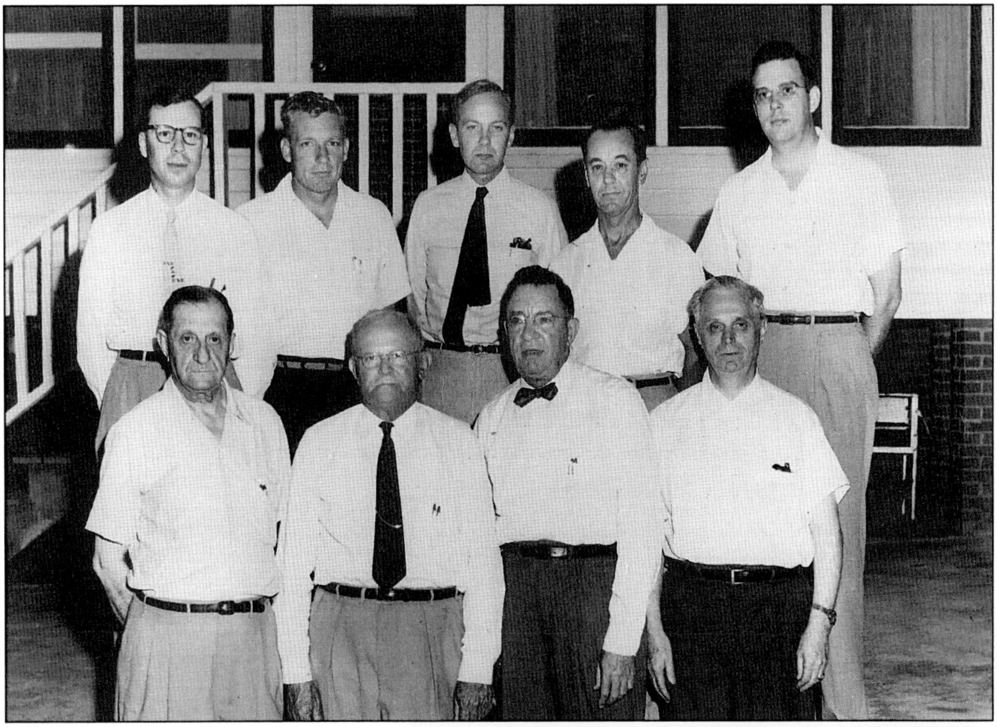

LAURENS GLASS EXECUTIVES. Laurens Glass executives, shown from left to right, are identified as follows: (front row) Ernest Easterby, H. Douglas Gray, Robert H. Roper, and Robert Erwin; (back row) Paul McAlister, James Ferguson, John Faris, Carl Davis, and Robert H. Roper Jr. (Courtesy of Mrs. Harriett Easterby Faris.)

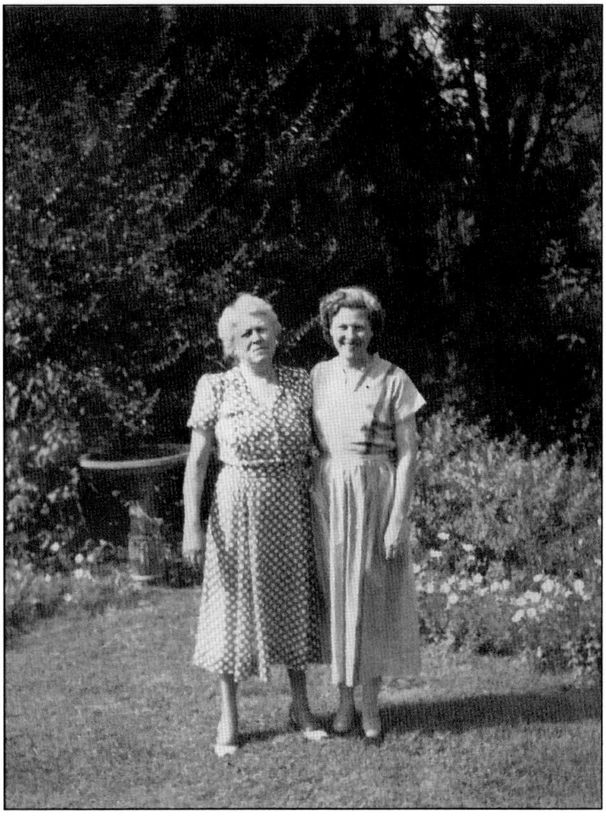

MOTHER AND DAUGHTER. Mrs. H. Douglas Gray and her daughter, Mrs. Harriett Gray Hunter, are in the garden surrounding the Gray home on South Harper Street. (Courtesy of Mrs. Harriett Gray Hunter.)

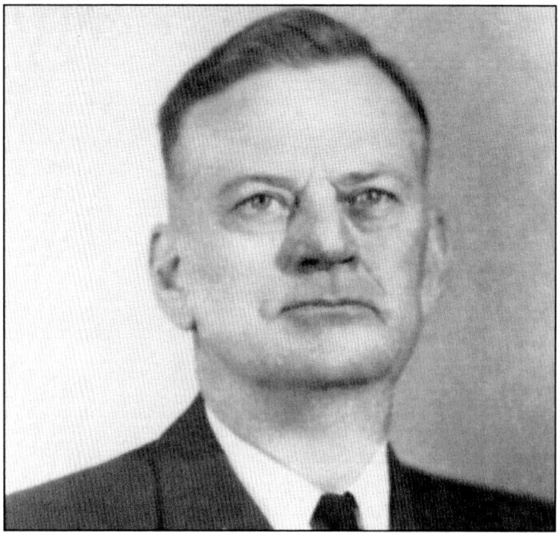

School Superintendent. C.K. Wright served as superintendent of education for the Laurens schools. He was a respected member of educational circles as well as the community at large. The dedicated educator did much to improve the educational system of Laurens. (Courtesy of Laurens County Library.)

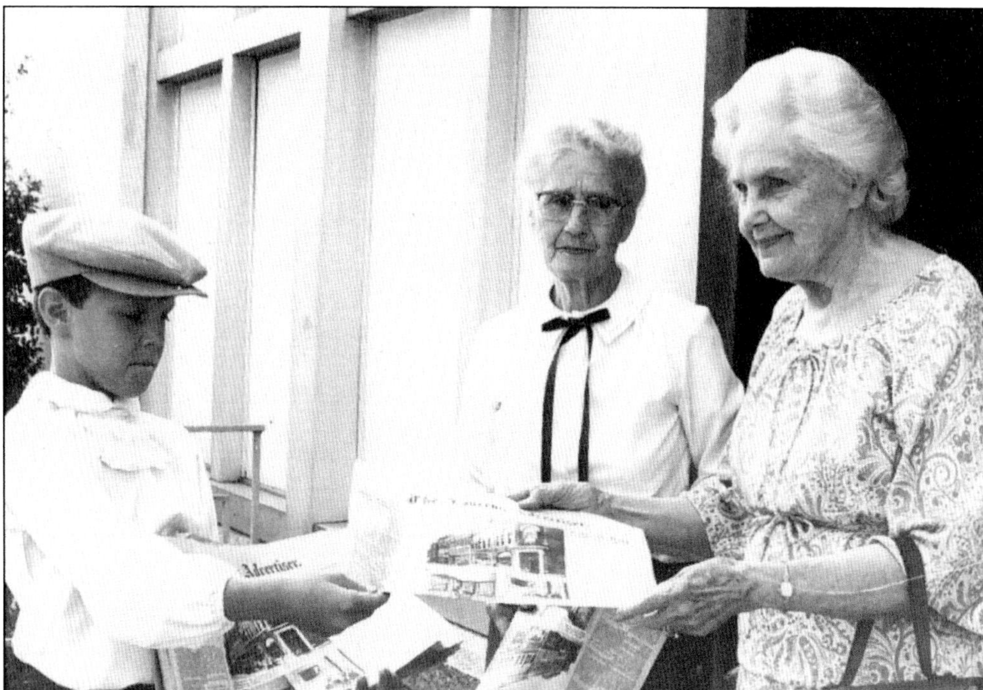

Writer and Teacher. Edna Riddle Foy and Ruth Riddle, daughters of Adolphus and Emily Owens Riddle, spent their childhood years on East Main Street and later moved to West Main Street. Edna was married to Groover Foy and upon his death returned to Laurens to live with her sister in the family home. The late "Miss Edna" (center) was known for her journalistic abilities, and "Miss Ruth," as an English teacher in the Laurens School System. In this photograph, the sisters are seen purchasing a newspaper from an unidentified lad. (Courtesy of Laurens County Library.)

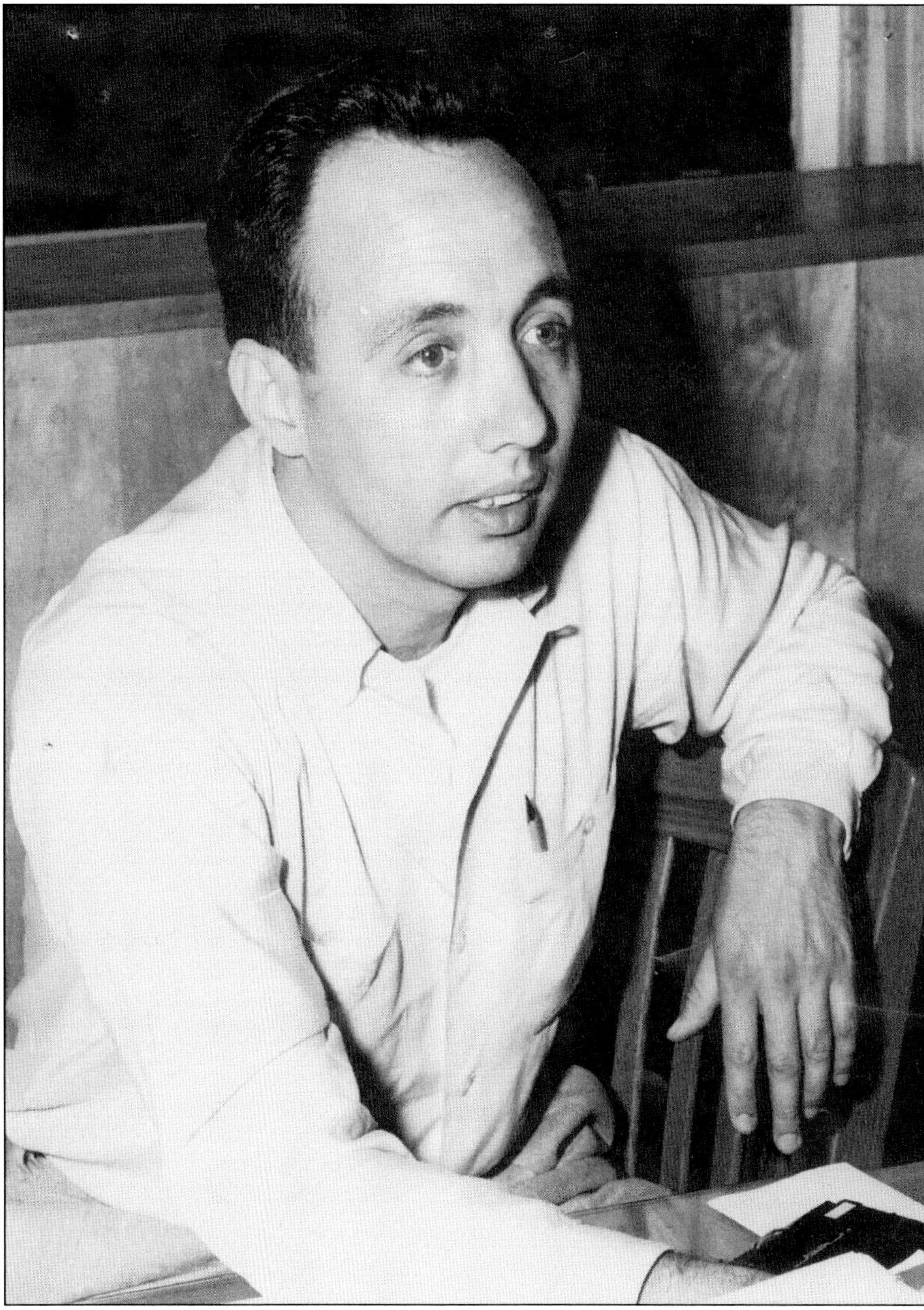

Editor and Publisher. William James Brown and David Harman purchased the *Laurens Advertiser* from Allison Lee in 1956. Brown later purchased Harman's interest and became sole publisher and editor of the weekly newspaper. Brown is shown here at the newspaper office, which at the time of his purchase, was located on Silver Street. (Courtesy of *Laurens County Advertise* files.)

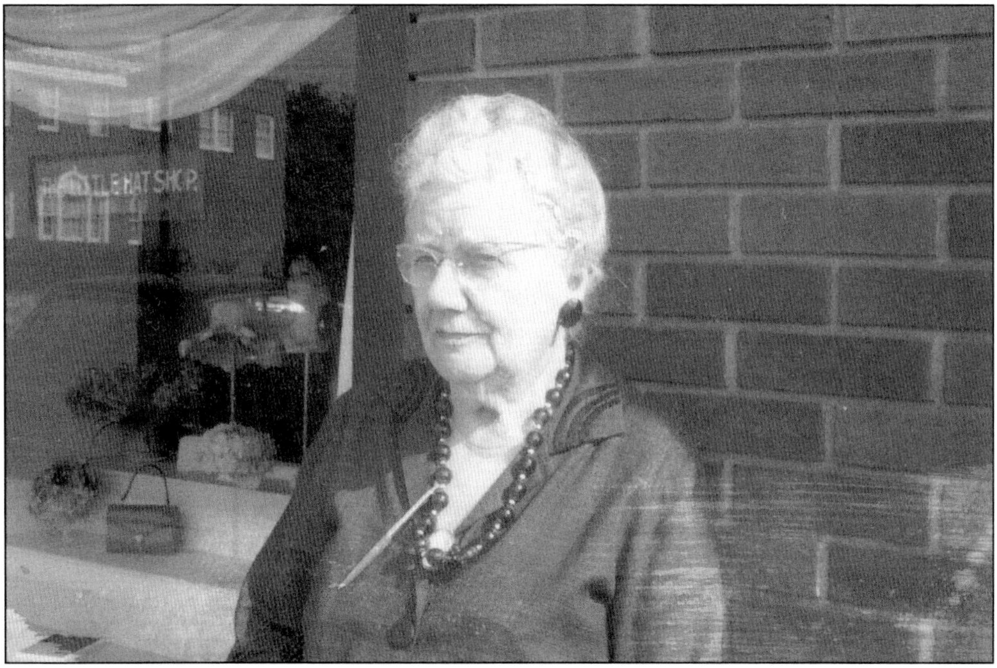

LITTLE HAT SHOP. Elizabeth Hance Crews was the daughter of Laurens police chief J.T. Crews. For many years, "Miss Bess" operated the Little Hat Shop, a millinery store for ladies on West Main Street. The talented and respected Laurens merchant was a charter member of the Laurens Business and Professional Women's Club. (Courtesy of the Rhodes collection.)

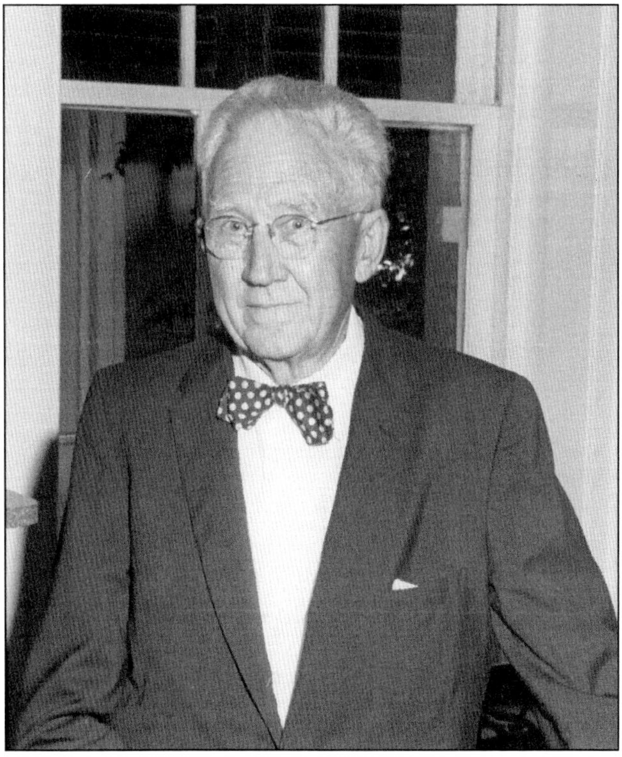

HISTORIAN AND ANTIQUE COLLECTOR. Clyde T. Franks was a native and lifelong resident of Laurens. The son of John A. and Sallie Henderson Franks and the husband of Sadie Fuller Franks, he was a representative of the Federal Land Bank for 35 years. An authority on early architecture and Laurens County history, Franks restored the Rose Hill Plantation house in Union County and the Villa in Laurens. He was also an avid collector of antiques, amassing quite a collection in his lifetime. (Courtesy of the Rhodes collection.)

Four

HOUSES OF WORSHIP

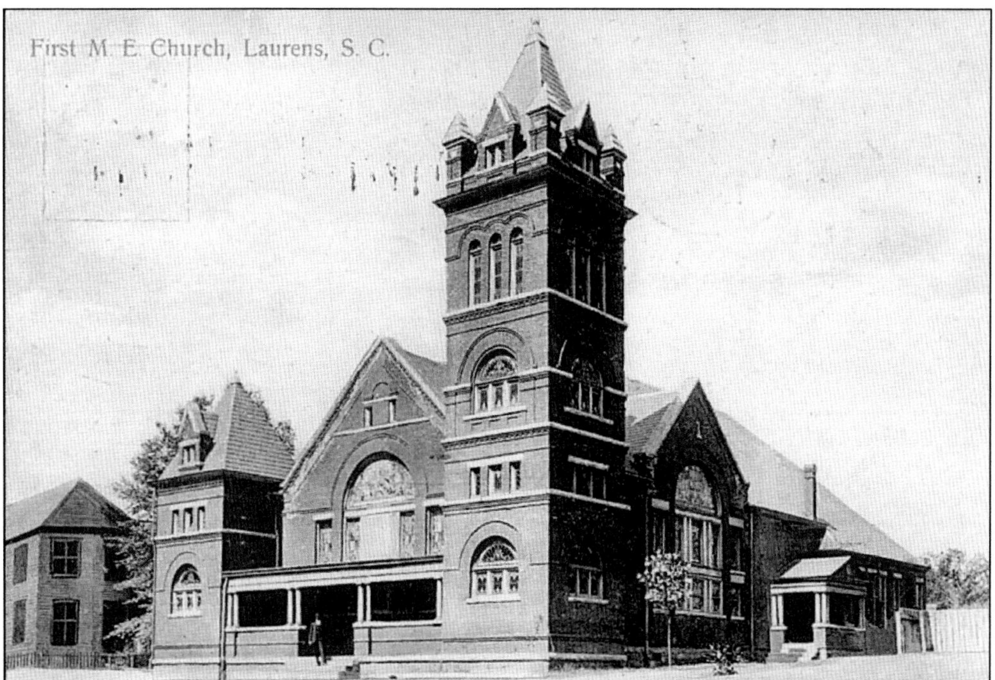

FIRST UNITED METHODIST CHURCH. The present church, located on West Main Street, was built in 1897–1898. The first service was held on Christmas Day, 1898. The first infant to be baptized in the new facility was Hattie Dunklin Gray. The brick church replaced the old Methodist church located at the railroad overpass. (Courtesy of Laurens County Library.)

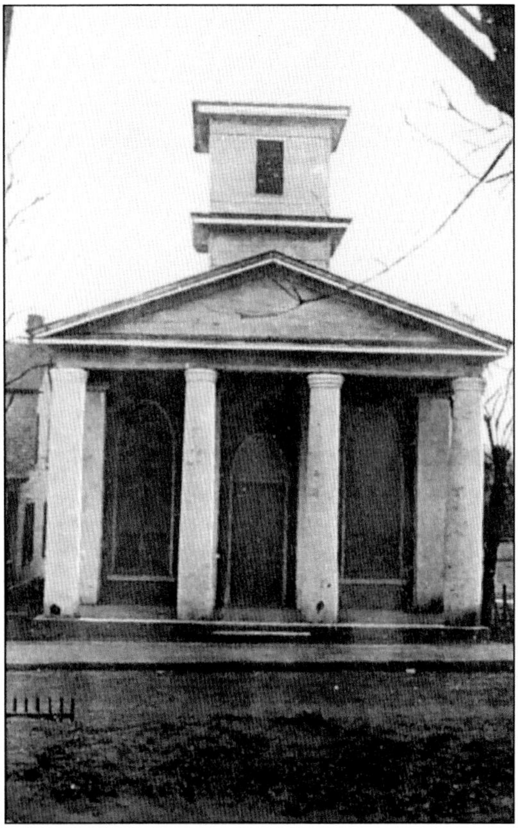

Church of the Epiphany. Located on West Main Street, the Church of the Epiphany is the oldest church building still standing in the city of Laurens. The church was built in 1846 on land given by Colonel James H. Irby, a prominent Laurens citizen. T.R. Badgett, a local builder, constructed the church with brick made in his brickyard near Wattsville. Refugees from the Lowcountry came to Laurens during the Civil War and worshiped in the Episcopal church. (Courtesy of Laurens County Library.)

Old Methodist Church. A simple house of worship was constructed by the Methodist congregation in 1852. Epworth Methodist Children's Home in Columbia was organized in the church. "Chief" J.T. Crews recalled helping his sister wash the lamps in the old church located at the railroad bridge. When a member of the church died, it was his job to climb into the loft and toll the "death bell." At the time of his death, the chief was still the proud possessor of a key to the old Methodist church. (Courtesy of the Rhodes collection.)

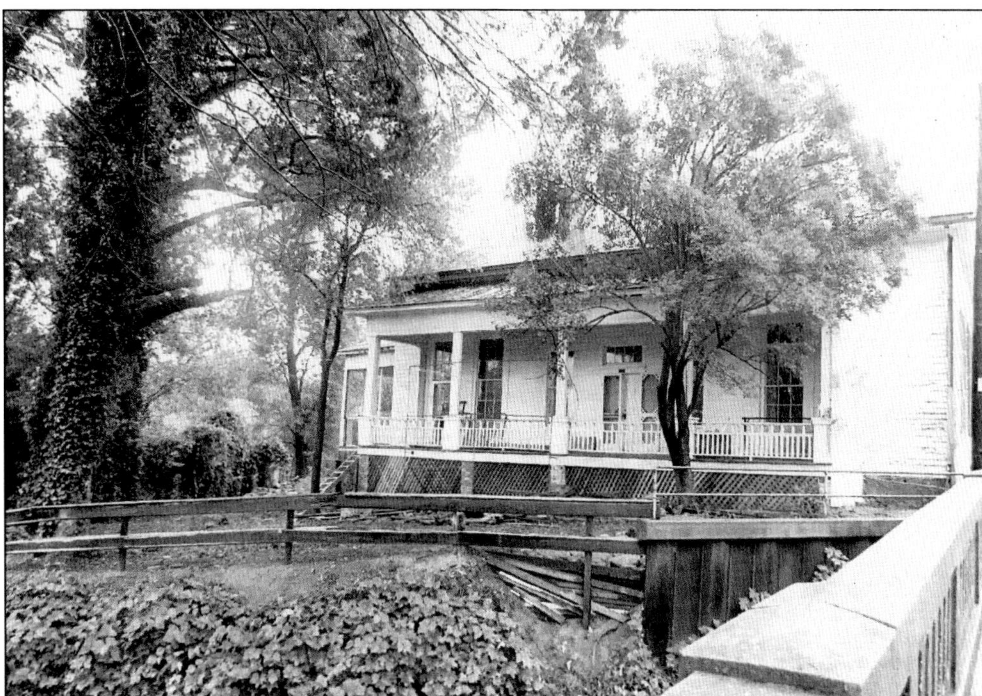

LANDMARK OF LAURENS. Built in 1895, the First Presbyterian Church, located on West Main Street, is a landmark of Laurens. The church was organized in 1832 by Reverend Samuel Lewers with 14 charter members. In the beginning, there was not a building; therefore, the congregation met on East Main Street near the depot. The first church building was constructed on Church Street in 1850. By 1860, the church membership reached 176. (Courtesy of the Rhodes collection.)

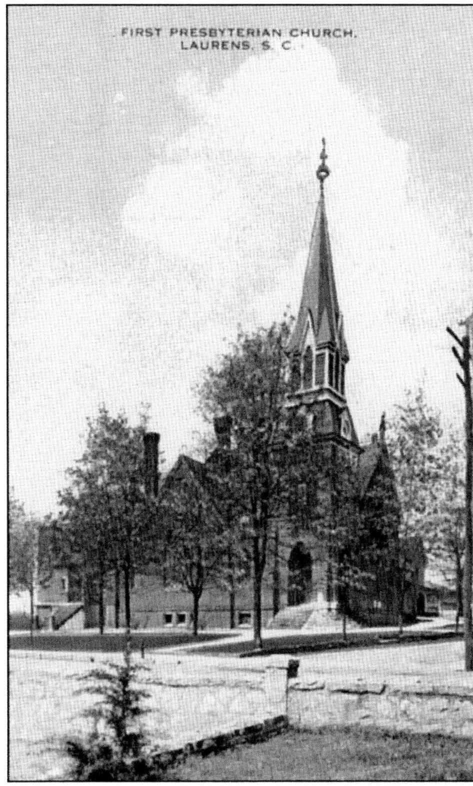

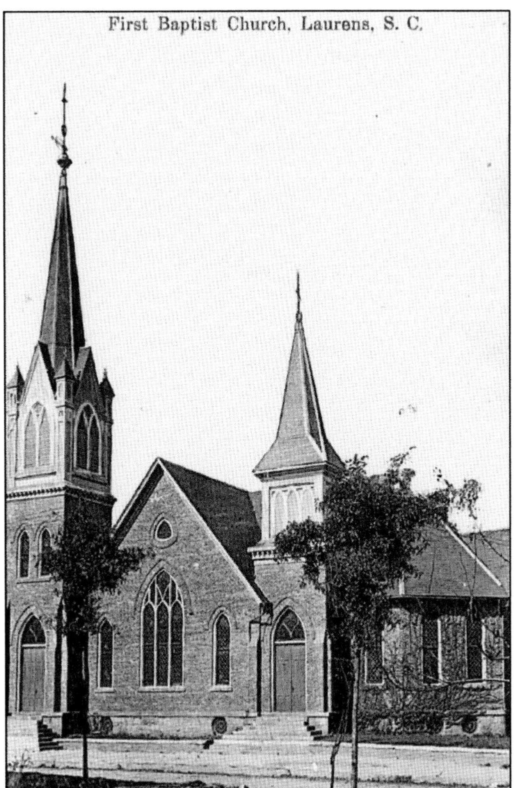

FIRST BAPTIST CHURCH. In 1834, 16 members organized the Laurensville Baptist Church. The first structure was wooden and built on the corner of Church and College Streets in 1850. Several brick buildings were constructed during the years as the congregation grew. This postcard shows the First Baptist Church in 1909 on the corner of West Main and Church Streets. (Courtesy of Laurens County Library.)

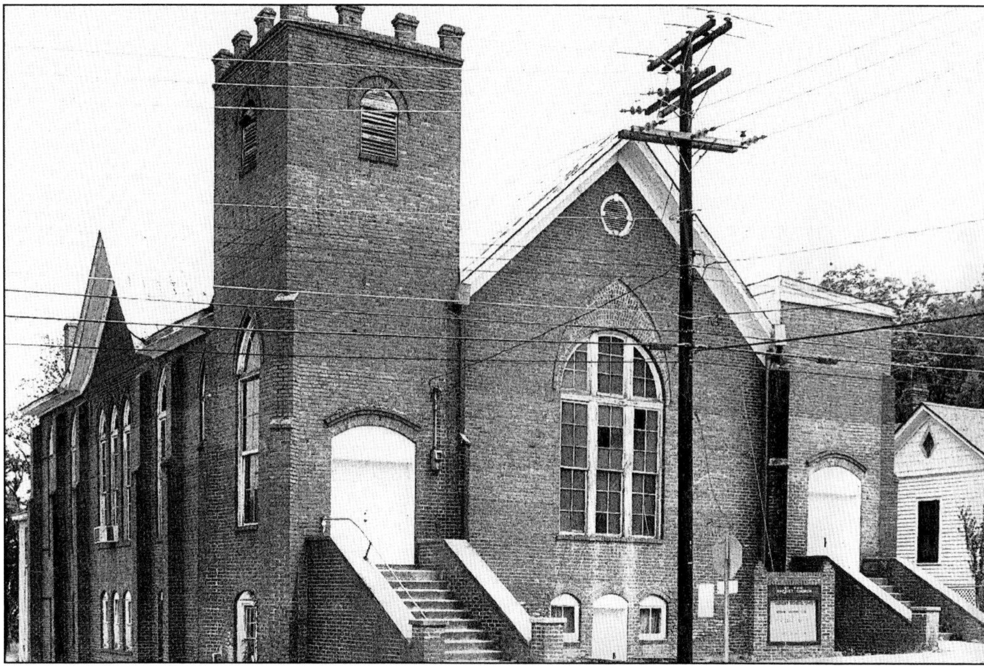

FIRST AFRICAN-AMERICAN CHURCH. Standing on the corner of Caroline and Hampton Streets, St. Paul First Baptist Church was the first African-American Baptist church in the town of Laurens and served as the first public education center for African Americans. The original church was destroyed by fire in 1910. Parts of the basement and foundation were incorporated into the brick structure built in 1912. The windows with center-pointed arches and a tower with battlements reflect the late Gothic-Revival style. (Courtesy of the Rhodes collection.)

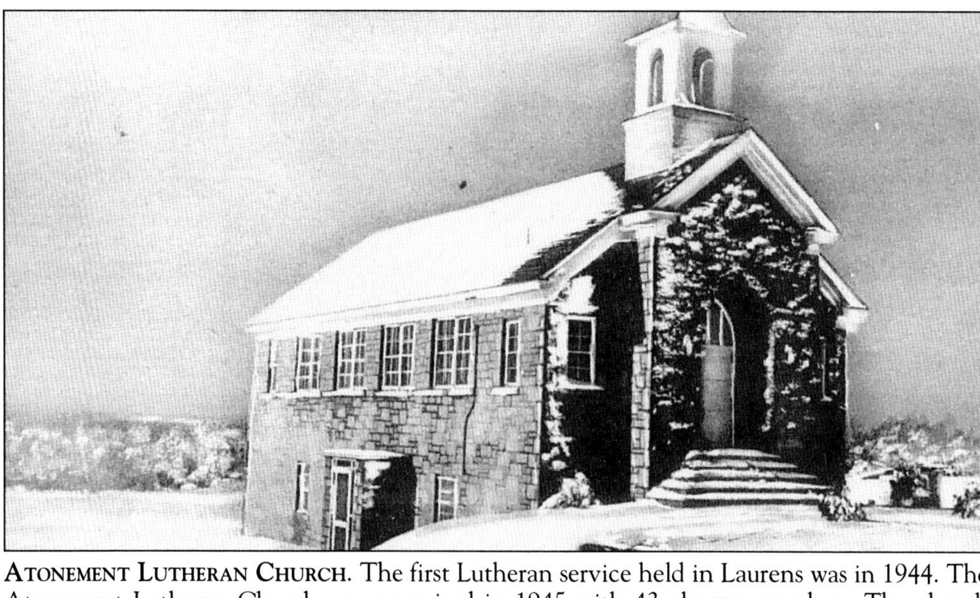

ATONEMENT LUTHERAN CHURCH. The first Lutheran service held in Laurens was in 1944. The Atonement Lutheran Church was organized in 1945 with 43 charter members. The church property fronted Farley Avenue directly across from the Laurens County Hospital. (Courtesy Mrs. Katherine Weathers Johnson.)

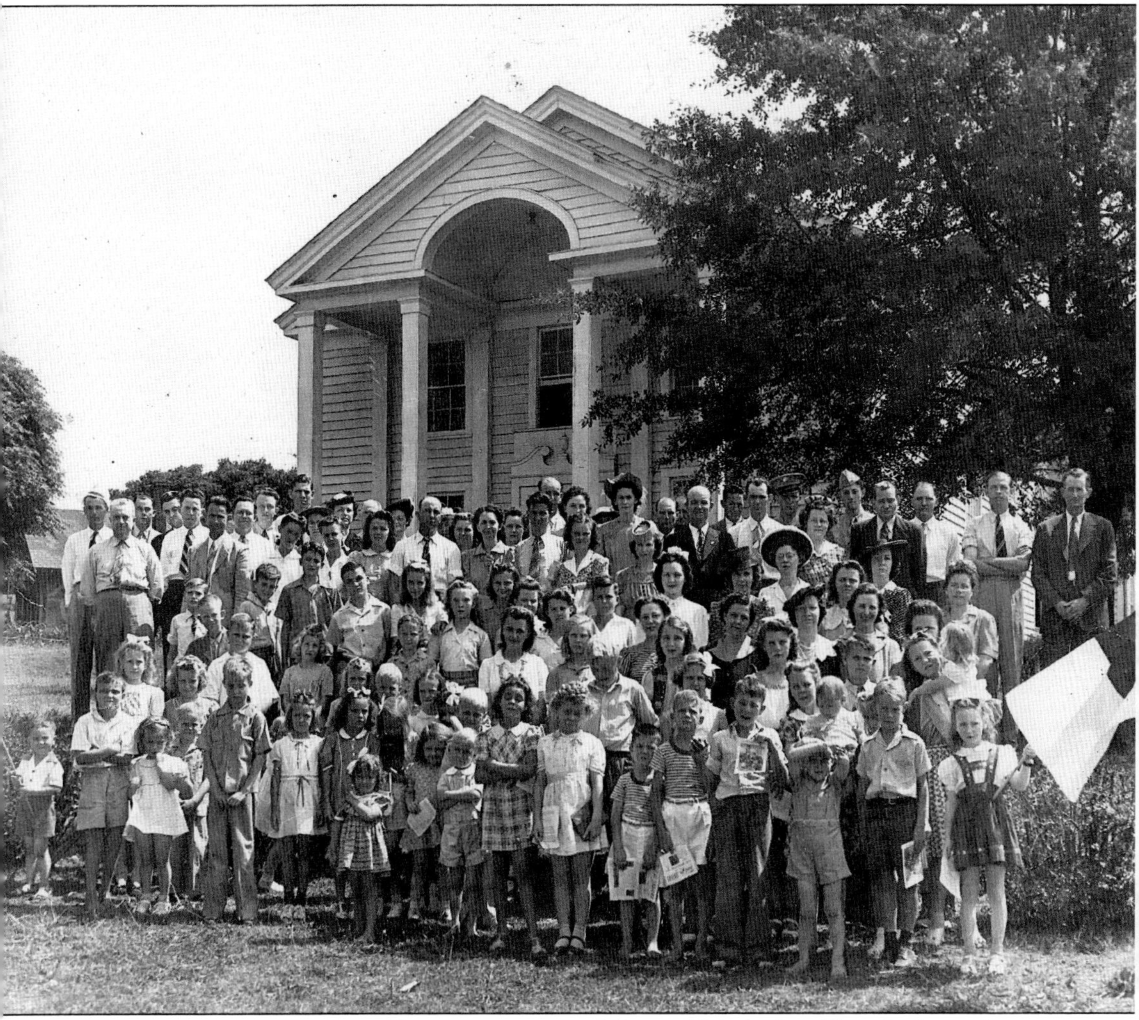

CENTRAL METHODIST CHURCH. The congregation of Central Methodist Church, located on Fleming Street at the Laurens Cotton Mill, gathered on the front lawn of the white frame church in 1938. The church was replaced with a brick structure in later years. (Courtesy of *Laurens County Advertiser* Files.)

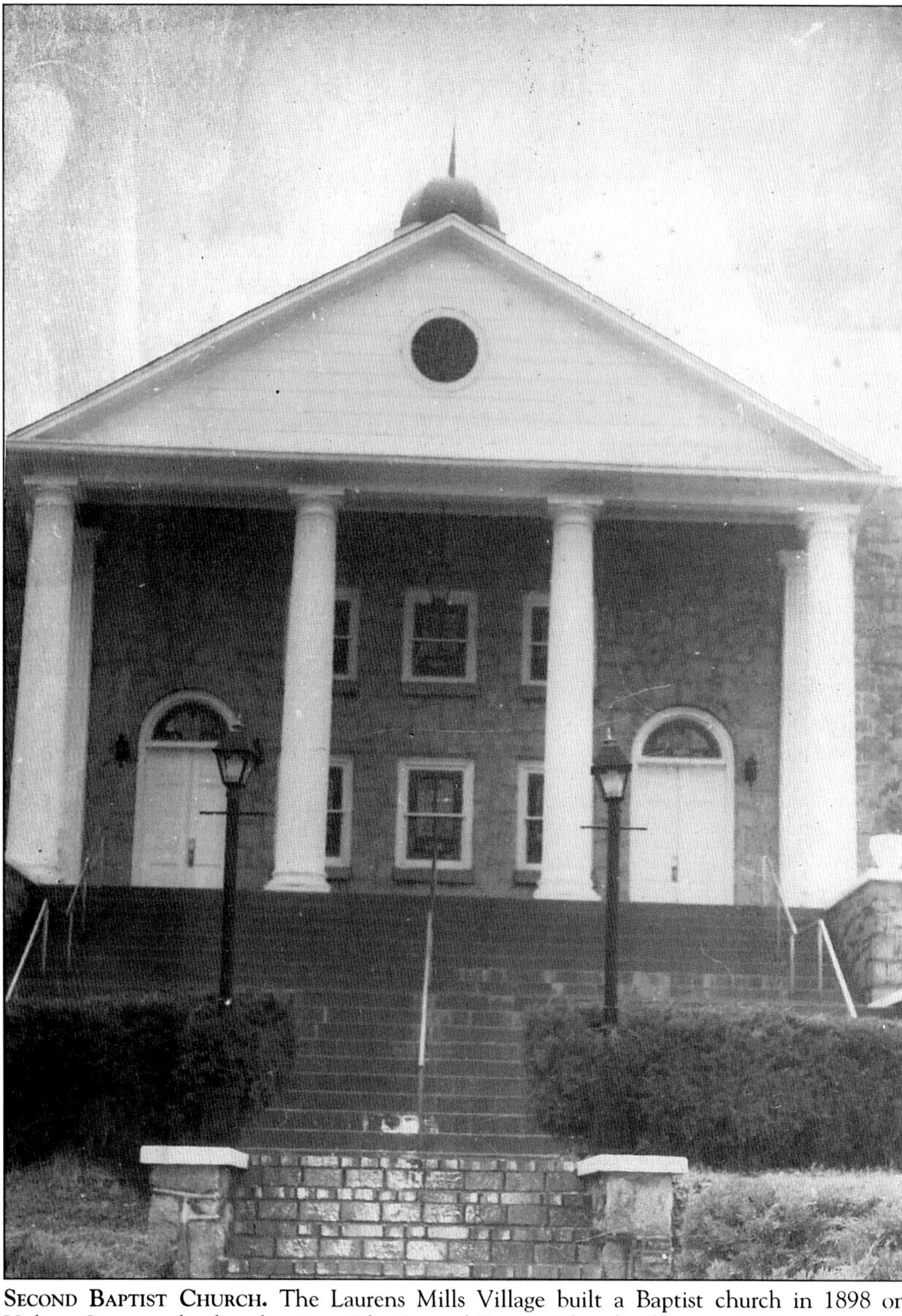

SECOND BAPTIST CHURCH. The Laurens Mills Village built a Baptist church in 1898 on Holmes Street and referred to it as "the Second Baptist Church of Laurens." The new name was officially carried in the annual report to the Laurens Baptist Association in a session on September 28, 1902. Some years later, a granite church was constructed on Fleming Street in Laurens. (Courtesy of the Rhodes collection.)

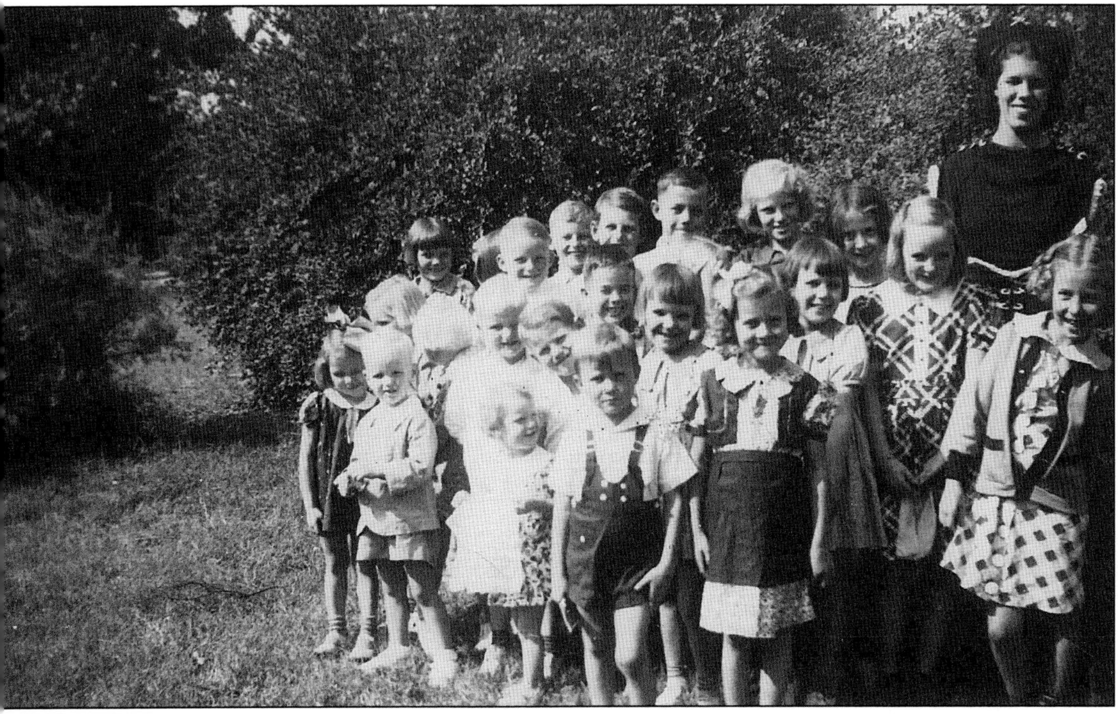

Second Baptist Sunbeams. Seen in this *c.* 1938 photograph of the members of Second Baptist Sunbeam Band and its leader, Louise Rogers, are the following: Carolyn Bobo, Ted Mahaffey, Merita Barett, Tommy Reames, Frances Reames, Arnell Mahaffey, Edna Jennings, Wayne Campbell, Tommy Barett, Johnny Bobo, Audrey Chumley, Jewel Chumley, Betty Campbell, Barbara Bolt, Alice Nelson, Lois Barrett, Larry Campbell, Bruce Jennings, Jack Barrett, James Rogers, Jessie Mae Barrett, and Joyce Wardel. (Courtesy of Mrs. Louise Rogers Hall.)

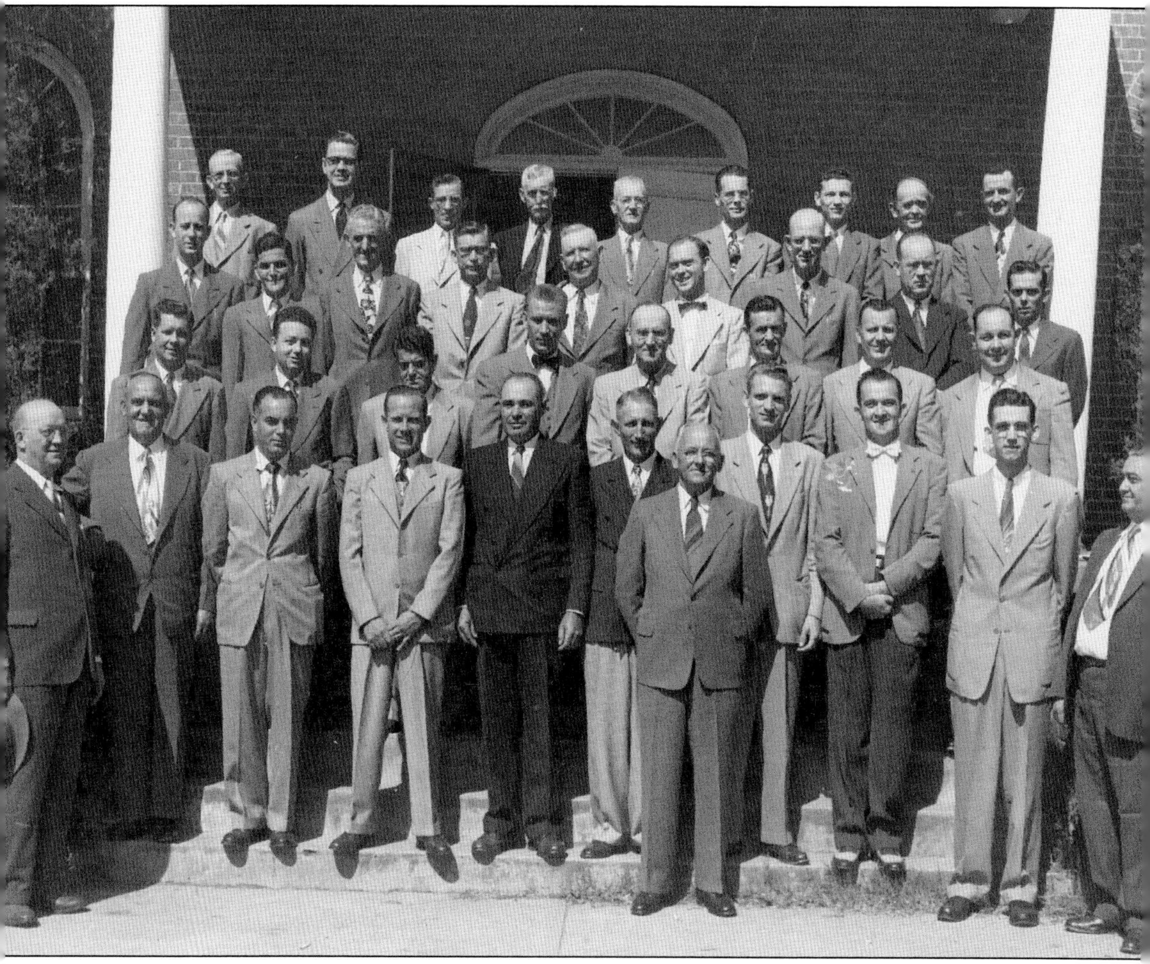

St. James Methodist Church. In the early 1950s, the E.B. Proctor Bible Class of St. James Methodist Church was the largest class in the church with an average attendance of 30 members each Sunday. The class was named after Mr. E.B. Proctor, a former teacher. Reverend J.A. Grigsby was pastor. (Courtesy of Mrs. Myrna Benjamin Self.)

Five

Educational Facilities

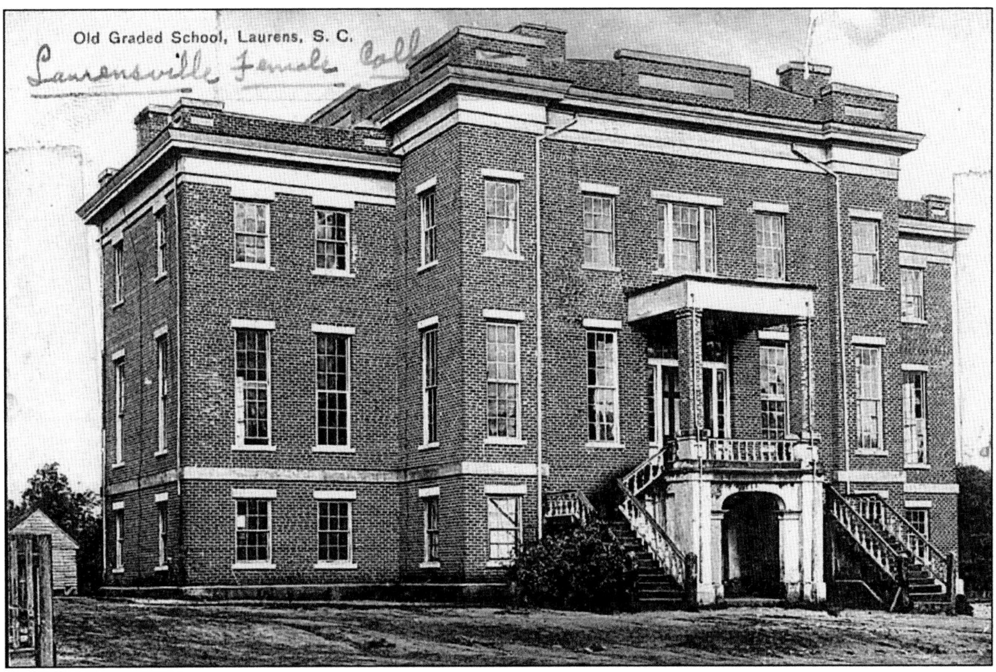

Celebrated Female Institution. The Laurens Female College was situated on the corner of West Main and Church Streets. The three-story brick building contained 15 classrooms, a museum on the third floor, and a library containing approximately 1,000 volumes. Founded in 1858, the curriculum compared favorably with other female institutions in the South. It was considered the most celebrated female institution in Upper State South Carolina. (Courtesy of Laurens County Library.)

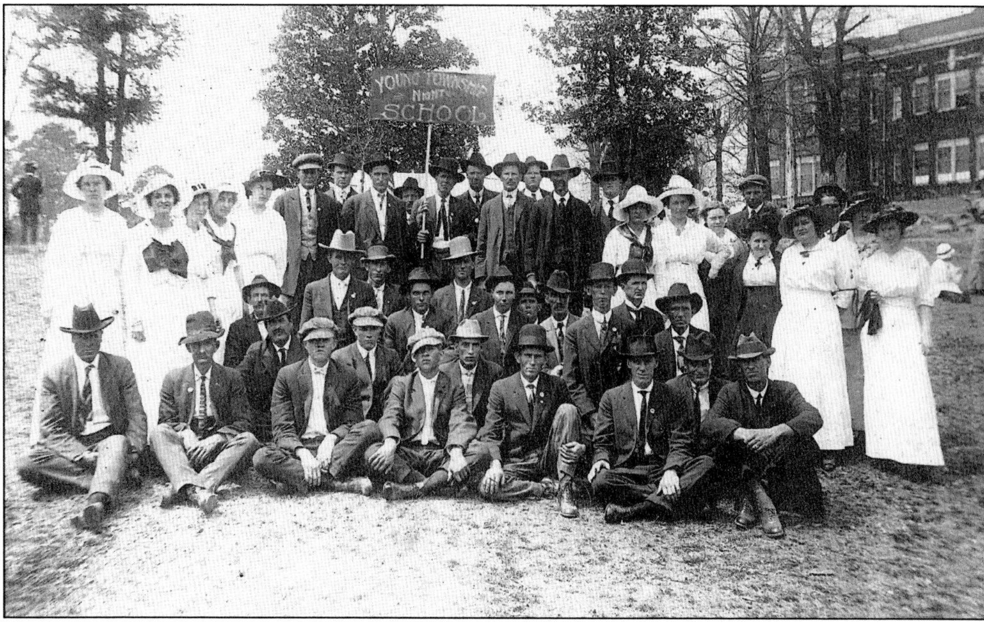

Adult Education. Dr. Wil Lou Gray was a pioneer in adult education. In 1912, she refused a professorship at Louisiana College in order to accept the position of school supervisor for Laurens County. During this time she developed an experimental adult education program in seven communities of Youngs Township. The students were taught by volunteer teachers. Dr. Wil Lou Gray is pictured (short lady in black dress) with a group of adult students. (Courtesy of Laurens County Library.)

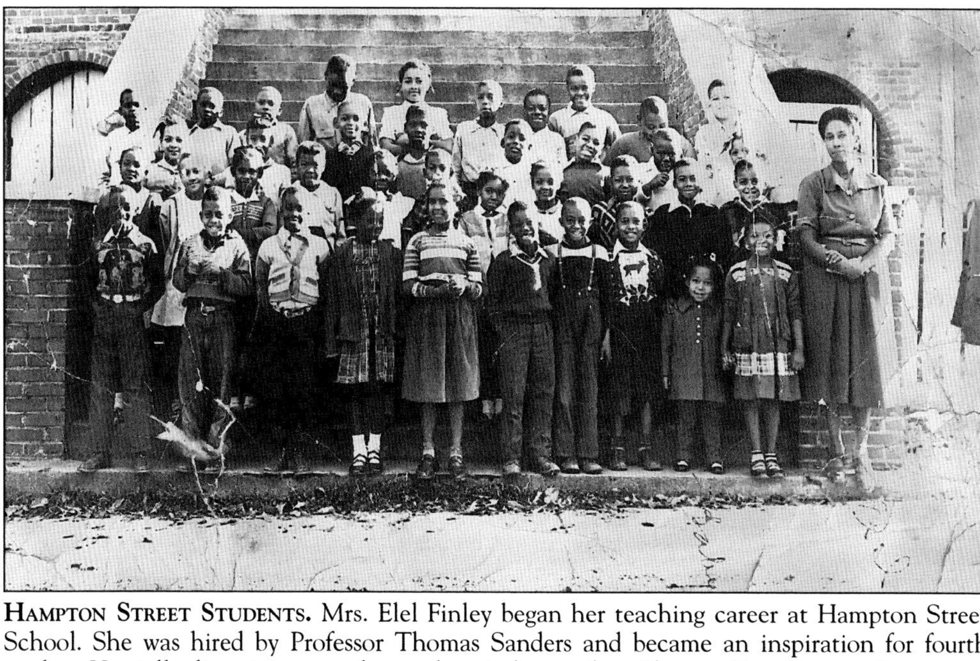

Hampton Street Students. Mrs. Elel Finley began her teaching career at Hampton Street School. She was hired by Professor Thomas Sanders and became an inspiration for fourth graders. Her jolly disposition won her a place in her students' hearts. Standing on the steps of Bethel A.M.E. Church and preparing for a field trip, the Laurens teacher poses with her class. (Courtesy of Mrs. Elel Finley.)

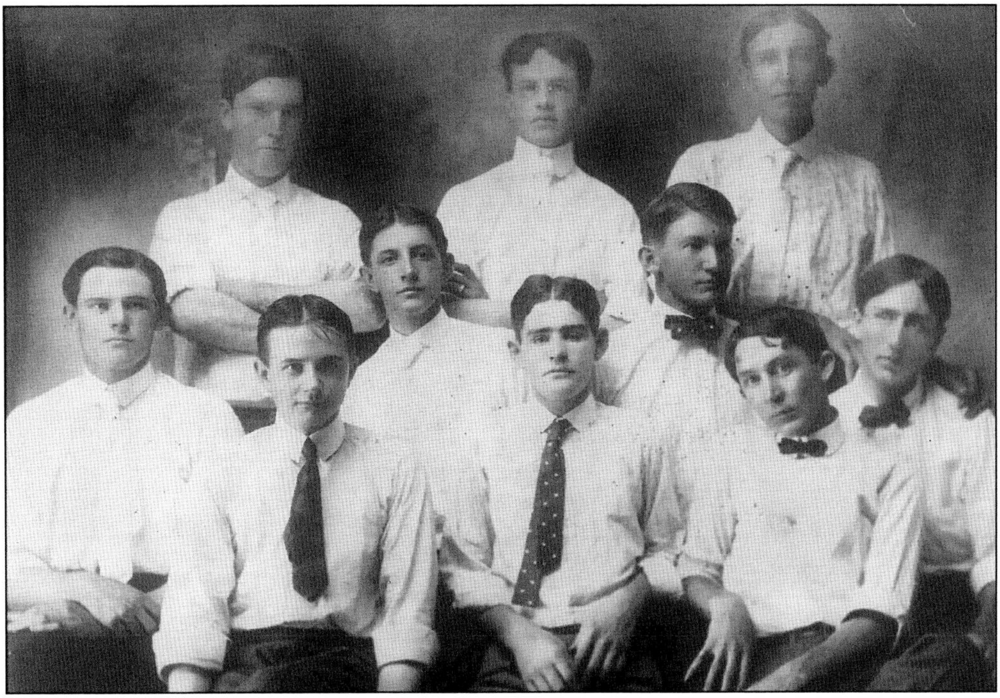

Schoolboys. Included in this class of Laurens young men are Ernest Easterby and H. Douglas Gray. The location and date are unknown. (Courtesy of Mrs. Harriett Easterby Faris.)

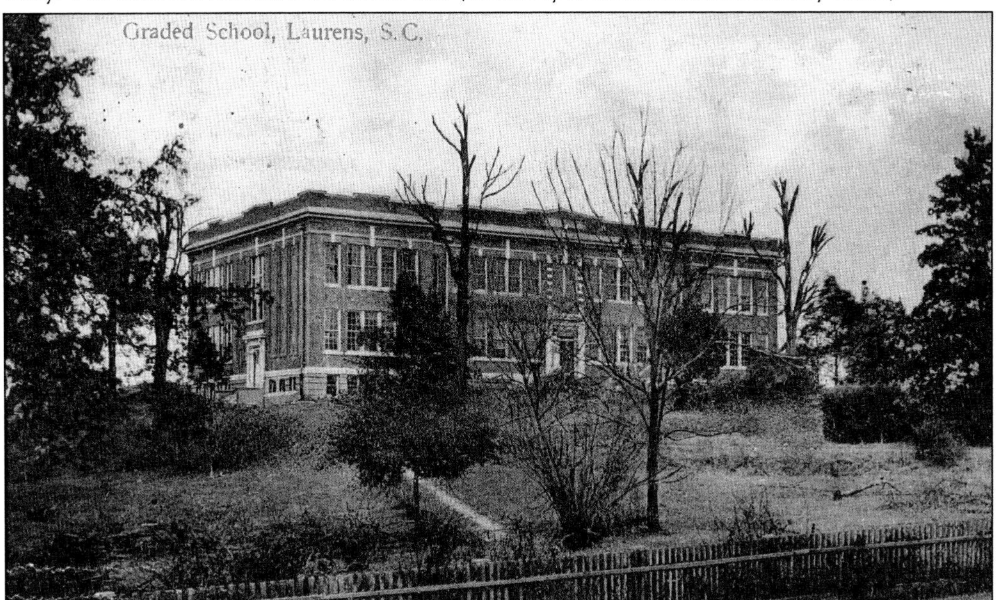

Laurens Graded School. Originally, the public school for the town's children met in the Courthouse on an interim basis. In 1892, children moved into a building located on College Street that had previously housed the Female College. In 1908, the Central School, a two-story brick structure, was built on the corner of Church and Laurens Streets. The Laurens Police and Fire Departments replaced the "Old Central School." (Courtesy of Mrs. Agnes Brownlee Sherer.)

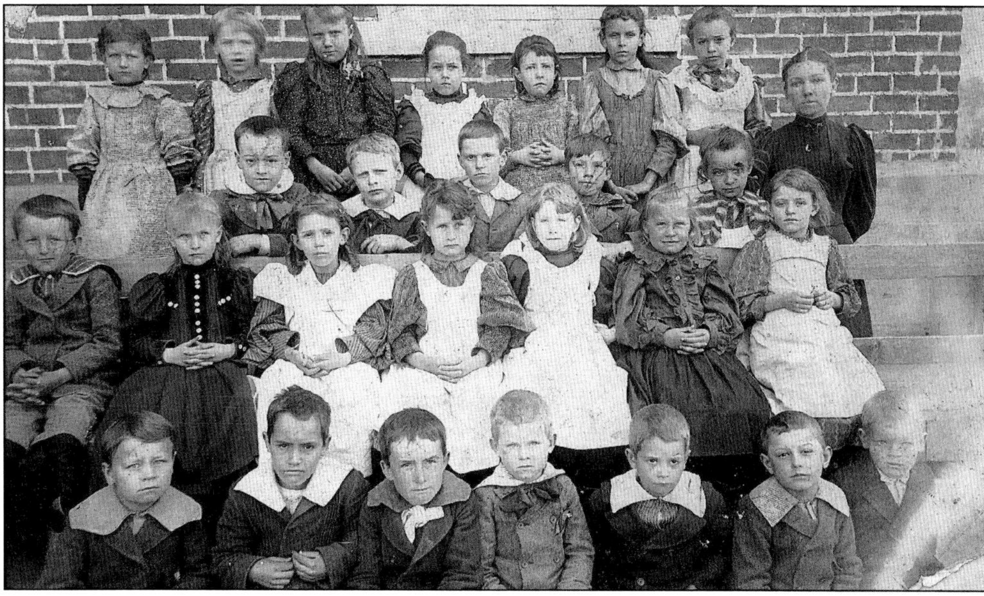

LAURENS GRADED SCHOOLCHILDREN. In 1895, Laurens children attended school in a building on College Street that had previously housed the Female College. Miss Mary Miller was the teacher for this group pictured at the old school. From left to right are the following: (front row) Lloyd Langston, ? Snow, Allen Barksdale, Albert Dial, John Wells Todd Jr., Calhoun McGowan, and Dunklin Sullivan; (second row) Albert Simpson, Helen Hix, unidentified, Ida Taylor, Lila Mae Dial, Aliene Crews, and Willie Mae Childress; (third row) Mitchell Dial, Coke Gray, Hugh Hill Wallace Webb, and Pearle White; (fourth row) Eloise Boyd, Bessie Goggans, Bess Crews, Rosalie Franks. Frankie Beeks, Hattie Hill, Ruby Whitten, and Miss Miller. (Courtesy of John Wells Todd IV.)

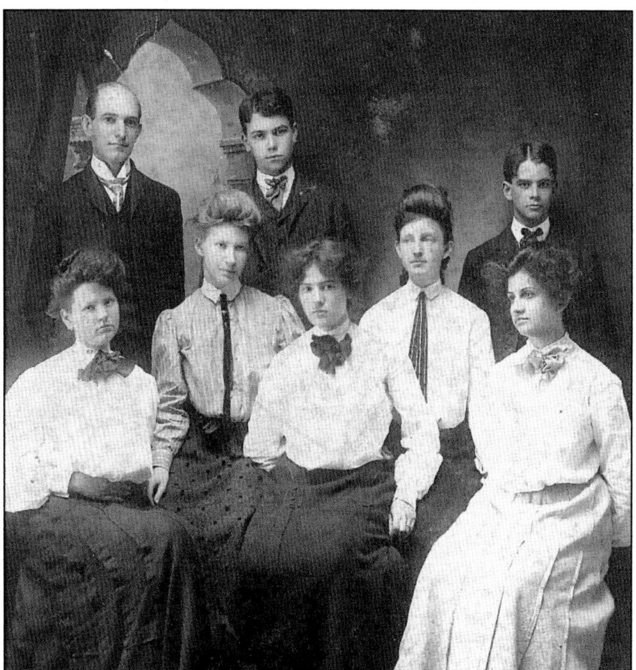

LAURENS CITY SCHOOL GROUP. Shown here are Laurens students in the early 1900s. They are, from left to right, as follows: (seated) Lily Armstrong (Nash), Ollie Adams, Zelene Gray (Dunklin), Beth Shell, and Miss Fitz (teacher); (standing) Mr. B.L. Jones (teacher), Charles Simpson, and John Wells Todd Jr. (Courtesy of John Wells Todd IV.)

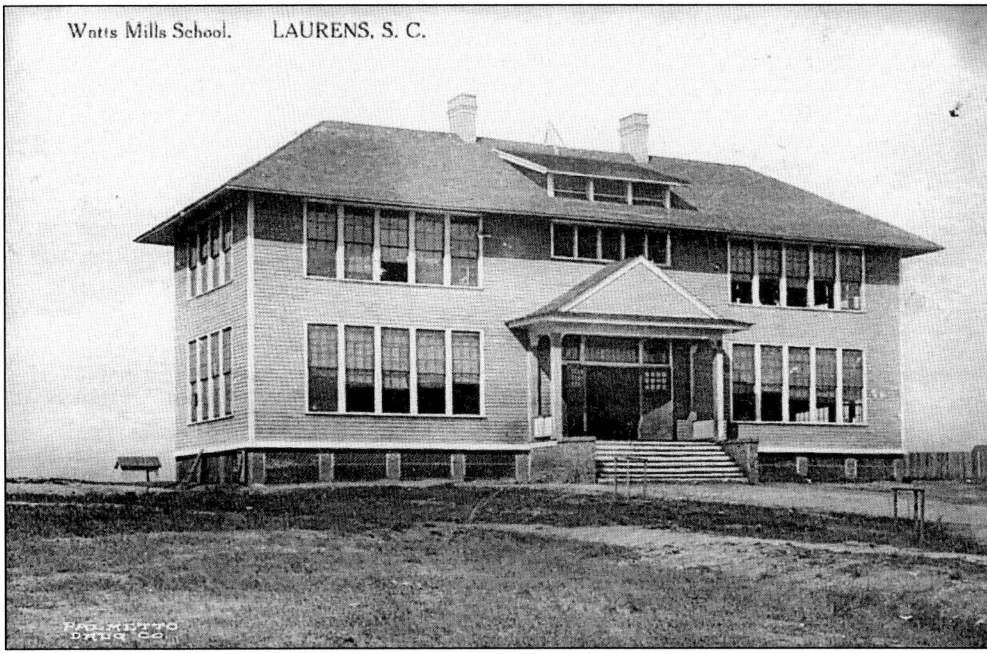

INTEGRAL PART OF THE TEXTILE VILLAGE. The Watts Mill School was built in the early 1900s. The two-story frame building stood on Lucas Avenue, the street named for one of the mill's founders. The "Watts Mill Old School" met the needs of countless Watts Mill children through the years. (Courtesy of Mrs. Frances Weathers.)

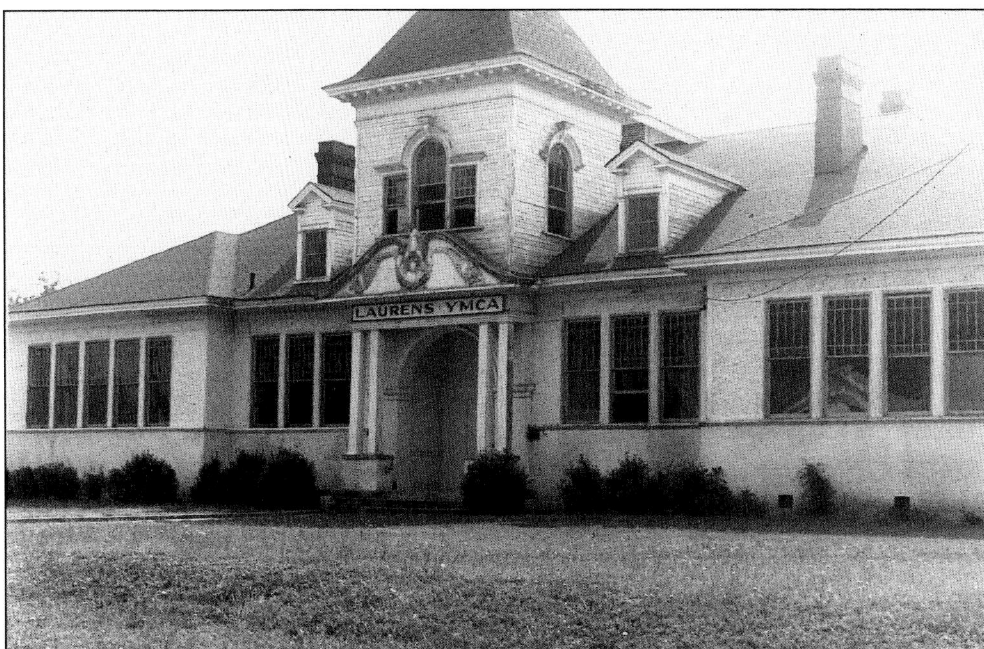

LAURENS MILL SCHOOL. Located on Holmes Street on the east side of Laurens, the Laurens Mill School provided education for students in the Laurens Mill Village. In later years the building was torn down. (Courtesy of the Rhodes collection.)

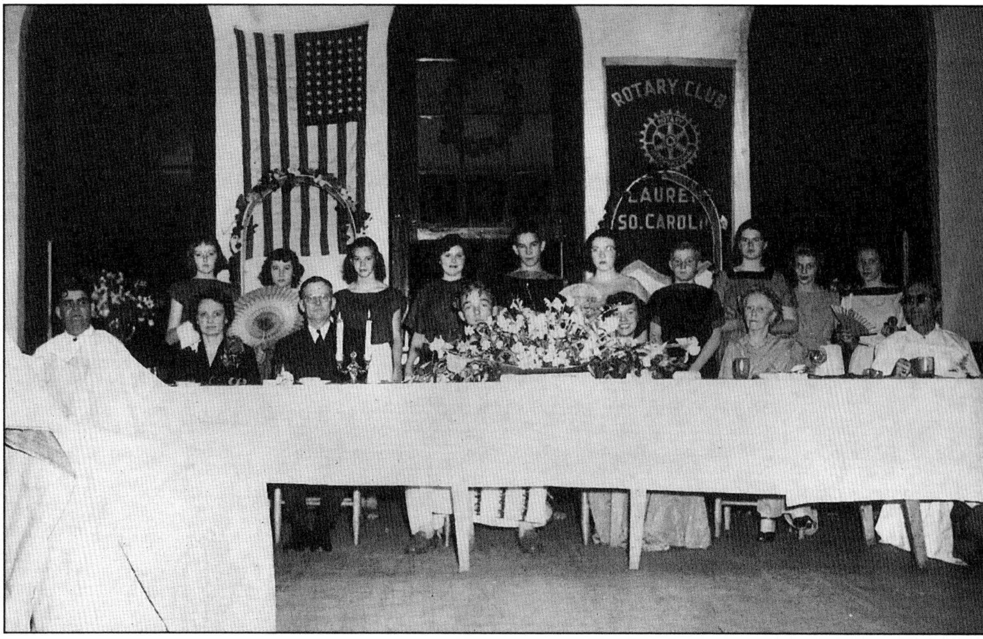

UPSTAIRS CITY HALL. A Laurens school group, the Junior Classical League, met for a banquet at the Laurens City Hall. The picture was taken on the third floor with an arched window fronting the square. The large upstairs room was used for civic, school, professional, and social functions. (Courtesy of Mrs. Beatrice Babb Bradley.)

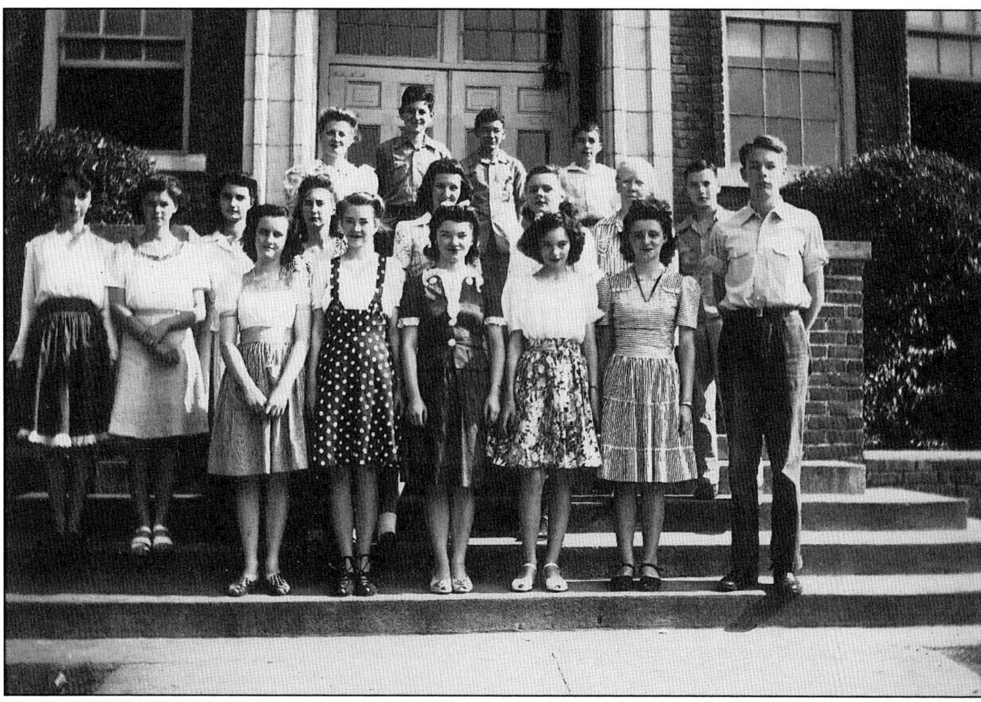

IN FRONT OF GRADED SCHOOL. A class of the Laurens Graded School stands at the front entrance of the school with teacher Miss Sara Babb. They are probably either Latin or English students. (Courtesy of Mrs. Beatrice Babb Bradley.)

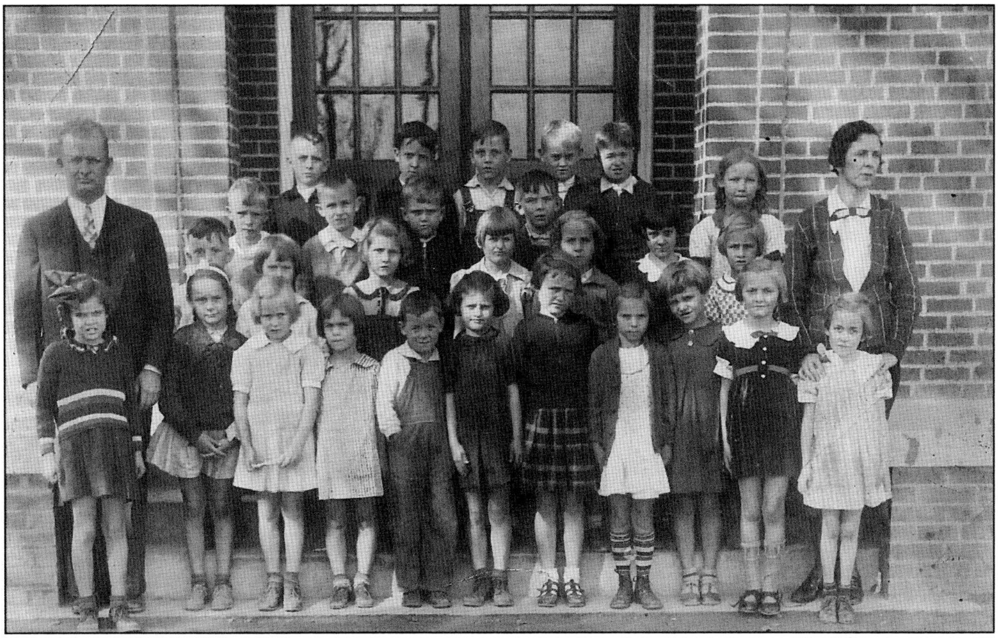

FORD HIGH SCHOOL. A brick two-story school building located on Lucas Avenue replaced the old wooden Watts Mill School. The school was named in honor of its principal and later superintendent: J.E. Ford. A second grade class in 1935 stands with Ford and teacher Miss Curry at the entrance of the school building. (Courtesy of Mrs. Elizabeth Tumblin.)

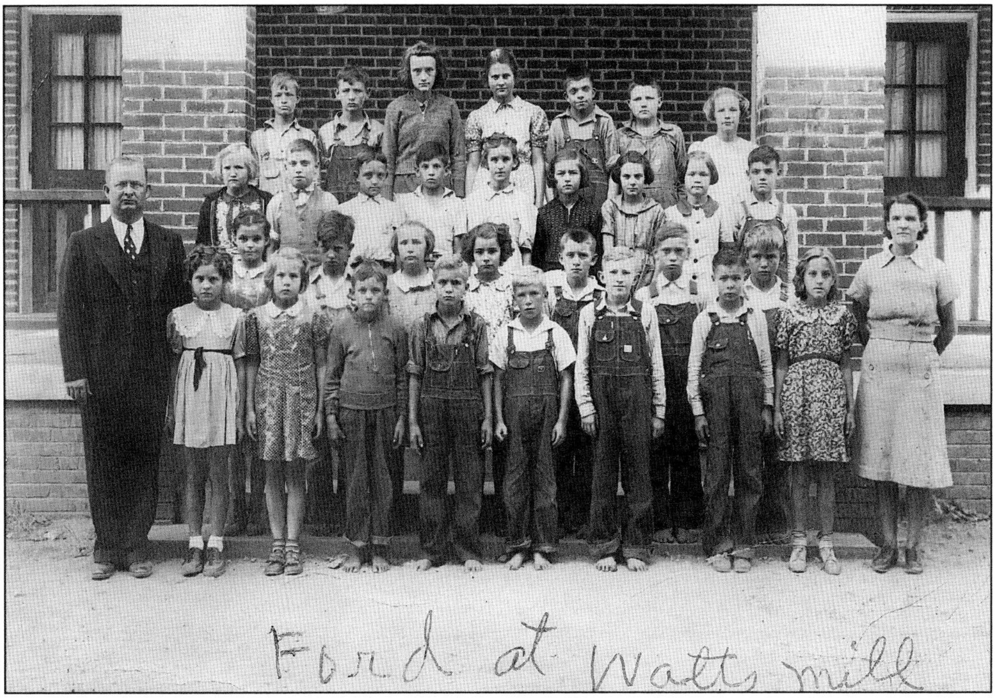

1937 FOURTH GRADERS. Ford High School was a vital part of the Watts Mill community and provided an education for both elementary and high school students. A group of fourth graders stand with their teacher and Principal Ford in 1937. (Courtesy of Mrs. Elizabeth Tumblin.)

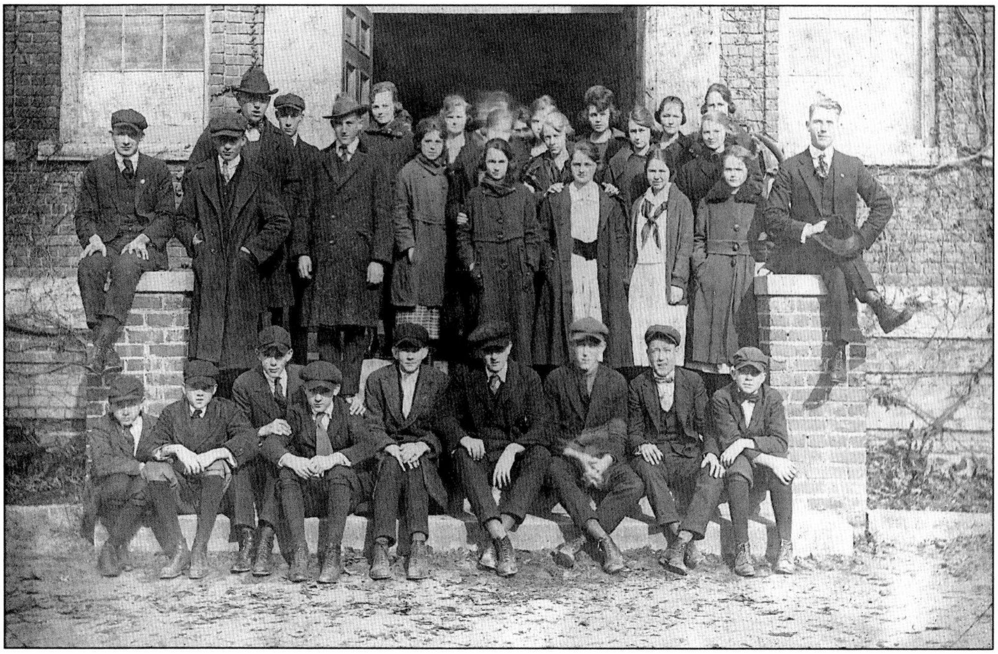

TENTH GRADE. Students pose for a class picture with members of the faculty of the Laurens Graded School. The only identification was "tenth grade," written on the back of the photograph. (Courtesy of Mrs. Beatrice Babb Bradley.)

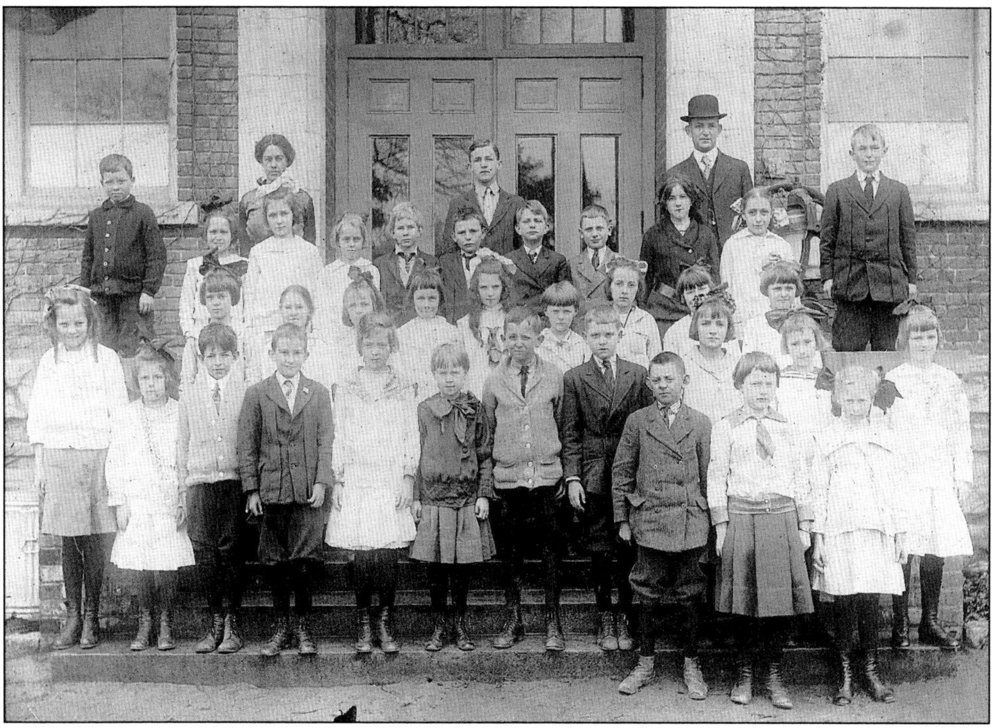

FOURTH GRADERS. Schoolboys, schoolgirls, and their teachers stand on the steps at the entrance of the Laurens Graded School. (Courtesy of Mrs. Beatrice Babb Bradley.)

Six

TEXTILE MILLS AND INDUSTRY

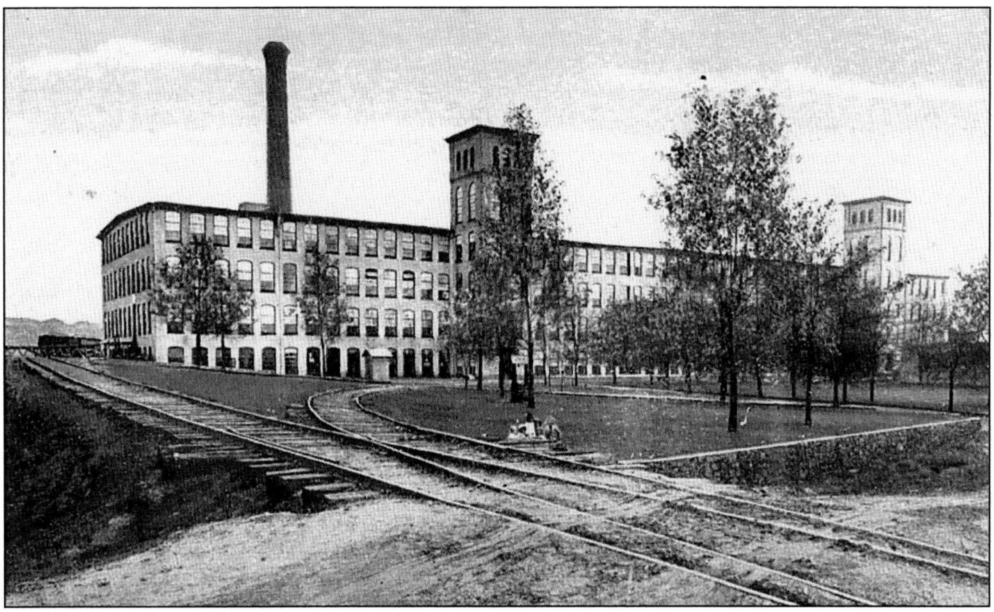

THE OLD MILL. Laurens Cotton Mills, often referred to as "the Old Mill," was organized on February 13, 1895, and a charter was granted August 7 in the same year. John Ferguson, N.B. Dial, and W.H. Martin incorporated the mill. W.E. Lucas, Dr. J.P. Simpson, J.W. Todd, Captain Albert Dial, Colonel J.O. Fleming, J.W. Ferguson, and M.V. Montgomery made up the board of directors. W.E. Lucas was instrumental in organizing and building the mill, therefore he was elected president and treasurer. (Courtesy of Laurens County Library.)

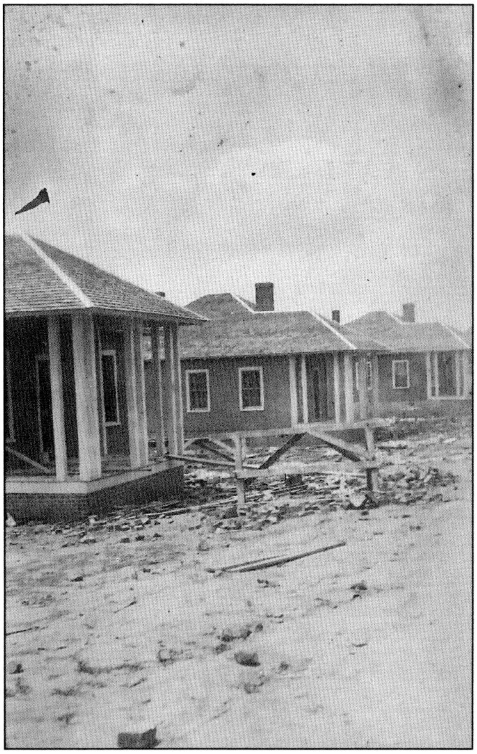

Mill Houses Constructed. Numerous sites in and around Laurens were considered for the construction of Laurens Cotton Mills before the decision to build on Mill Street was made. This location was chosen because of the topography of the ground, the proximity to the railroads, and the supply of water. The mill employed 150 people with a one-shift operation in the beginning. Mill houses were built for employees along with a community building. (Courtesy of Mrs. Agnes Brownlee Sherer.)

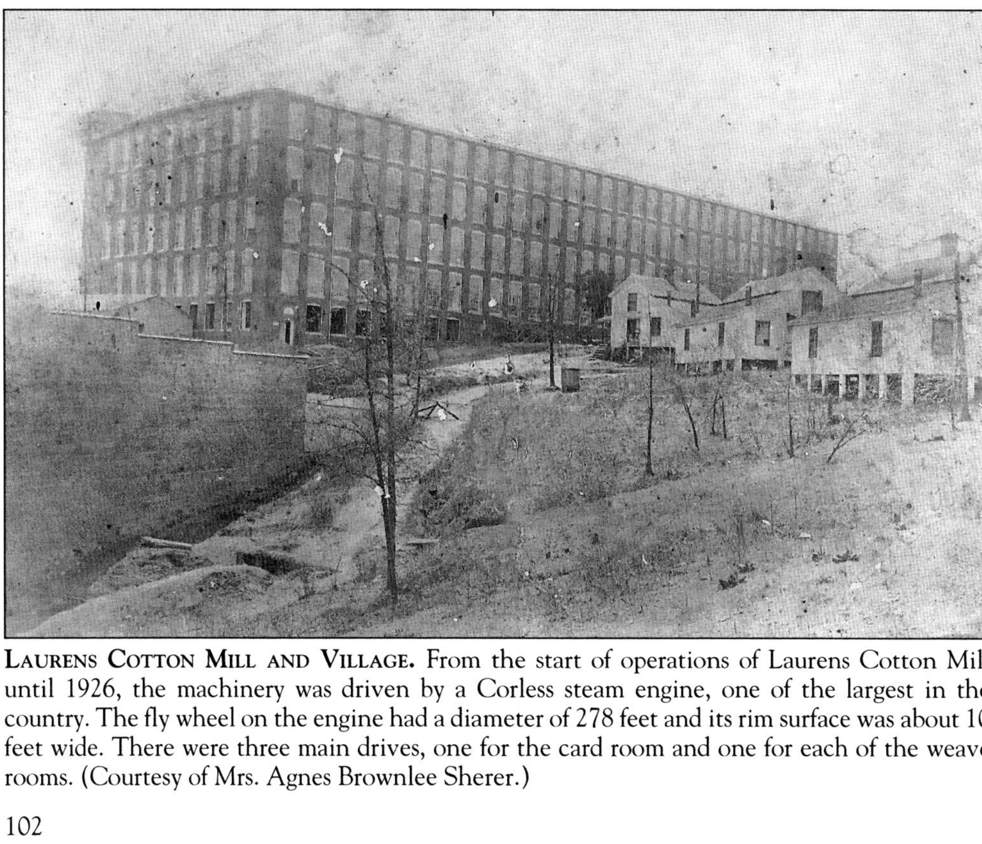

Laurens Cotton Mill and Village. From the start of operations of Laurens Cotton Mill until 1926, the machinery was driven by a Corless steam engine, one of the largest in the country. The fly wheel on the engine had a diameter of 278 feet and its rim surface was about 10 feet wide. There were three main drives, one for the card room and one for each of the weave rooms. (Courtesy of Mrs. Agnes Brownlee Sherer.)

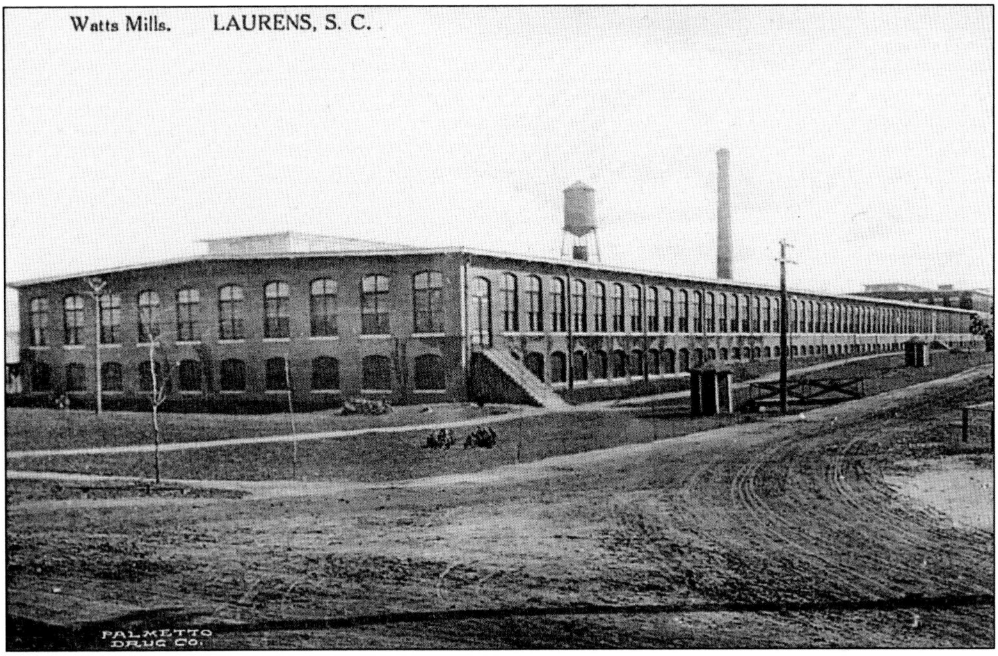

WATTS MILLS. A group of Laurens businessmen met in 1902 to officially organize Watts Mill. At the meeting W.E. Lucas was elected the first president and treasurer of the mill. Actual production began in 1904. The mill was originally housed in a two-story building and wove strictly cotton cloth, making "fancies," including ginghams and handkerchiefs. The mill continued to produce cotton cloth until the 1930s with the advent of rayon. At this time they produced synthetic fibers as well as some cotton. (Courtesy of Mrs. Frances Weathers.)

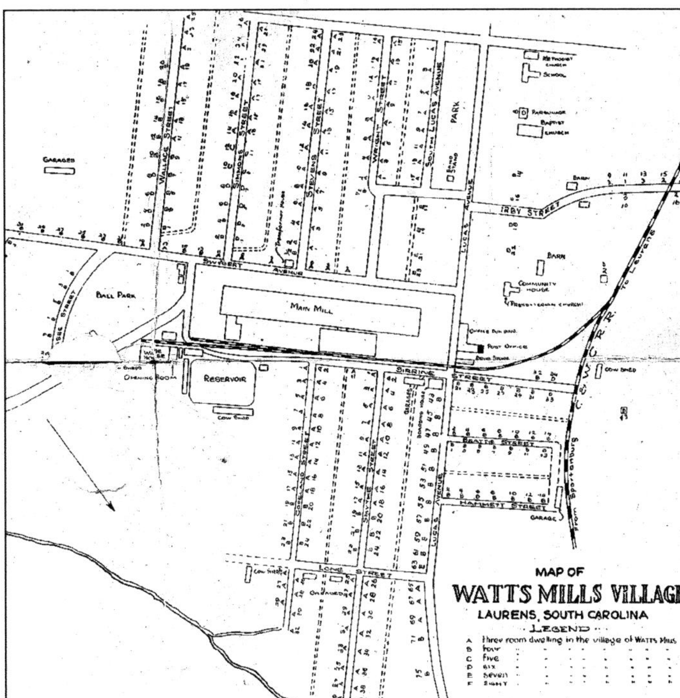

MAP OF WATTS MILL VILLAGE. Printed on a pamphlet, "Instructions Governing Watts Mills Property," and passed out when the mill began operation in 1904, are rules to be followed by Watts Mill tenants and a map of the newly laid-out village. It reads, "Learn the name and location of all the streets in your village. This may prove of value in case of an emergency," and "See your overseer if you are bothered with stray chickens or dogs or if you want screen doors hung." (Courtesy of the Rhodes collection.)

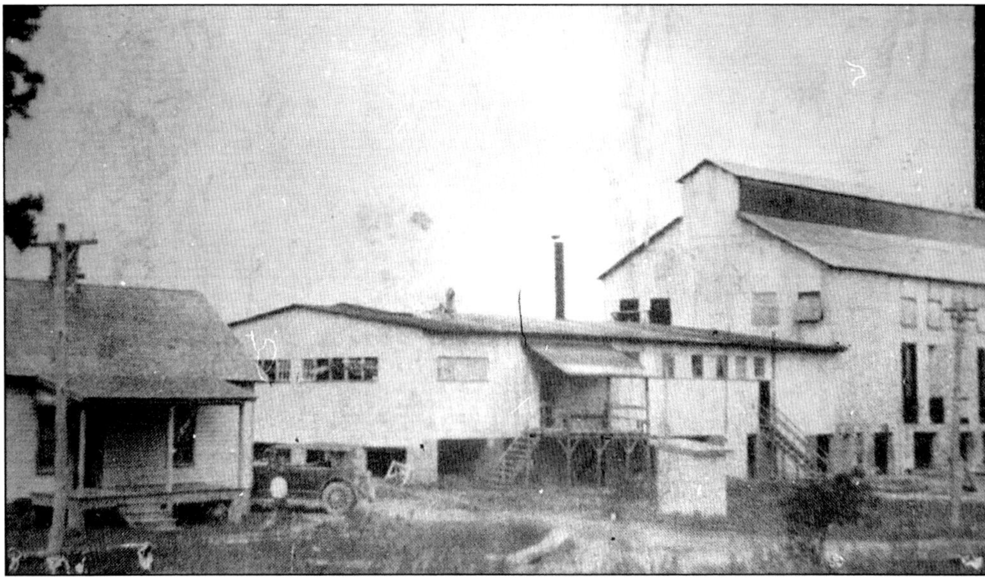

Laurens Glass. Colonel N.B. Dial and a group of Laurens businessmen organized and built the first glass plant in 1910. The first glass was produced in 1910 with 50 to 75 workers in the plant. The proper techniques of glass-blowing were not known, and the quality of the first glass produced was poor. The operation stopped in 1911. The company was reorganized in 1913 with Albert Dial named as president. Mr. Dial obtained the first license in the United States to manufacture Coca-Cola bottles. (Courtesy of Larry Weathers.)

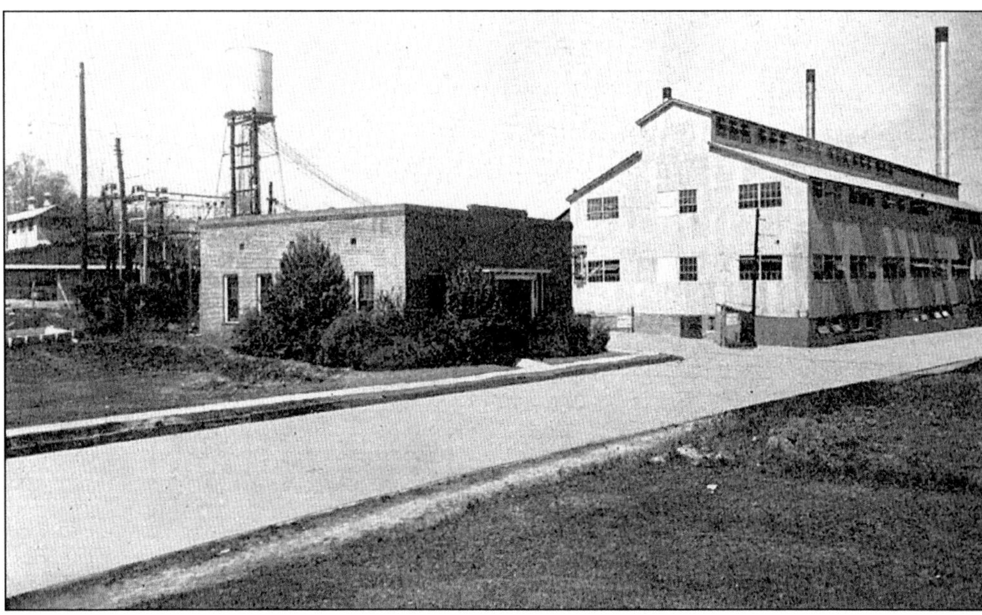

Reorganization. Albert Dial served as the president of Laurens Glass until his death in 1928. Ernest Easterby then assumed the office. Easterby, along with H. Douglas Gray, was a partner with Albert Dial in the company that emerged after the 1913 reorganization. (Courtesy of the Rhodes collection.)

Seven

Entertainment, Sports, and Social Events

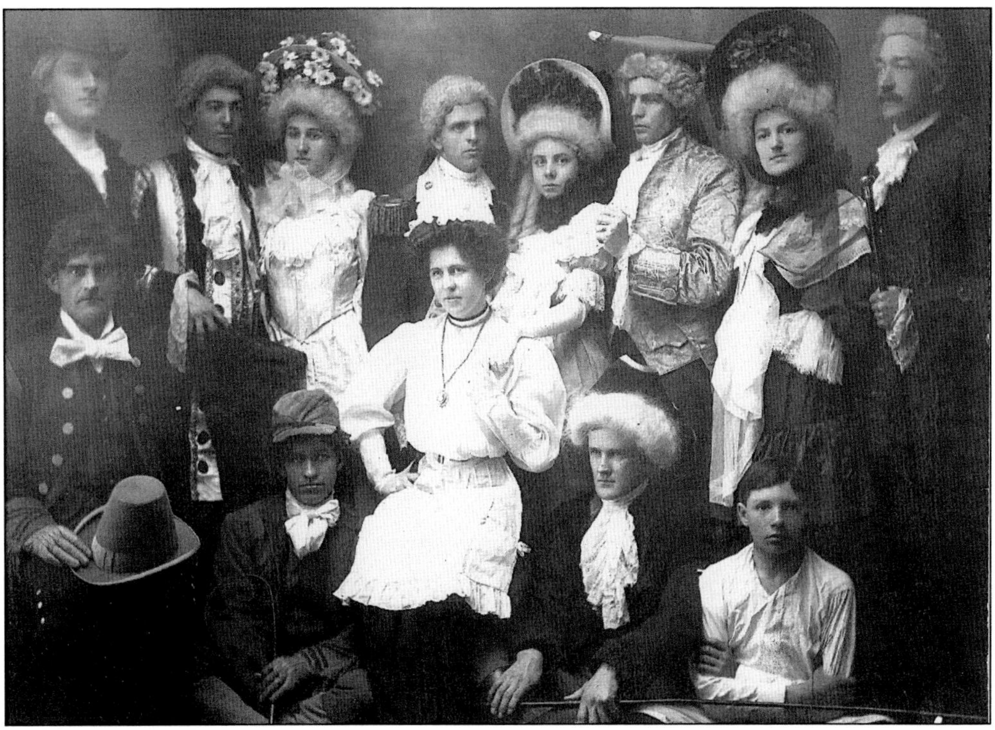

Theatrical Production. Laurens thespians often thrilled audiences with their renditions of popular plays of the day. Amateurs bedecked in wigs and costumes presented the *Rivals* in 1907. They are, from left to right, as follows: R. Vance Irby, L. George Balle, Eva Brownlee, E.O. Anderson, and Robert Roper; (back row) unidentified, ? Lancaster, Helan Goggans, Albert Todd, Emily Meng, Dr. Hughes, unidentified, and unidentified. (Courtesy of Laurens County Library.)

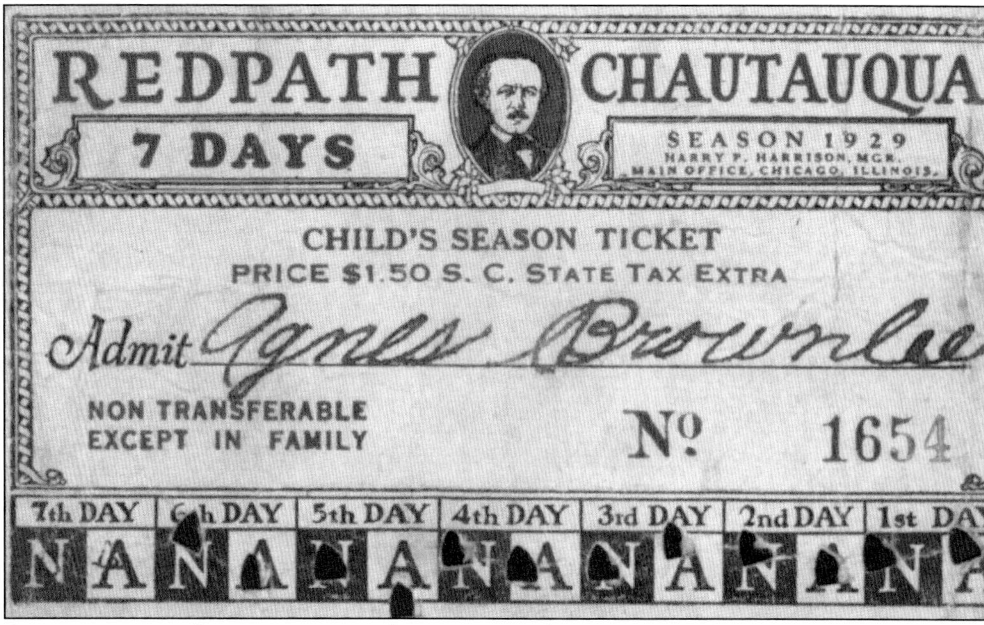

Chautauqua. When spring arrived Laurens residents awaited the arrival of Chautauqua. Traveling by train, the troupe pulled into the Laurens Depot. With spectators lining the streets and a brass band playing, they traveled by wagon to Garlington's Pasture, where a huge tent was set up. The annual event later moved behind the graded school. Spectators purchased tickets to see programs, plays, and musicals. On the seventh and final day, local talent performed with the traveling company. (Courtesy of Mrs. Agnes Brownlee Sherer.)

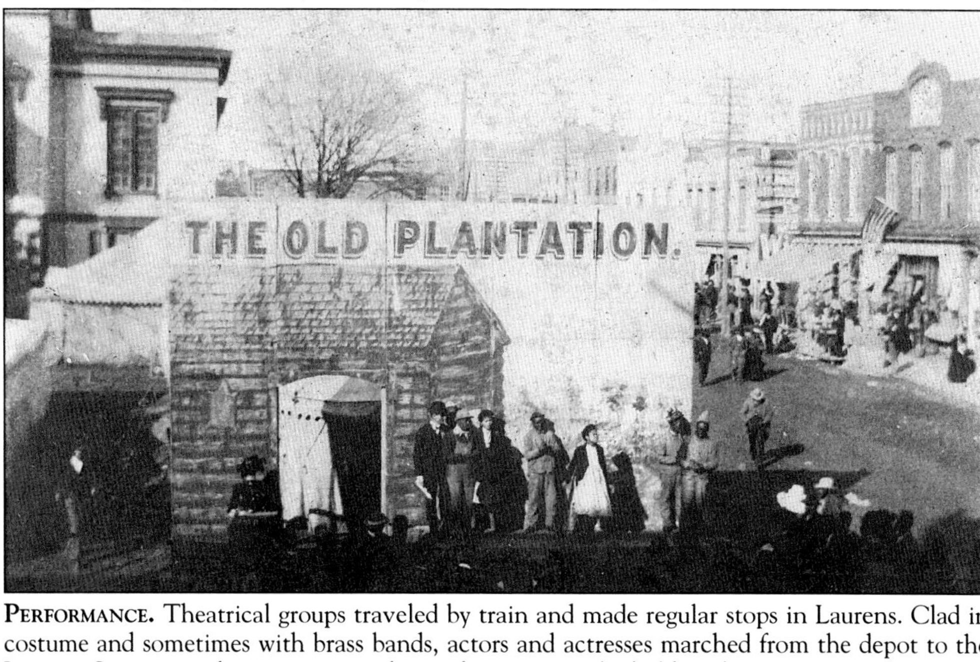

Performance. Theatrical groups traveled by train and made regular stops in Laurens. Clad in costume and sometimes with brass bands, actors and actresses marched from the depot to the Laurens Square to advertise spectacular performances to be held at the Laurens Opera House. On some occasions aspiring thespians from the community received roles in the theatrical productions. (Courtesy of Mrs. Beatrice Babb Bradley.)

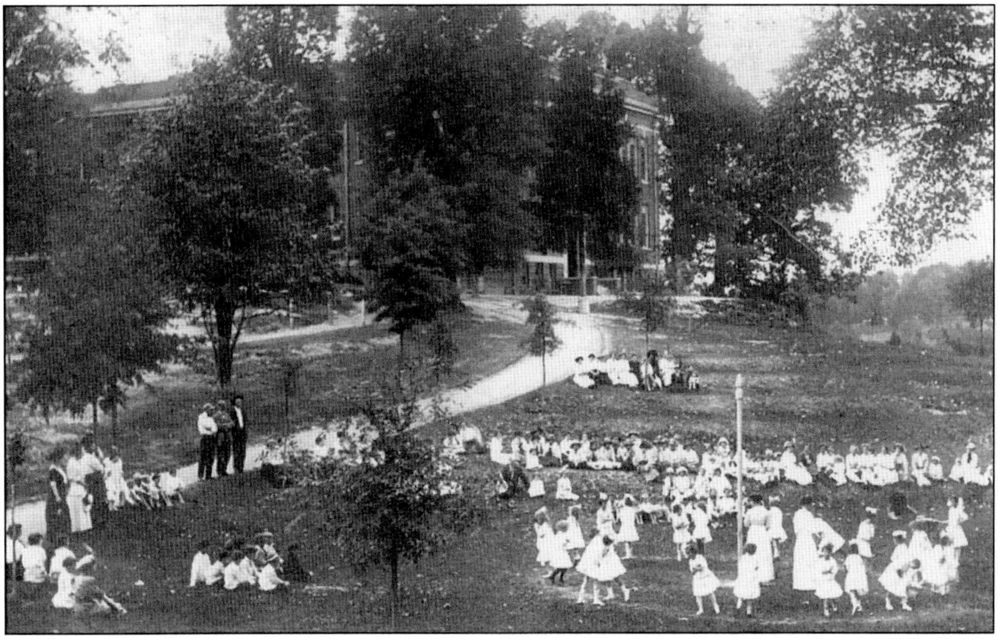

May Day Festivities. Wearing ruffled dresses of lawn and lace, schoolgirls weave intricate patterns with colored ribbons as they dance around the Maypole at the Laurens Graded School May Day Festival. Parents and teachers watched as the youngsters welcomed the arrival of spring to the Laurens Village. (Courtesy of Laurens County Library.)

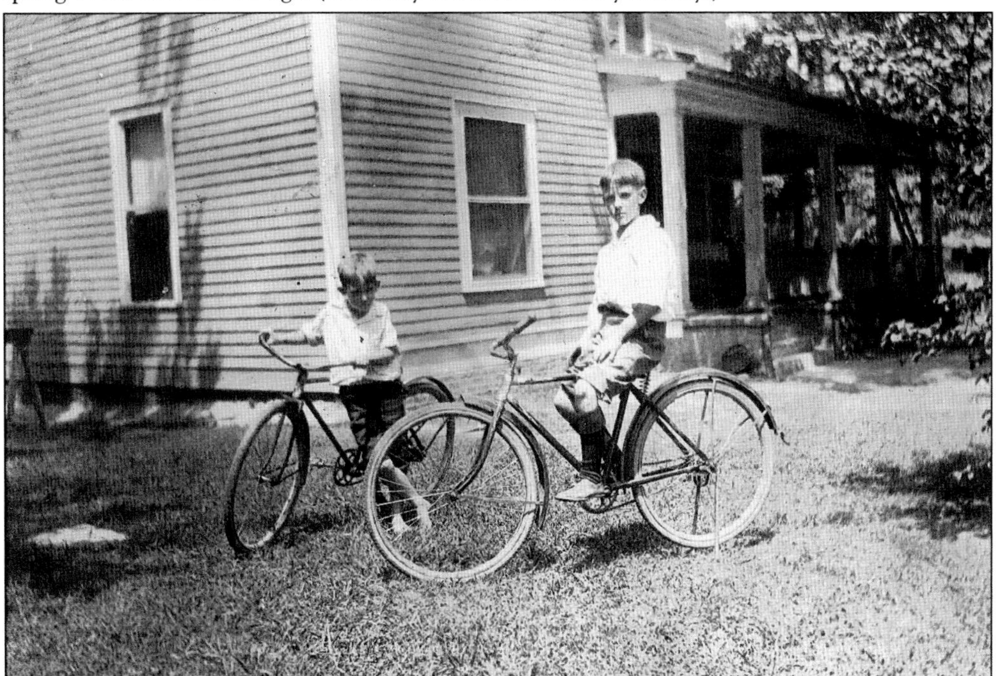

Babb House. Thomas A. "Buck" Babb idles away the afternoon with a friend at the home of his parents, Mr. and. Mrs. R.E. Babb, on West Main Street. (Courtesy of Mrs. Beatrice Babb Bradley.)

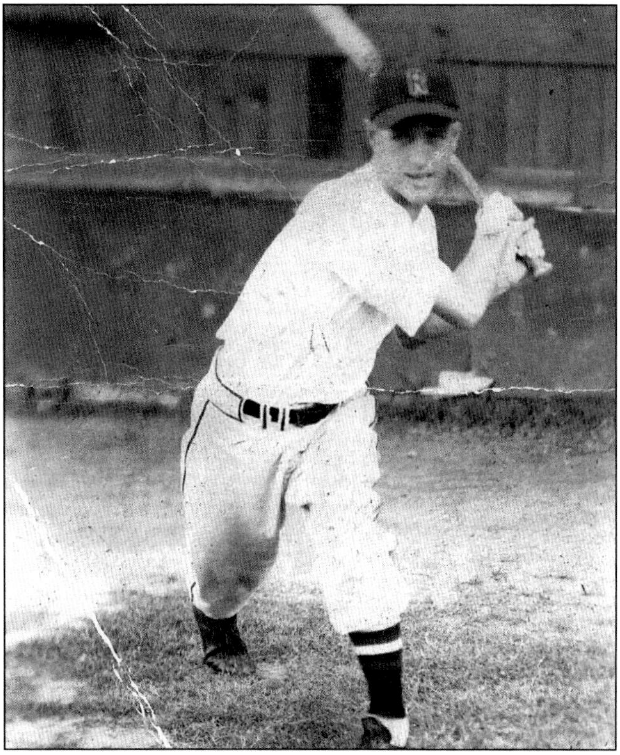

BASEBALL, A PART OF MILL VILLAGE LIFE. An idol to many children and baseball fans and possessing a winning personality, Dan Kirby played catcher for several baseball teams. He also served as the manager for the Riverdale Mill team in Enoree, the Joanna team, and for both Laurens and Watts Mill textile teams. Textile baseball was very much a part of mill village life. (Courtesy of Julian Coats.)

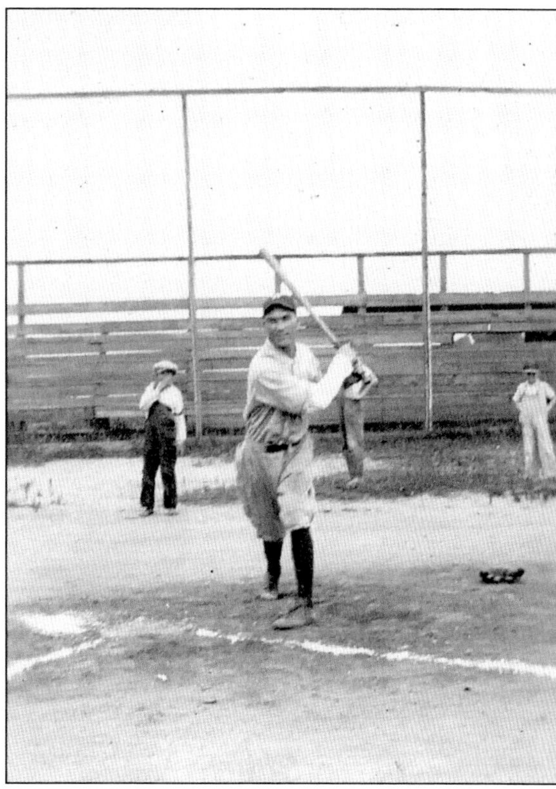

PLAY BALL. James "Trim" Taylor was a third baseman for the Watts Mill textile team. The young boy clad in overalls was one of many young fellows that hung around the ballpark located behind the mill. (Courtesy of Julian Coats.)

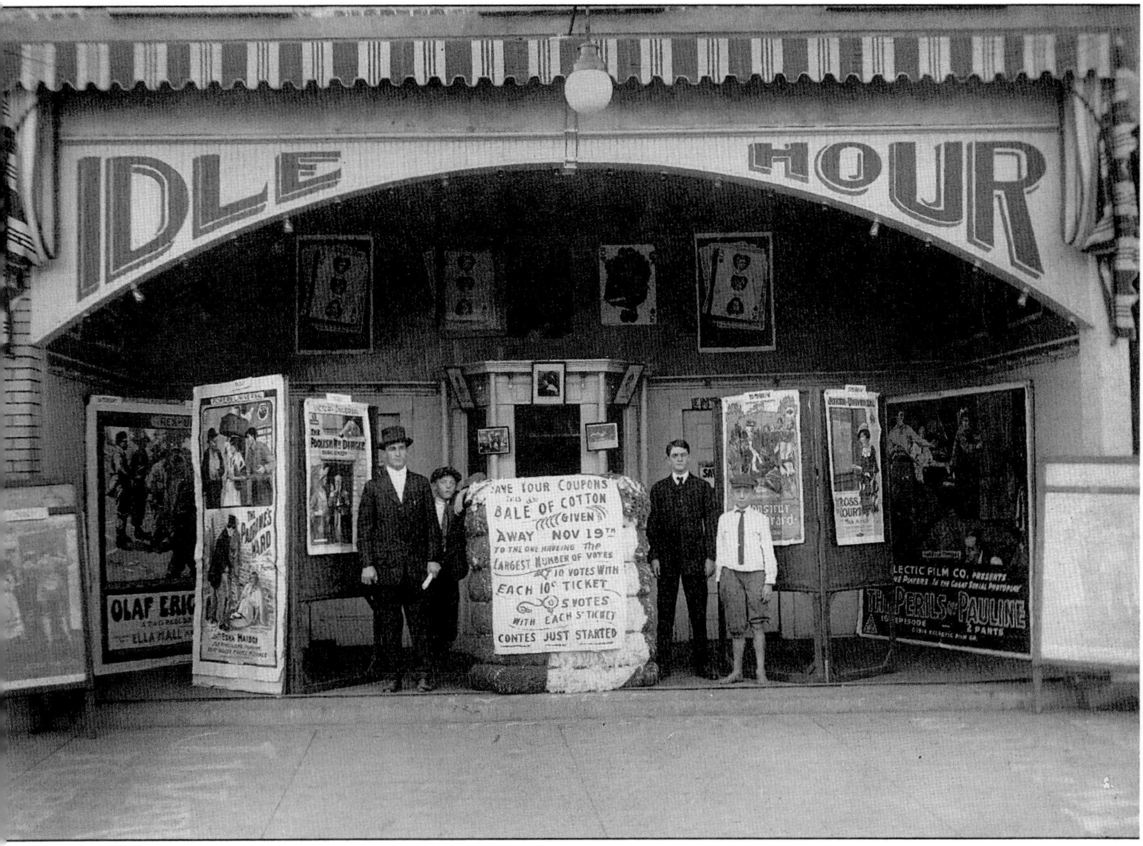

The Idle Hour. Both young and old enjoyed watching the big screen of the Idle Hour Theater, located on the north side of the Laurens Square. Standing in front of the theatre from left to right are A.S. Perry, manager; unidentified; Pack Childress; and A.M. Easterby. (Courtesy of Mrs. Agnes Brownlee Sherer.)

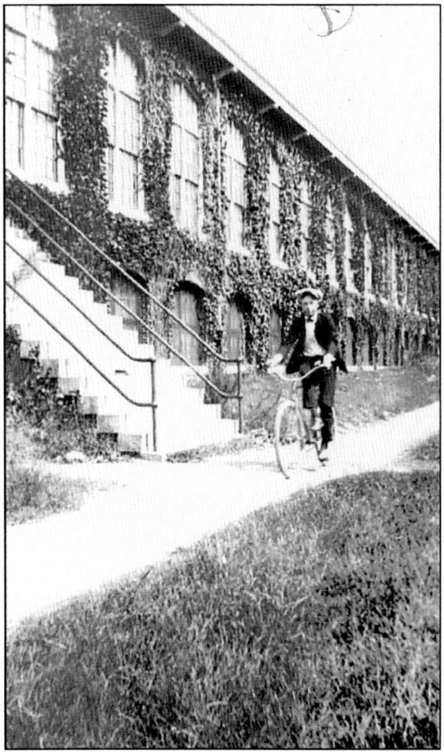

Sunday Afternoon Delight. Dressed in his Sunday best, Brooks Weathers pedaled his "wheel" *c.* 1920 alongside the ivy-covered south entrance to Watts Mill. Weathers was the son of Watts Mill residents Desse and Cordia Weathers. (Courtesy of Mrs. Frances Weathers.)

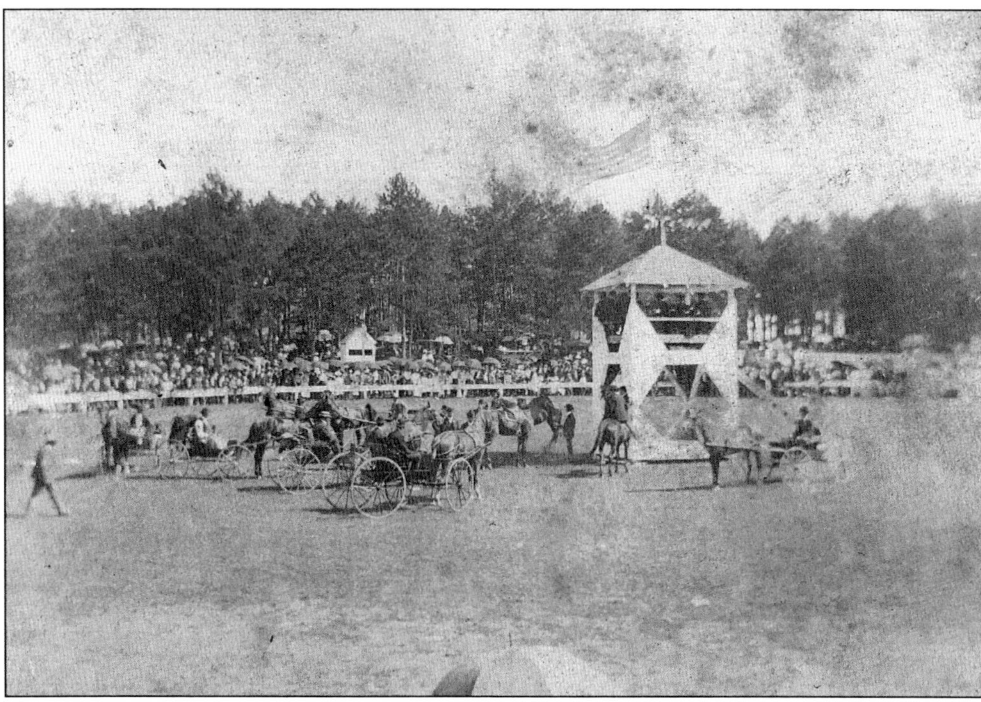

Race Day. Laurens residents often traveled to the Fairview Race Track in Fountain Inn to watch horse racing. The exact location and date of the picture is not known. (Courtesy of Mrs Beatrice Babb Bradley.)

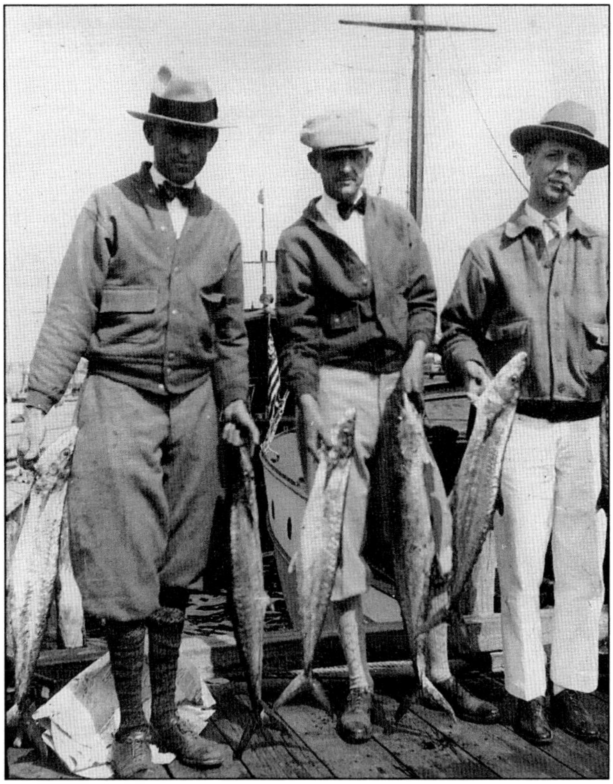

CATCH OF THE DAY. Laurens businessmen Albert Dial, Ernest Easterby, and George Wright (from left to right) pose for the camera with the "catch of the day." Dial and Easterby were executives with Laurens Glass, and George Wright, with Laurens Cotton Mills. (Courtesy of Mrs. Barbara Dial McAlister.)

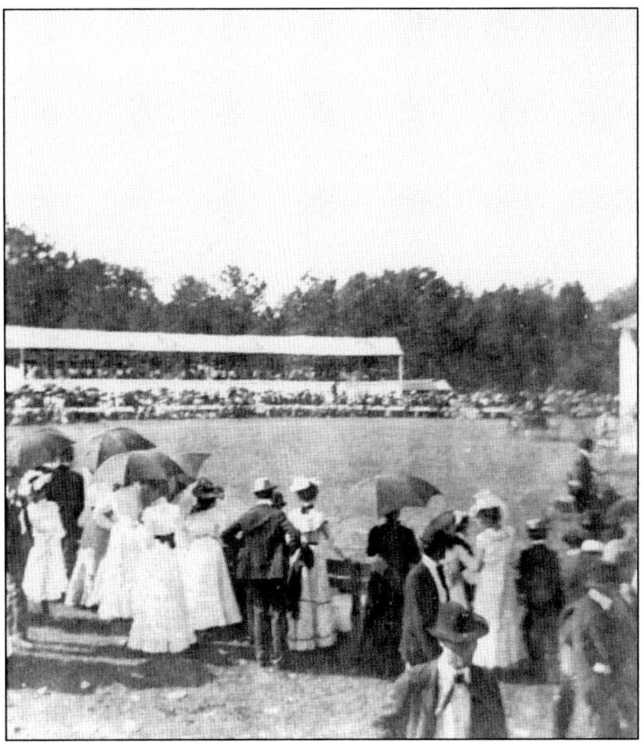

I'LL BET MY MONEY ON THE BAY. Horse racing was a popular sporting event for the young men of Laurens. They gathered at the "Race Track," an extension of Todd Avenue, to place wagers on their favorite steed. Dressed in the fashions of the day and wicker lunch baskets packed, Laurens residents would travel by horse and buggy to attend horse events. (Courtesy of Mrs. Beatrice Babb Bradley.)

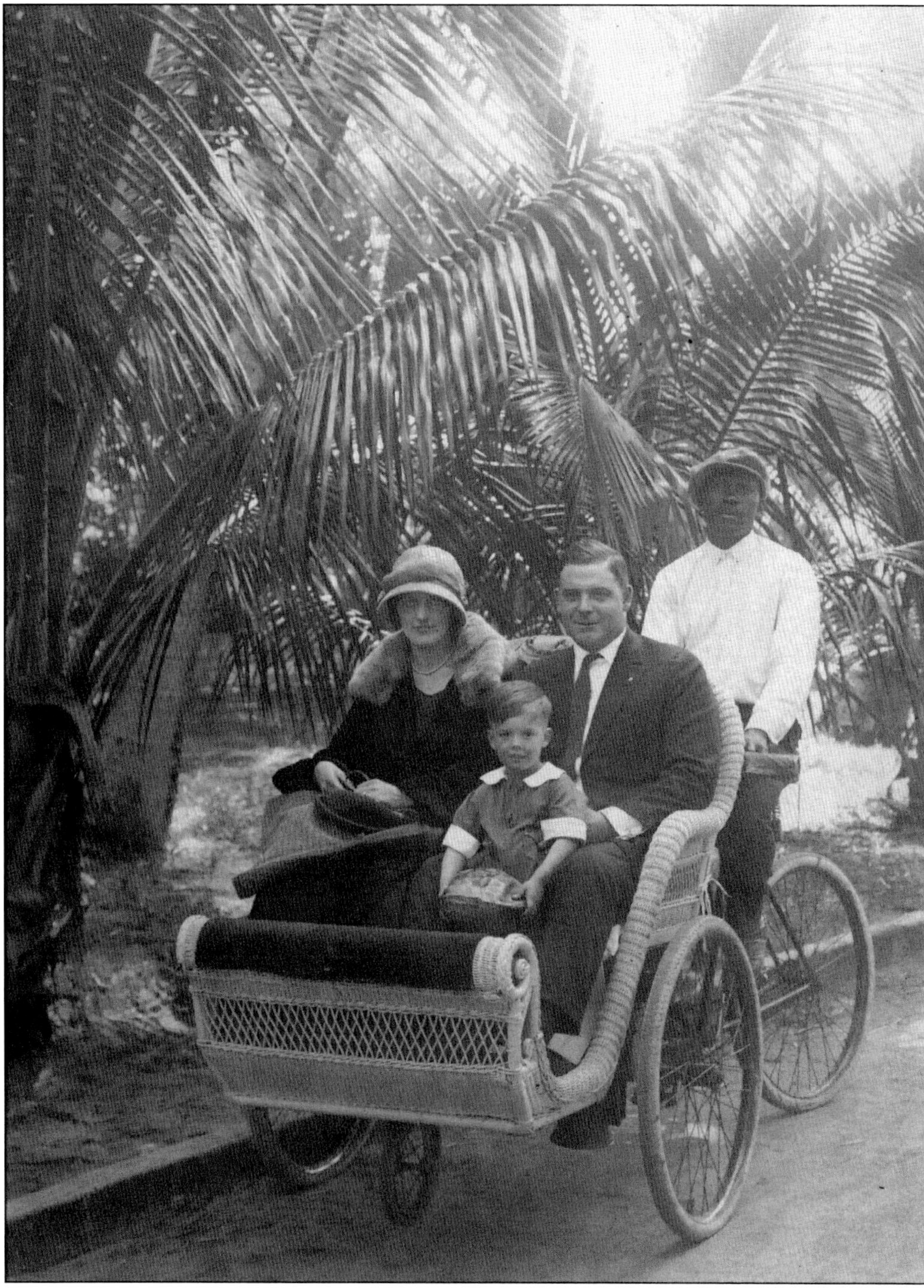

FLORIDA VACATION. In 1924, Claudia Darlington and James Conway Todd vacationed in Florida with their young son, James C. Todd Jr. James Todd was the son of Hattie Garlington and John Wells Todd. He was educated in the Laurens schools and Davidson College and was an elder in the First Presbyterian Church, a member of the board of trustees of Presbyterian College, a veteran of WW I, and the owner of Spratt Grocery, a wholesale grocery concern in Laurens. (Courtesy of Dr. James C. Todd III.)

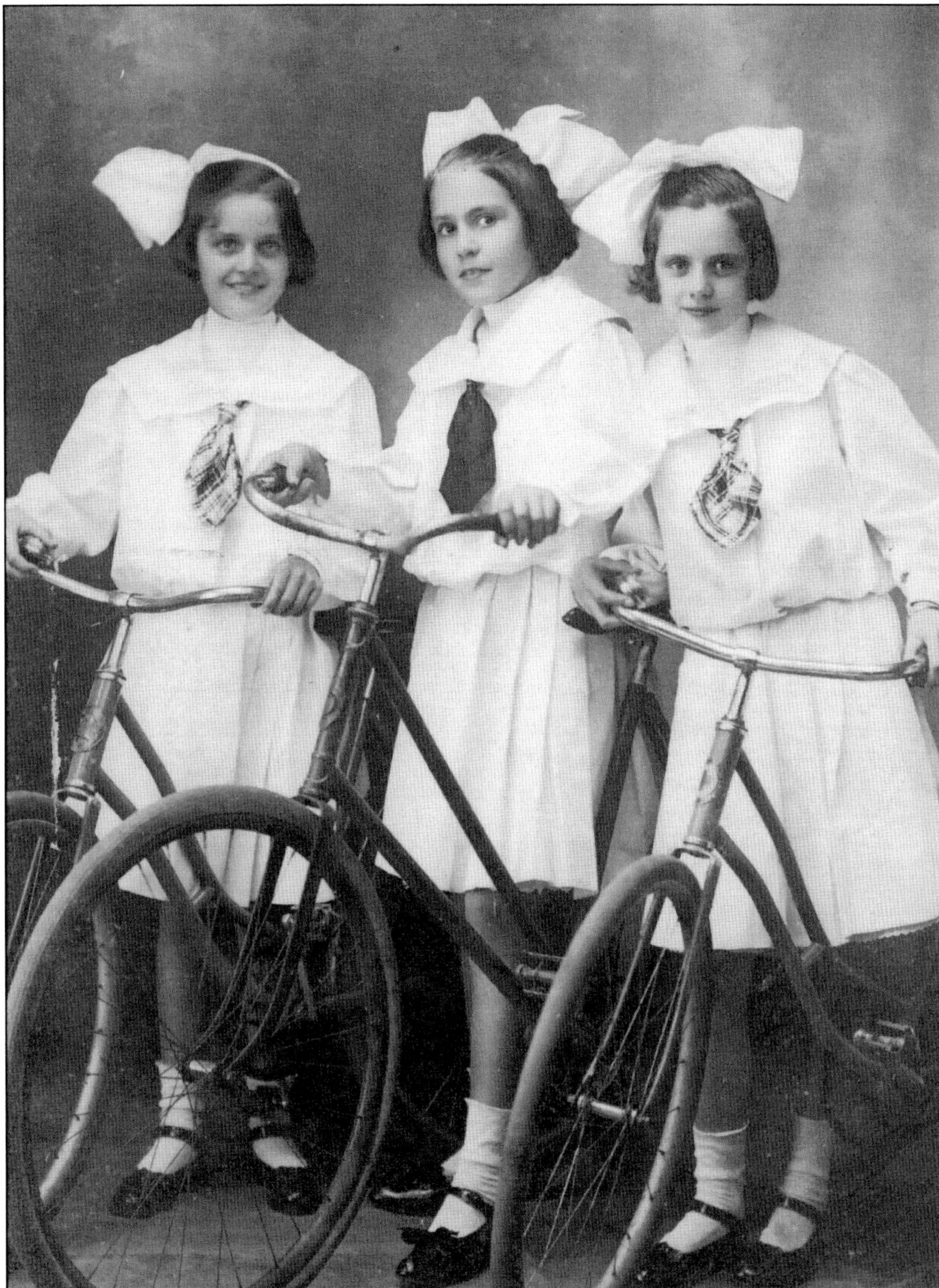

Bicycling, a Favorite Pastime. In 1910 young ladies found bicycling to be a favorite pastime. From left to right are Claudia Irby Darlington, Elizabeth Hood, and Lucy Vance Darlington. The Darlington sisters were the daughters of Colonel. Thomas and Lyde Irby Darlington and the granddaughters of Dr. W.C. and Laura Vance Irby. Both the Darlington and Irby families lived in Victorian houses on Irby Avenue. (Courtesy of Mrs. Mary Herndon Davis Todd.)

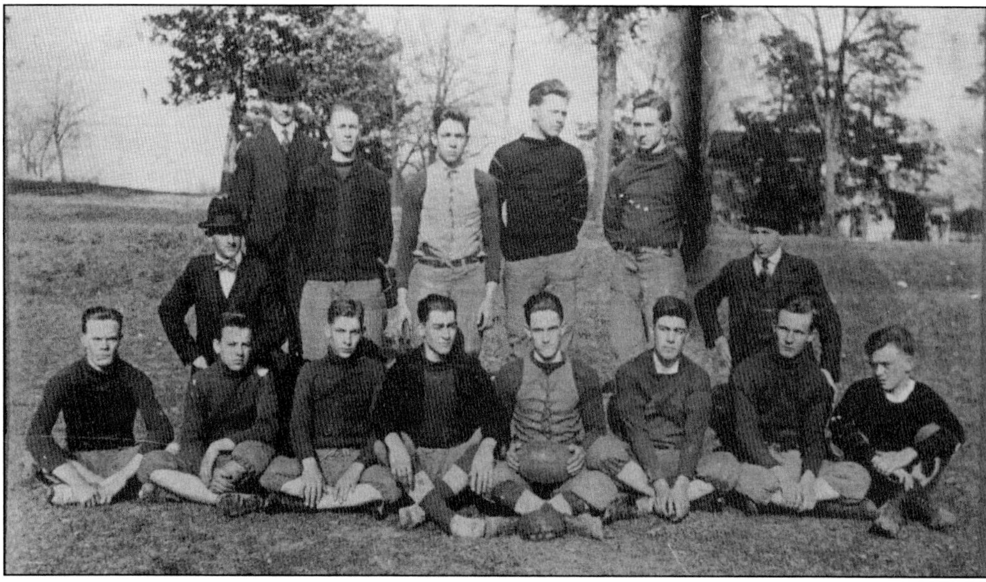

EARLY FOOTBALL TEAM. A group of Laurens High School football players are shown with their coaches on the grounds of the Graded School on Laurens Street. Football provided recreation for Laurens families, and from the earliest days it was supported by the town. (Courtesy of the Rhodes collection.)

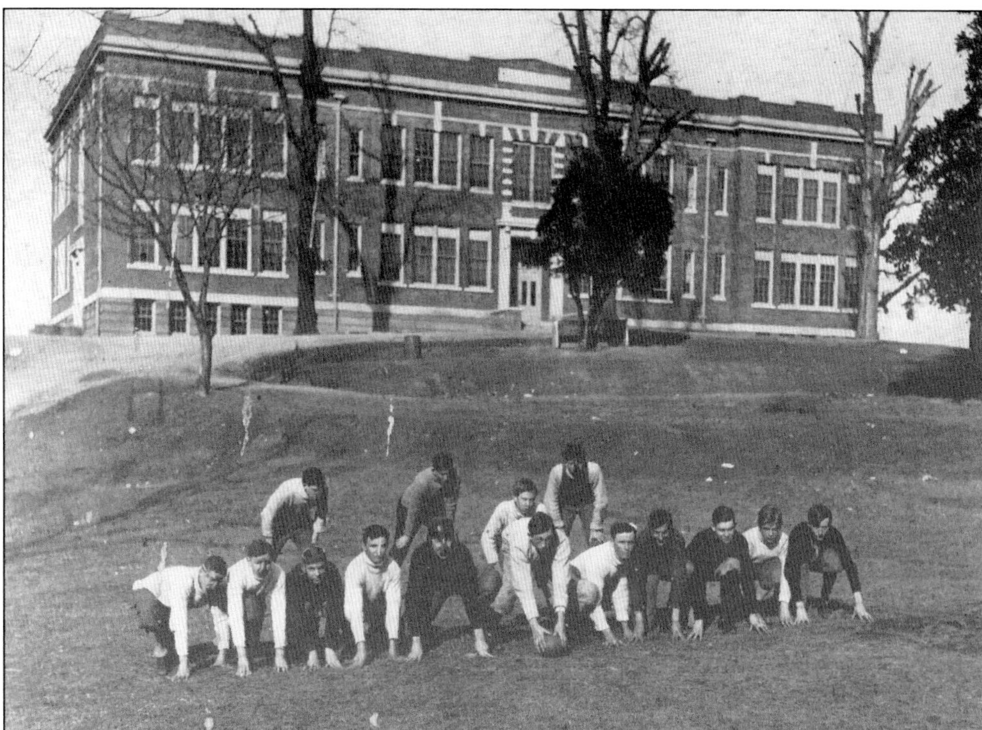

FOOTBALL PRACTICE. The 1909 Laurens football team is pictured in front of the Laurens Graded School, located on Laurens Street. It is interesting to note that many of the players later became leaders of the Laurens community. (Courtesy of Mrs. Mary Herndon Davis Todd.)

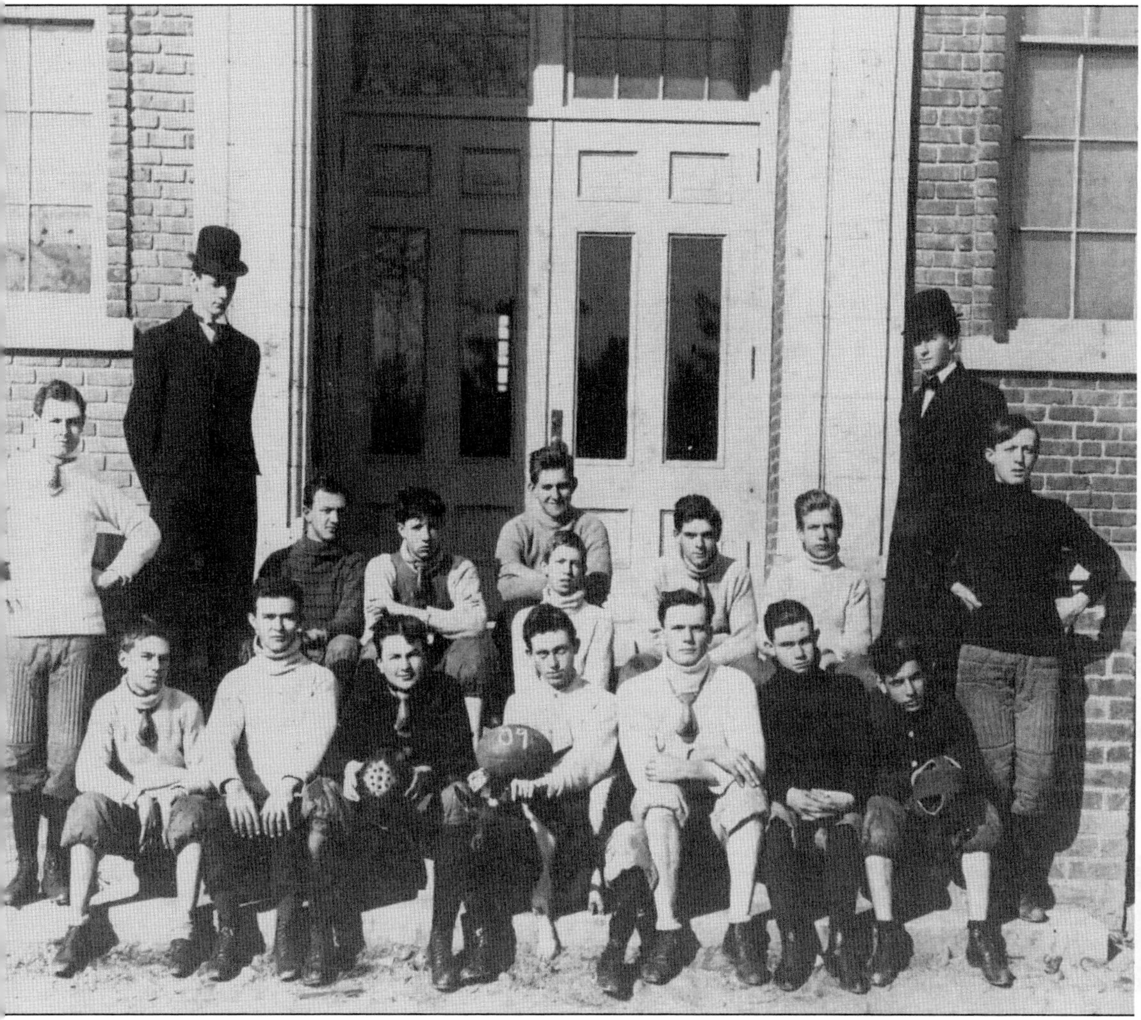

First Football Team. The first football team for Laurens was organized in 1909. The team members posing in front of the Laurens Graded School include the following: Charles Fleming, Sam Bolt, William Byrd, Hastings Dial, Carl Roper, Tom Bennett, Grover Richey, Douglas Featherstone (standing at right, white sweater), Robert H. Roper, William B. McGowan, James C. Todd, Job Little, Professor B.L. Parkinson (standing at left, with derby), Coach Montgomery (standing at right, with derby), and Tom Lake (standing at right, dark neck sweater). (Courtesy of Mrs. Mary Herndon Davis Todd.)

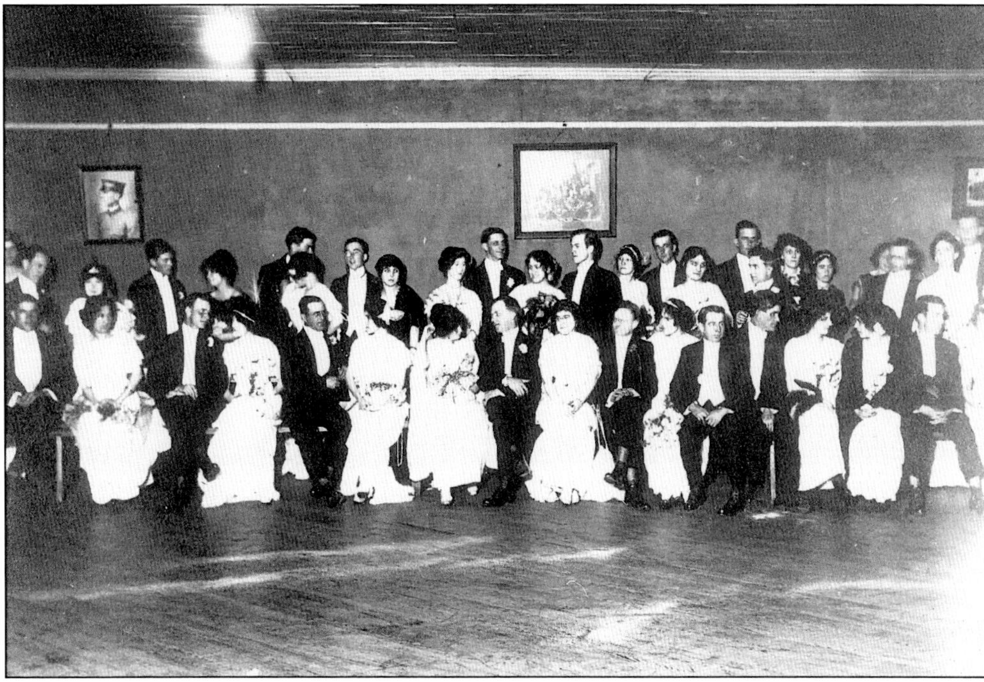

Social Event. A group gathered in formal attire is pictured at a party held upstairs in city hall c. 1910. The large room on the third floor was used for dances, parties, and other social events. (Courtesy of Mrs. Barbara Dial McAlister.)

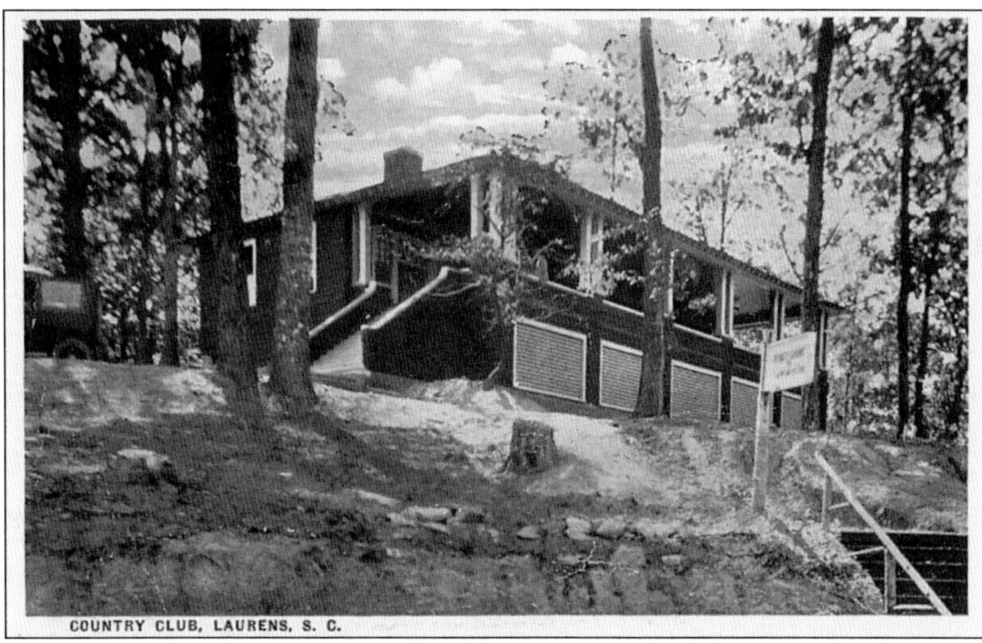

Country Club. Even though it was not located within the city limits, the Laurens Country Club, located between Laurens and Clinton, is worthy of mentioning because numerous Laurens citizens held memberships. Members enjoyed golfing and attending social functions held in the clubhouse. (Courtesy of Mrs. Harriet Easterby Faris.)

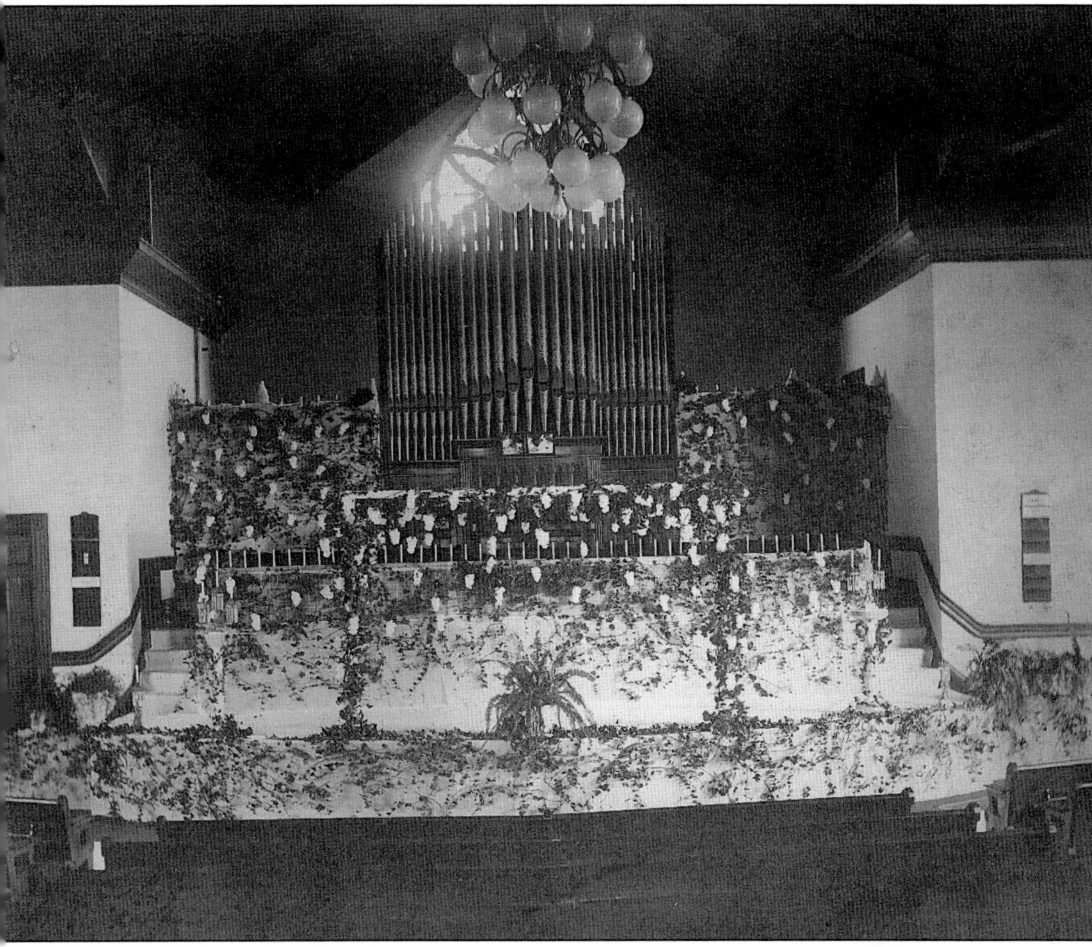

DECORATED FOR A WEDDING. The sanctuary of the First Presbyterian Church is swathed in white, entwined with ivy and other trailing vines, and complemented with white blossoms and ferns. The chandelier, organ, and stately sanctuary complete the wedding scene. However, the bride and groom are missing. The photograph was not labeled and leaves one to guess at the names of the betrothed couple and the year of their marriage. (Courtesy of Dr. James C. Todd III.)

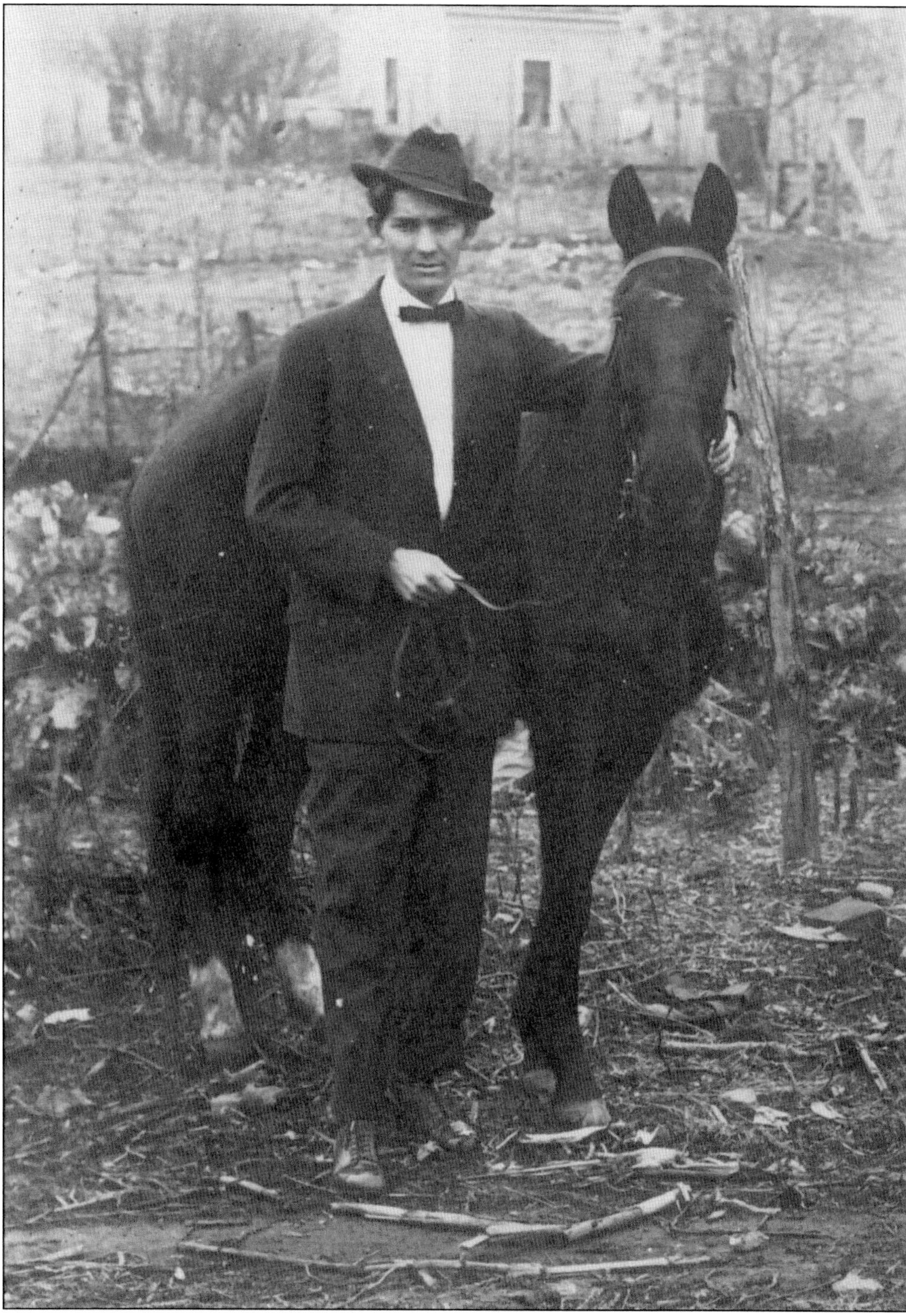

Horses Providing Entertainment. Many young men and sometimes ladies enjoyed riding "about" the town of Laurens on horseback. Riding was a favorite pastime for many. (Courtesy of the Rhodes collection.)

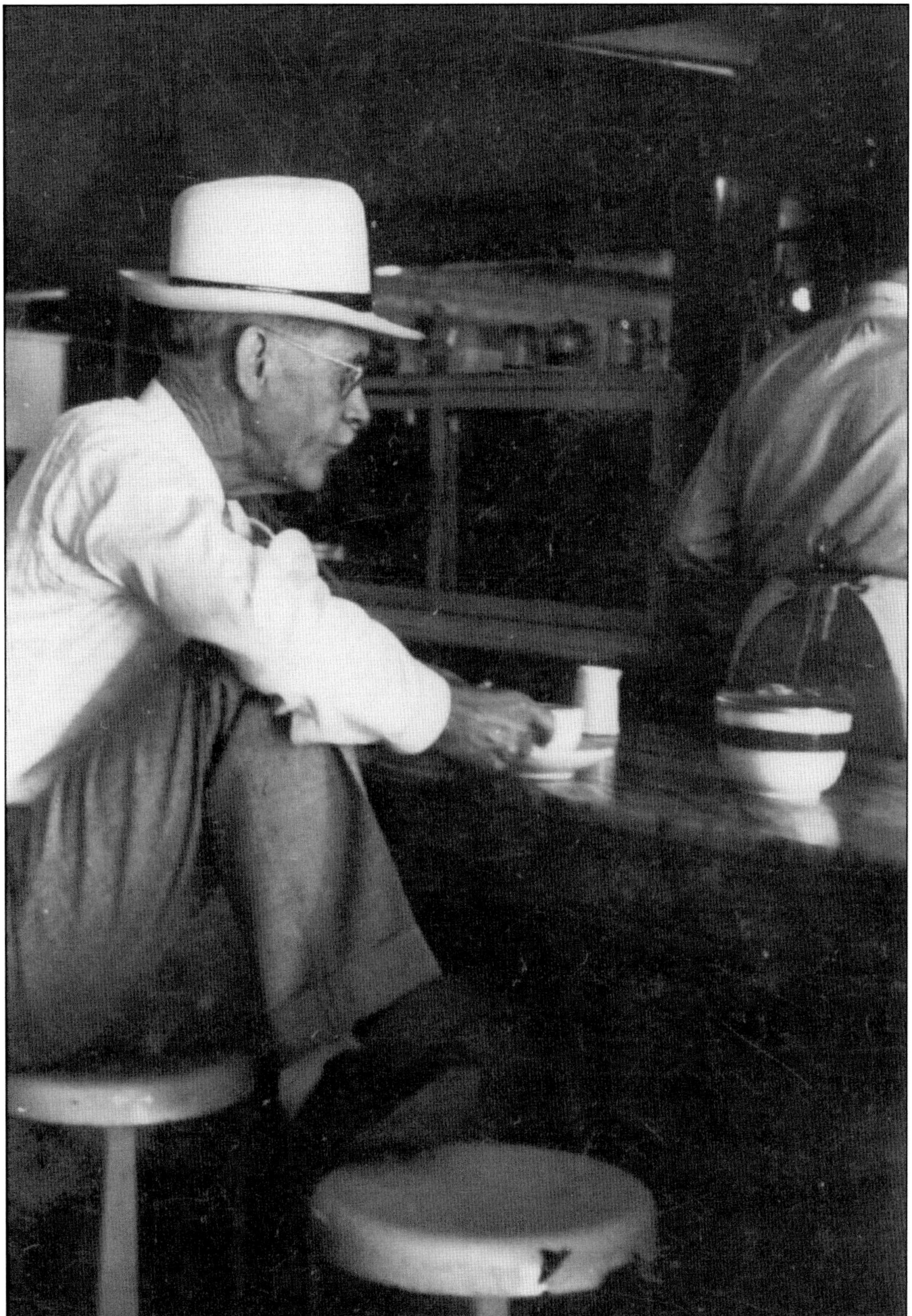

TOWN TALK OVER COFFEE. Robert E. Babb, along with other gentlemen of Laurens, often gathered at drugstores, or as in this photo, at Pete Mitchell's cafe for discussions on politics and other town matters. (Courtesy of Mrs. Beatrice Babb Bradley.)

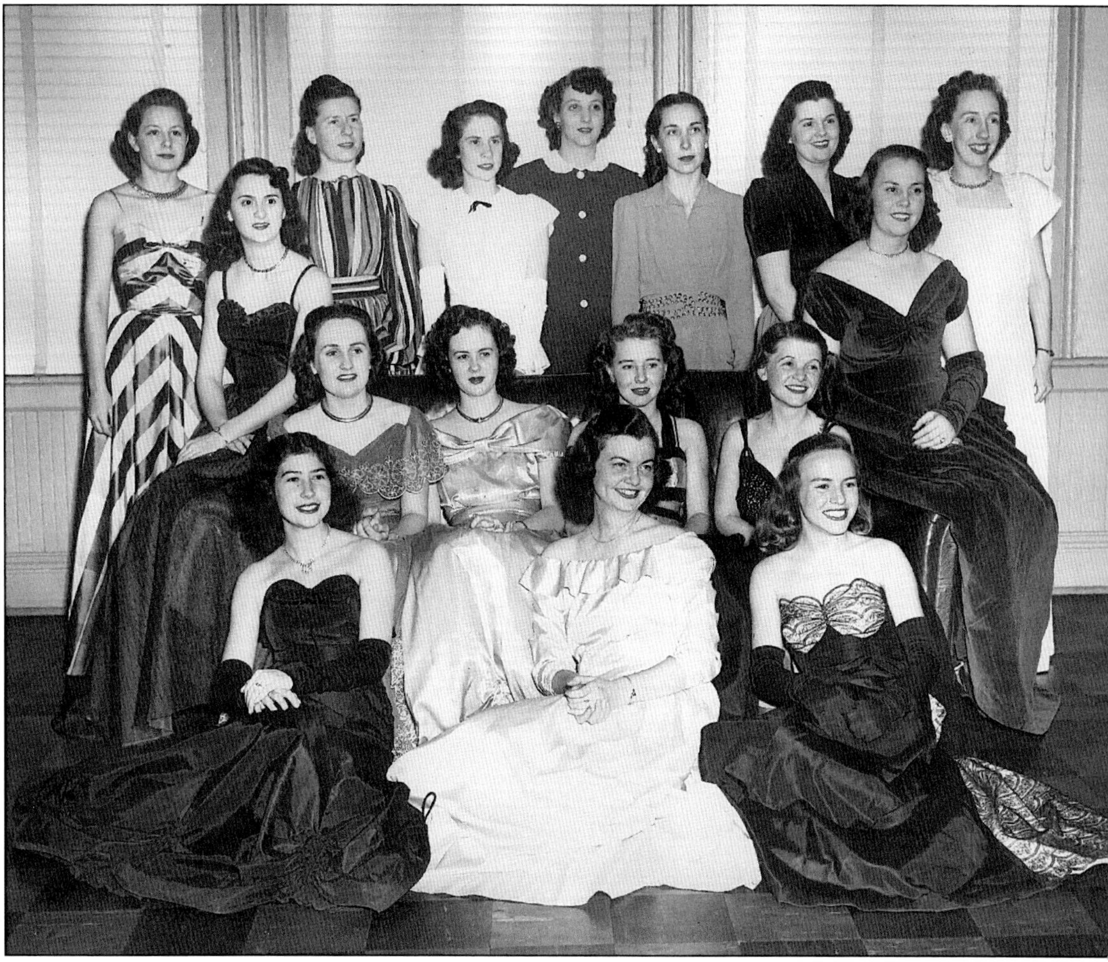

Sorority. Young Laurens ladies became members of various social clubs and sororities, and enjoyed the functions they provided. (Courtesy of *Laurens County Advertiser* files.)

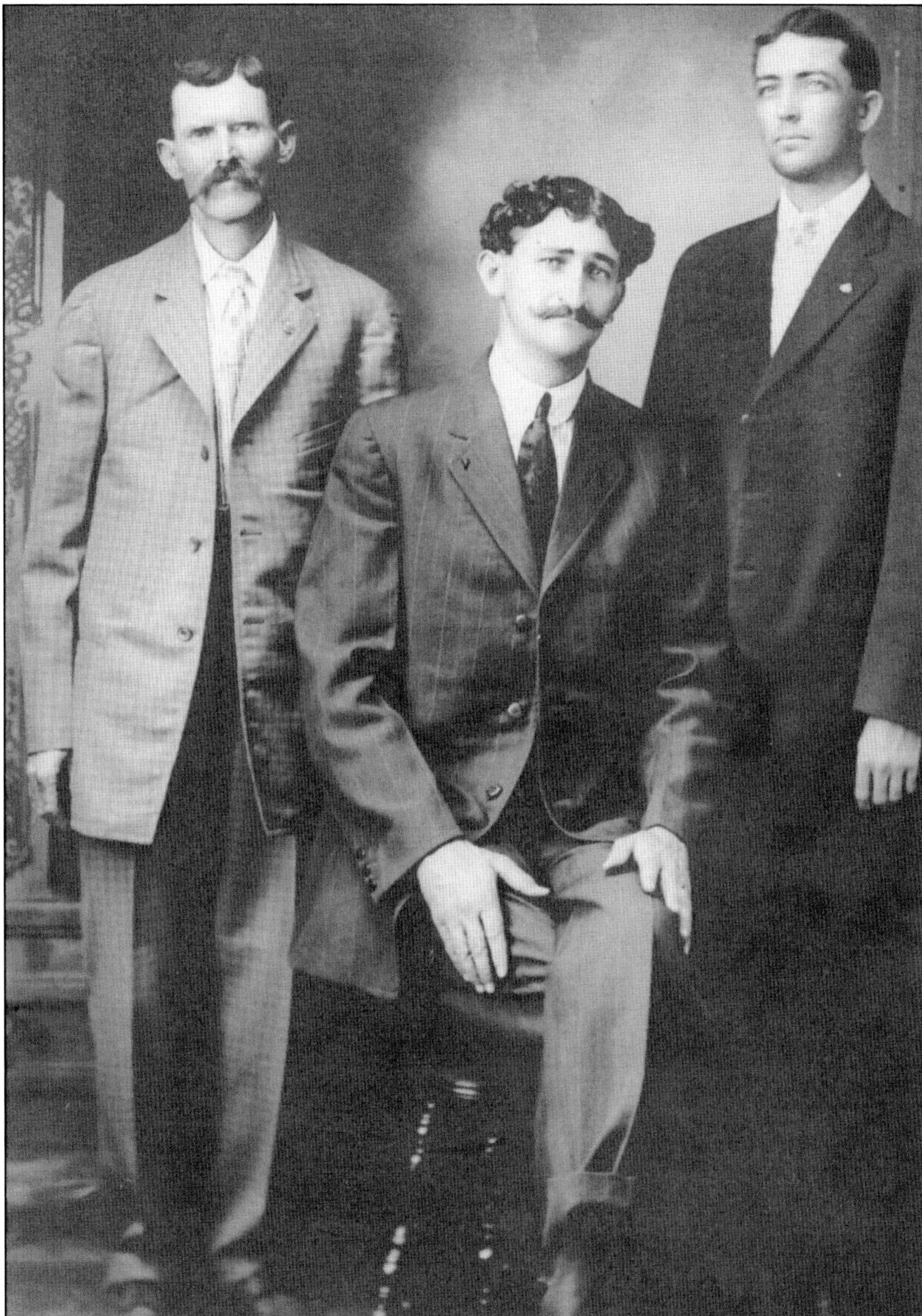

VISITING THE PHOTOGRAPHER. Young working men often dressed in their Sunday best and visited the photographer on Saturday afternoons. These men from the Wattsville area gathered in the studio and are identified, from left to right, as Lucious Brown, Burley Langston, and Tom Brown. (Courtesy of Julian Coats.)

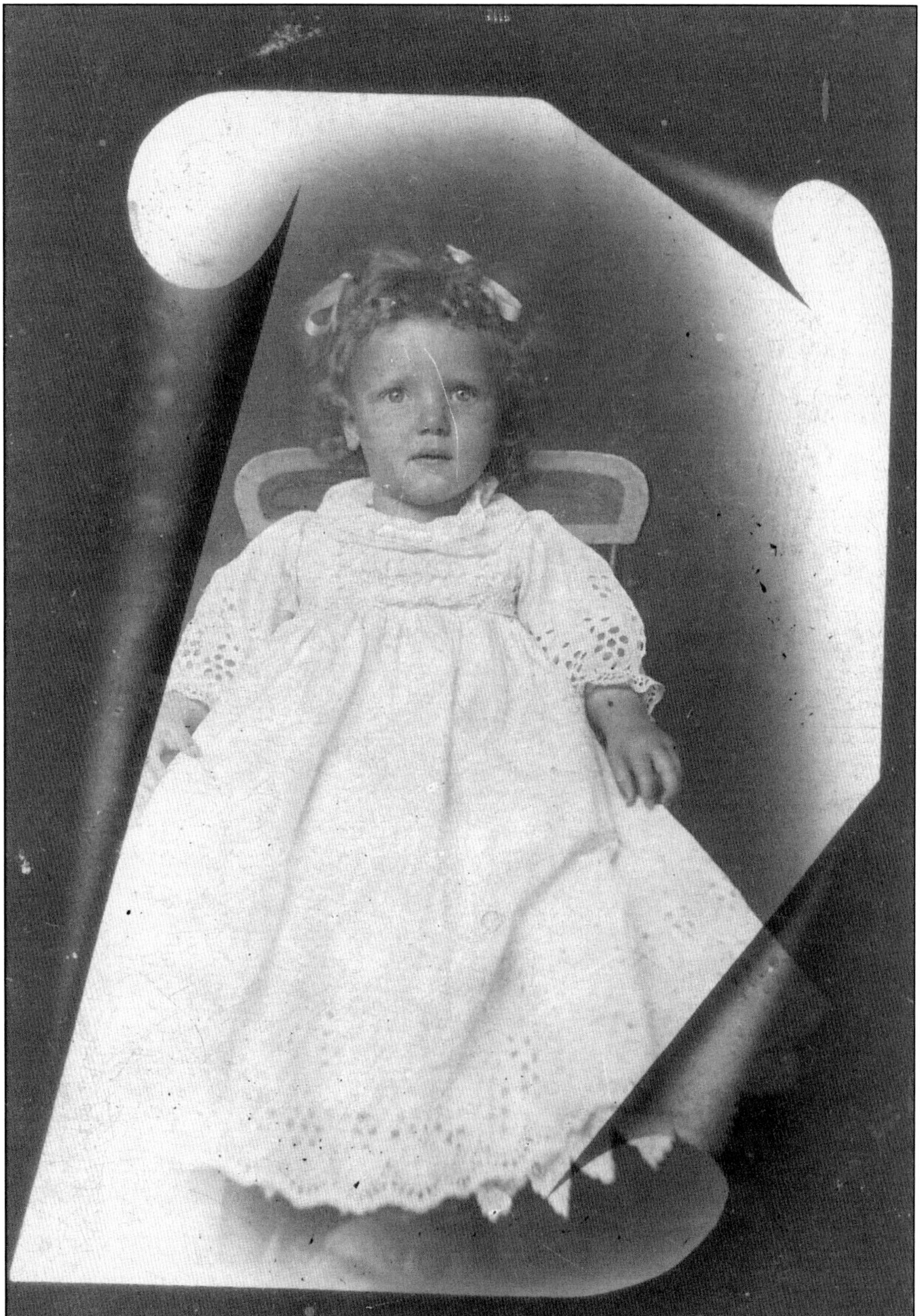

Smile. Mothers also dressed their children in ruffles and lace at the beginning of the 1900s and visited the local photographer. With blond curls and blue eyes, Alice Brown made a charming subject. (Courtesy of the Rhodes collection.)

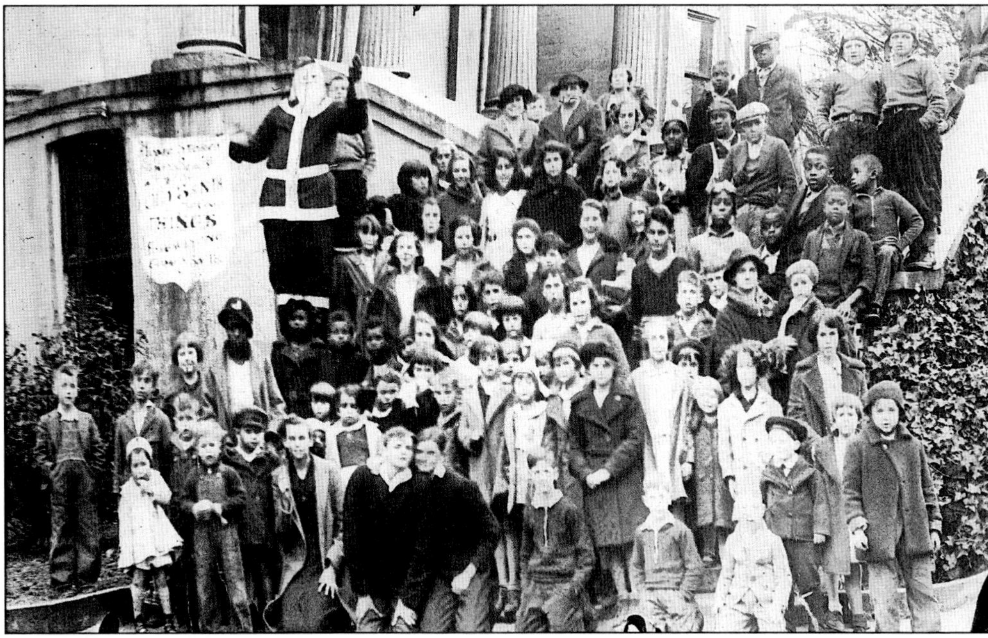

Annual Christmas Parades. Young and old enjoyed the annual Christmas parade, as it officially opened the Christmas season in Laurens. Children watched Santa arrive from the Courthouse steps. (Courtesy of the Rhodes collection.)

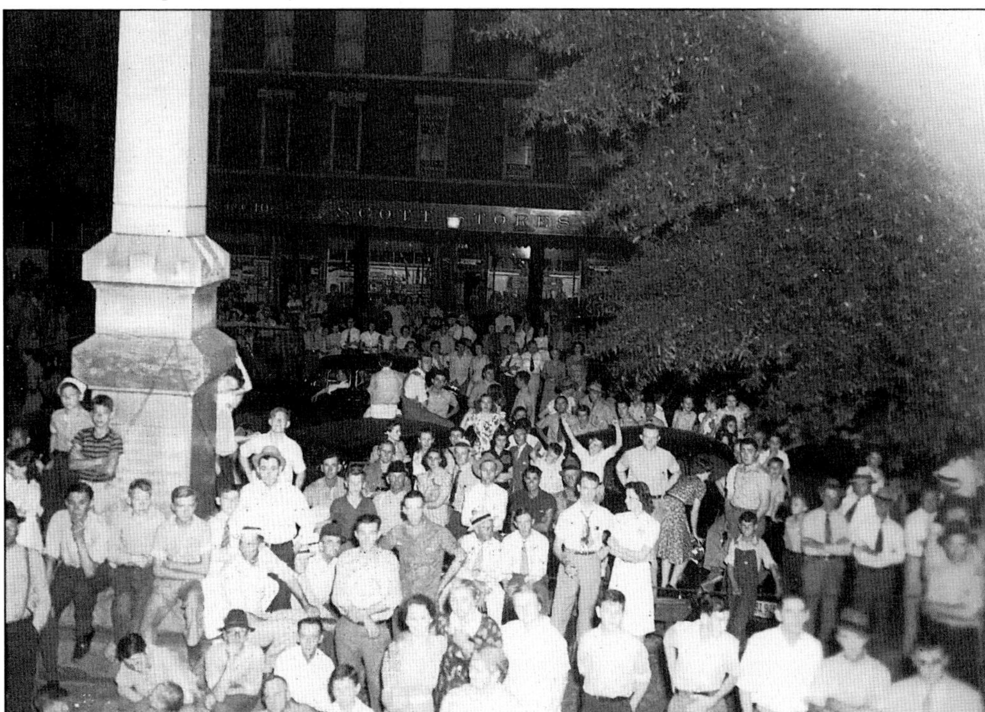

Political Speeches. Laurens residents found a favorite pastime in gathering for political speeches. They also gathered at the Courthouse on election night to hear results announced. (Courtesy of the Rhodes collection.)

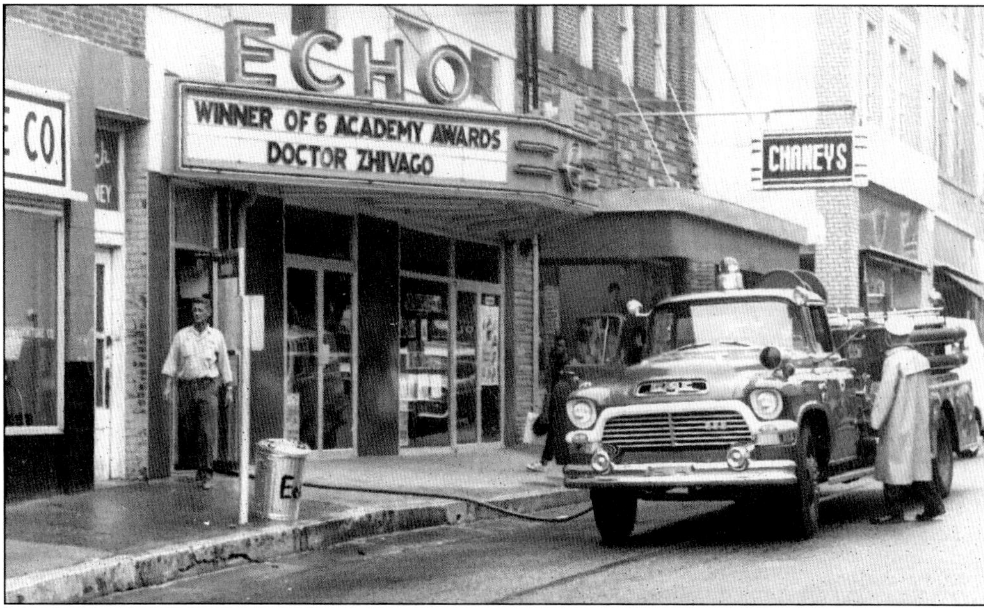

Theatres. The Echo and Capitol Theatres were two popular theatres enjoyed by Laurens residents. Both are now closed. (Courtesy of *Laurens County Advertiser* files.)

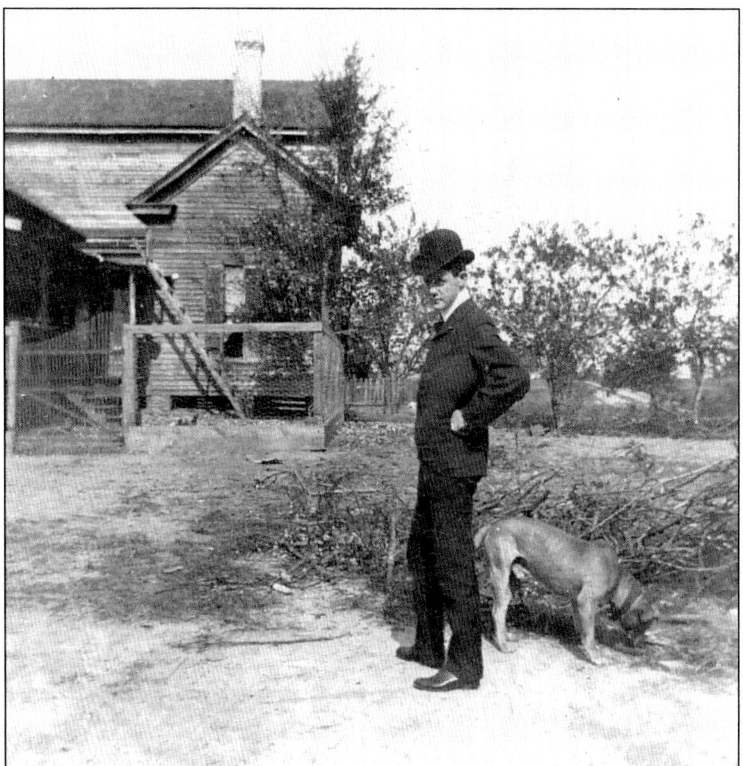

A Man and His Dog. A son of Messar Babb spends time with his dog at the rear of the Babb house on Farly Avenue. As with many other Laurens families, horses and dogs provided entertainment for the family. (Courtesy of Mrs. Beatrice Babb Bradley.)

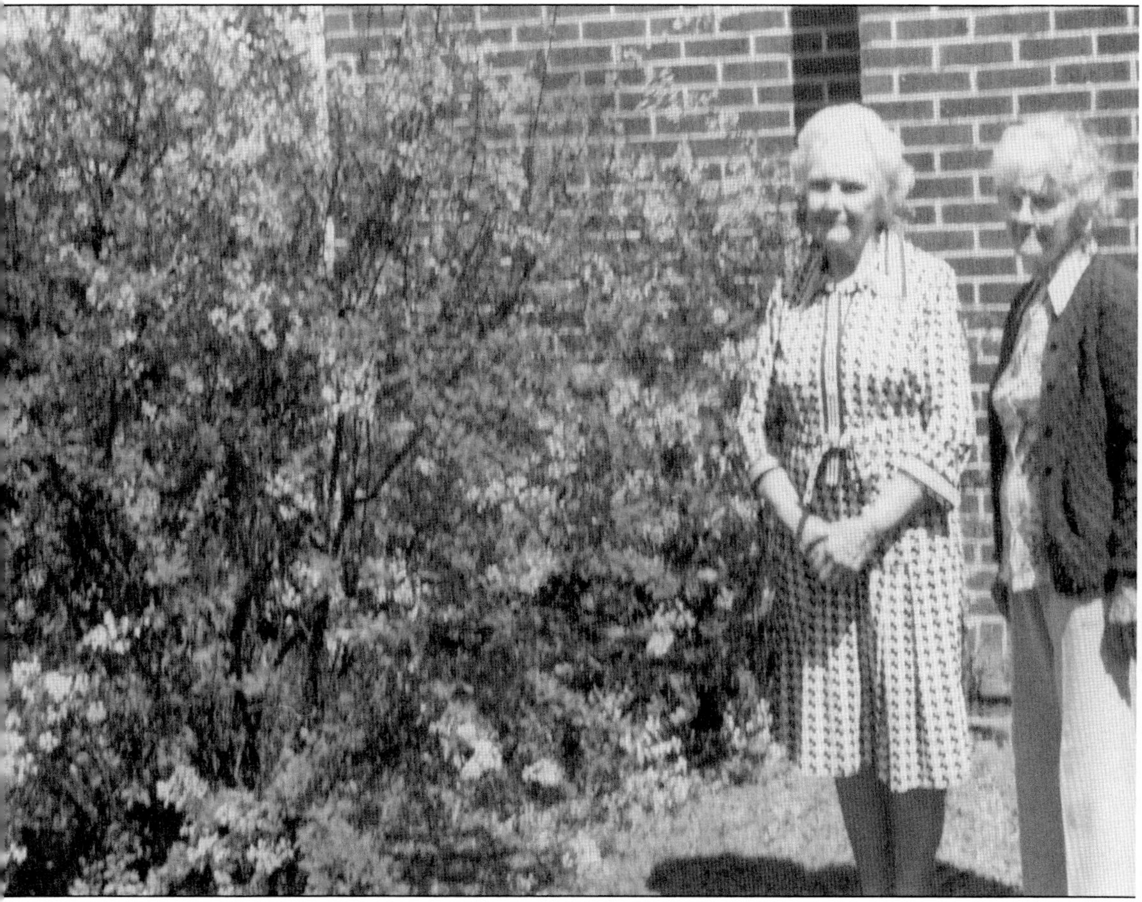

GARDENING. Mrs. Edna Foy was an active horticulturist and found untold pleasure in growing plants in the West Main yard that she shared with her sister, Ruth Riddle. Many Laurens ladies like Mrs. Foy found satisfaction and entertainment provided by garden clubs. (Courtesy of Laurens County Library.)

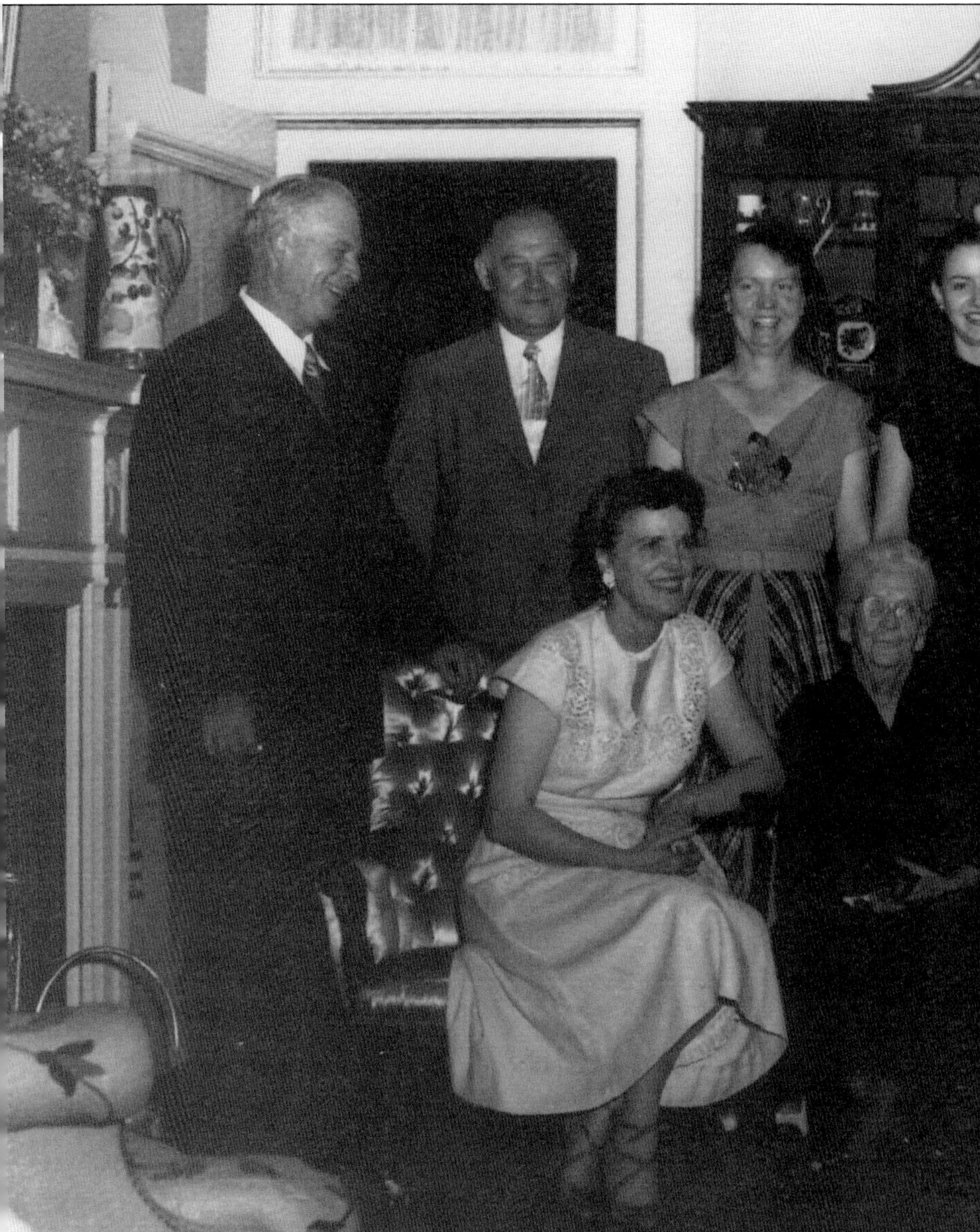

Dinner Party. Guests of Mr. and Mrs. James C. Todd gathered for a dinner party in 1948 at the Todd home on West Main Street. They are identified, from left to right, as follows: (seated) Claudia Darlington Todd, Hattie Garlington Todd, Albert Creswell Todd, and Eva Brownlee

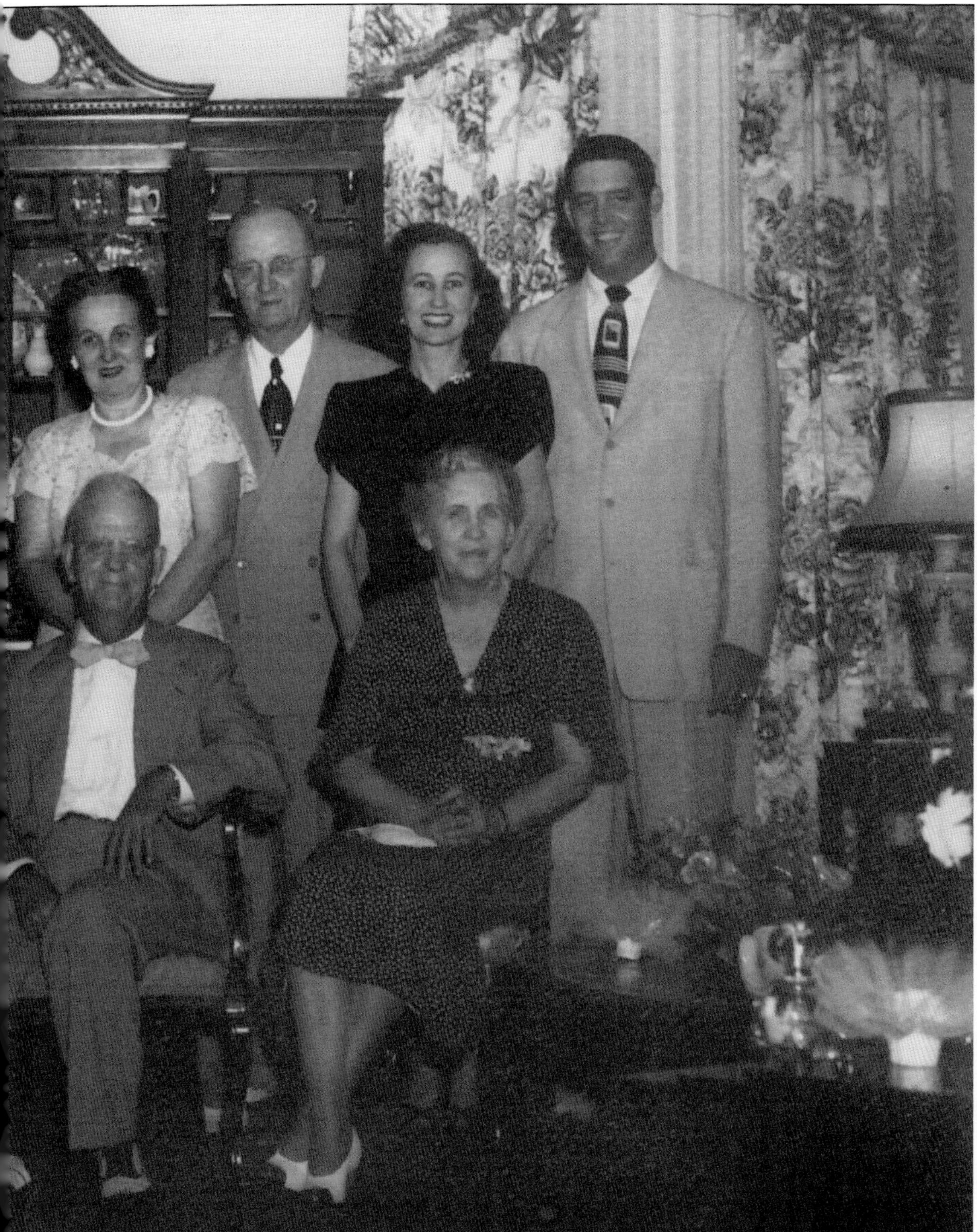

Todd; (standing) James Conway Todd, Paul Gallant, Harriet Todd Gallant, Jane Harney, Mary Sullivan Davis, James Robert Davis, Mary Herndon Davis Todd, and James Conway Todd Jr. (Courtesy of Dr. James C. Todd III.)

Acknowledgments

The research in *Laurens* has been aided by many people who have told me stories, allowed me to look through scrapbooks of clippings and mementos, and have "dug deep" into trunks, attics, and photo boxes and shared family photographs, documents, and genealogical research of their ancestors. To these people, I wish to express my appreciation for their enthusiasm about the book and their willingness to trust me with valued treasures of the past. Because the town of Laurens that we know, love, and call home was made great by a fusion of devoted men and women, it was impossible to picture all of the citizens, homes, businesses, and churches. Perhaps at a later date, a second volume can be compiled.

I am grateful to my parents, Betty Cleveland and James Julian Coats Jr., for their support, encouragement, and for always being there. To my father, thank you for a lifetime of captivating stories that allowed me to return to the past and inspired me to become a writer. I would like to believe that my writings are as enchanting as your tales. To my mother, thank you for your everlasting patience and prayers and for constantly keeping Daddy and me focused on the present and future. To "Aunt" Betty Waldrip Irwin, I express gratitude for teaching me to appreciate genealogy and to savor books from an early age.

Thanks are also extended to Jim Brown, owner and publisher of the *Laurens Advertiser*, for handing me a pad and pencil at the age of 13 and encouraging and critiquing my writing efforts through the years. This book would not have been possible without his allowing me to use back issues of the *Laurens Advertiser* for research.

Grateful acknowledgment is given to Elaine Martin of the Laurens County Library for providing access to photographs, books, documents, and other materials from the library's South Carolina Room Collection. With her vast knowledge of Laurens, Elaine assisted in choosing people and places, and in verifying dates and locations.

Without the "go ahead and do it" from my oldest and dearest friend, JoAnn Johnson Ross, I probably would have never undertaken the project. Early on, she assisted me in determining the chapters and patiently listened to "stories" as I uncovered new information. Carol Chambers proved to be a valuable assistant by helping me "keep up" with materials and photographs, calling in search of photographs, and organizing information.

Mrs. Ineze Motes Royster was always "a phone call away," day or night, to answer questions about houses, citizens, locations, and events in early Laurens. By feeding the horses and tending the barn, Nancy Suddeth and Joe Branin provided me with the necessary time to compile information and complete the book. Thanks also to my editor at Arcadia Publishing, Mark Berry.

Last and definitely not least, to my husband, Danny Rhodes, who never complained about missed dinners or neglected household chores and who gave me the space and time needed to complete my research and writing; and to my son and daughter, Mason Motes and Kate Rhodes, for worrying about my late hours; and to my grandsons, Mason and Johnson Motes, for "giving up Grandma" for a few months—I especially thank you for your constant support and inspiration; I am thankful for your love and belief in me. *Laurens* has been written with the heartfelt desire that the book will bring pleasure to those who turn its pages.